BROTHERHOODS
OF
FEAR

BROTHERHOODS
OF
FEAR

A HISTORY OF VIOLENT ORGANIZATIONS

PAUL ELLIOTT

BLANDFORD

A BLANDFORD BOOK

First published in the UK 1998 by Blandford

A Cassell Imprint

Cassell plc
Wellington House 125 Strand London WC2R 0BB

Text copyright © 1998 Paul Elliott

Distributed in the United States by Sterling Publishing Co. Inc.
387 Park Avenue South, New York, NY 10016–8810

A Cataloguing-in-Publication Data entry for this title is available
from the British Library.

ISBN 0-7137-2687-3

Jacket design based on an illustration by Alexis Liasotos

Printed and bound in Great Britain by
MPG Books Ltd, Bodmin, Cornwall

'They had traded the false gods of fear and blind piety for those of license and anarchy'

H.P. LOVECRAFT *The Silver Key*

Author and Publisher's Note

Brotherhoods of Fear is not *just* a history of violent organizations, but also of terror groups who have inspired fear, hatred and paranoia across the pages of history.

Contents

Preface

A seemingly endless array of death and pain assaults us from the television news each night. Among the perpetrators are governments and armies fighting border wars; guerrillas fighting civil wars; killers driven by passion or revenge; serial killers, thugs and gang members; road rage drivers; and terrorists. Yet in what seems to be a catalogue of chaos, there is some semblance of order. Depending on your viewpoint, those accused have motive and meaning or are deranged and irresponsible, and indeed, shifting patterns are commented on nightly by military analysts, criminologists or journalists.

Hiding away among these reports is a genuinely sinister criminal sub-group that defies all the norms while creating fear and panic in victims and onlookers alike. I term these groups 'brotherhoods of fear', for they are a community of individuals bound together to act out various unsavoury and repellent crimes. And for what purpose? This varies – widely – but what links these small – sometimes large – groups together, is their seeming phase-shift with reality. For these groups the normal standards of modern life do not apply, and they often feel free to act out abhorrent crimes with ease. Their motives are clear-cut and diverse. The Ku Klux Klan promotes a blatant policy of race hate; the Anarchists and the Baader-Meinhof group aimed to bring down modern society by assassinating key individuals; the Mafia pursues a ruthless and murderous regime of terror to further its profit margins and its security. Internally, the criminal activities of these clandestine groups are well worked out and usually consistent, but to the outside world they defy all the norms by which the civilized world defines itself.

Some of these motives are incredibly confusing. Why *did* the Aum Shinrikyo cult release nerve gas in Tokyo's subway system? If the Mafia killed President Kennedy, why did it do so? What evidence provoked the fanatical and murderous witch hunts? From where did the Nazis develop the belief that the German people were the 'master race'? The questions of where and how are easily answered, but when we look at *why* these groups have acted in the way that they have, we are faced with great difficulties. To penetrate the motives of such groups, it is necessary to delve deep into the esoteric beliefs of these organizations and to peel away the rhetoric to discover the truth that lies behind it. This is the purpose of *Brotherhoods of Fear.*

This is more than a catalogue of criminal syndicates and terrorist organizations. Where drug profits or illegal gambling provide an understandable and easily identifiable motive for business, I have ignored such criminal organizations. Similarly, where a terrorist group has allied itself with a cause one can readily identify, that, too, is left for other writers to discuss. Perhaps such a group is patriotic – the IRA or ETA, for instance – and is fighting on behalf of some minority or racial population. Perhaps it is the guerrilla army of a dissolved nation or the military wing of a political party that is committed to gaining control of the government at any price. But what about the anti-technology, hippie-inspired Unabomber, who spent over a decade executing a meticulous bombing campaign across the United States? Madman or terrorist? Religious fanatic or dangerous social revolutionary?

The 'brotherhoods of fear' seem to bend accepted definitions and defy traditional notions of bad guy/good guy. The neat distinctions of academics have become blurred. Evading easy categorization and pigeon-holing, many of these groups seem to cross boundaries, shifting from criminal activities to terrorism and into racial conflict, for example. We are left floundering for a meaning, for a motive, for an answer to these multifarious threats. Is there an answer? For that we must first identify a cause. Although I begin this discussion at the heart of the Middle Ages, and explore the breathtaking horror and mind-twisting double-think of the Inquisition, we shall see that the phenomenon is very much one of recent centuries. Yes, the human psyche does have within it the vital ingredients that go to create one of our 'brotherhoods of fear'. But it must also depend on social conditions and social pressure. To this subject we must return later on.

This book is in some ways a sequel to my earlier work, *Warrior Cults*. In that book I traced the history of numerous violent and arcane cults, but I restricted myself to ancient and medieval history, as well as to more recent primitive agricultural societies. Here I bring that story up to date, covering the period from the Middle Ages, through the Industrial Revolution and into the high-tech information age of the pre-millennial decade. Still, the criteria for selecting what should be included are the same, with an emphasis on organizations that merge violence, magic, revolution, religion and tradition in ever more intriguing and dangerous fashions.

I am indebted to both Stuart Booth and Roderick Dymott at Cassell for suggesting the unique theme of this book. Stuart in particular has been the thread connecting *Warrior Cults* with this project. Ian Howarth of the Cults Information Centre provided useful information and some food for thought, and 'Steve' provided more material on bike gangs than I could possibly use. My good friend Phil Parkes, who is energetically involved with the anti-Nazi movement in Wales, was able to fill me in on the recruitment activities of British neo-Nazis. Harvey Waring speculated with me endlessly on the subject of John F. Kennedy's assassination and convinced me not to write off the conspiracy theory altogether. From Mark Owen in Toronto I received a welter of useful research titles on the subject of masonic conspiracies for which I am very grateful. My gratitude is also warmly extended to Joseph Klein who spoke to me about his experiences in the Nazi concentration camps. His ordeal, which ended at Bergen-Belsen in 1945, brought home to me the true horrors of real-life hatred and fanaticism.

Without my wife, Christine, *Brotherhoods of Fear* might never have been written at all. Her constant support ensured the completion of the book in time, and her knowledge of the world's religions proved invaluable in debating various aspects of the project.

Paul Elliott
CANTERBURY, KENT

CHAPTER ONE

Hammer of Witches

If I knew what to say, I would say it. Oh Sir, I don't know what I have to say. Oh! Oh! They are killing me – if they would tell me what – Oh, Sirs, Oh, my heart ... loosen me and I will tell the truth; I don't know what I have to tell – loosen me for the sake of God – tell me what I have to say – I did it, I did it ... O wretched me; I will tell all that is wanted, Sirs – they are breaking my arms – loosen me a little – I did everything that was said of me ... What am I wanted to tell? I did everything – loosen me for I don't remember what I have to tell.

This statement was faithfully recorded as it was heard by a scribe working for the Spanish Inquisition. It provides us with a terrifyingly graphic and immediate window into the world of medieval witchcraft and its cruel and violent suppression. The pain of the tortures, the overwhelming panic and the bewilderment of the poor man are evident. As a victim of the witch-finders, he would have been accused by friends or neighbours who had done so under similar tortures. He would be made to confess to any crime the interrogators put to him and would accordingly suffer the death penalty. And yet most of these unfortunates were clearly free from guilt.

The incredible phenomenon that was to become known as the Great Witch Panic is one of the greatest mysteries of European history. Did witch cults really work their evil magic in towns and villages across the continent? Why were the authorities so afraid of these poor, misguided people? Why did these persecutions begin and end so suddenly? Who perpetrated this campaign of persecution? Why did they do so?

At its height, the Great Witch Panic saw incredible excesses of brutality and inhumanity – all in the name of the Christian faith. In the German town of Bamberg, for example, 600 witches were reputed to have been burned to death in a seven-year period. It was Germany, in particular, that rode the bloody climax of the witch panic, and Bamberg became the most notorious city in Europe for persecution. Its bishop styled himself as the *Hexenbischof* (witch-bishop), and his obsession led him to build a dedicated witch-house. This he had fitted with its own torture chamber for the interrogation of suspects, and while the victims – men, women and children – were subjected to all manner of terrifying tortures, they were supposed to draw comfort from the selected biblical texts that hung on its walls. Even the mayor of Bamberg could not evade the city's dedication to the cause: his body was smashed and mutilated to force a confession from him, and he was burned at the stake in front of the watching public.

The hunt for satanic covens of witches and their familiars did not end with individual stories of suffering and death; entire communities became caught up in the frenzy of fear. For years children were encouraged to provide testimony against their parents, while in some places whole families were marched into the torture chamber. Not only were many innocent people falsely accused of satanic worship, subjected to crippling tortures, made to confess and publicly burned to death, but they were sometimes forced to meet all of the costs incurred! Condemned victims or their grieving relatives were forced to remunerate the executioner for the cost of the stake and firewood and were, in addition, expected to pay for both the trial and the torture sessions.

The Great Witch Panic was blind panic, a real fear that the forces of darkness were at work in every town and village. At its heart was a new-found belief that there existed an occult conspiracy, a 'witch society', that threatened the survival of Christendom. The world of the late fifteenth century earnestly believed in both witches and the witch cult that bound them together. In more modern times some academics have found themselves with no alternative but to agree with that belief. As we shall later discover, the anthropologist Margaret Murray actually set down the customs and traditions of this secretive sect in her 1921 book *The Witch-Cult in Western Europe*. To a civilization that firmly believed in the existence of black or harmful magic (known to the witch-finders as *maleficium*), the suggestion of a secret cult of Devil worshippers with actual magical powers must have caused genuine fear. It was no less a person than Pope Innocent VIII (reigned 1484–92) who was to direct the energies of the Catholic Church towards eliminating this dangerous conspiracy. The witch cult had to be stopped. In 1484 a papal bull (an official proclamation by the pope) unleashed across the land an élite, international judicial force that was charged with achieving precisely this goal. It was the Inquisition.

The Origins of the Inquisition

In the early medieval period witchcraft was virtually ignored by the Church. Rural magicians, male and female, were considered to be practitioners of an established and tolerated craft, and only when they used their powers to an evil end would the authorities take note. The magnitude of any action taken, however, was based on the evil magic (the *maleficium*) that had been used and not on the theological basis for that magic. Witchcraft was part of life, a hangover from the superstitions and magical practices that had survived from Romano-Celtic times. Those individuals practising the simple rural magic of witchcraft were often isolated, penniless and powerless, and they were thus of little consequence to the ecclesiastical establishment. Moreover, the Christian Church faced far greater problems from a growing number of organized and well-supported religious sects.

Disenchanted with the hypocrisy of the Catholic Church and its authoritarian hold over the masses, breakaway Christian movements were gaining in both popularity and strength. The previously unchallenged power of Rome, the traditional seat of Christianity, was coming under threat from these 'heresies'.

The greatest of these heretical groups were the Cathars (or Albigensians) and the Waldensians. Of these, the Cathars, in particular, found wide support at all levels of society, seriously endangering the theological monopoly of the Catholic Church. From the south of France the movement reached northern parts of the country and across the border into Flanders and western Germany. Cathars were even found in northern Italy. Much of this new faith was based on the concept of dualism that had been filtering into Christianity from Persian cults in the Near East. Satan was the lord of the material universe and was, according to the Cathars, represented by the Hebrew god of the Old Testament. Thus all things earthly and material were 'evil'. Heaven and the higher spiritual world was ruled by the true Christian God. Cathars believed that the whole of mankind was involved in a cosmic struggle between good and evil, the spiritual and the material. Although the higher initiates of the sect (the 'Perfecti') lived austere lives, free from deception, sex, the eating of meat, the ownership of property and the committing of violence, they were often accused by the Church of sexual perversions. This belief sprang from the Cathar custom of sex outside marriage among the rank-and-file membership, since marriage and childbirth were condemned by the heretics as an invention of Satan designed to populate his world. Of course, the Cathar belief in sex for pleasure and not for procreation directly opposed the teachings of St Paul and the medieval Church. Both birth control and abortion are also believed to have been practised by the Cathars. Catharism quickly gained a sordid reputation for both 'unnatural sexual practices' and the practice of magic (*maleficium*).

Cathars went further than merely opposing the tenets of the Roman Church. Those being initiated as Perfecti ritually rejected the Catholic Church and their Catholic baptism. This, coupled with the sect's belief in another, 'higher' god, led the pope formally to charge the Cathars with heresy and Devil worship. Fear was growing that southern France would become engulfed by this powerful rival Church. Many of the people of Languedoc, the central principality of the region, were committed Cathars. It was from the Languedoc town of Albi in 1165 that a Catholic council sat in judgement over the heretical sect that flourished all around it. From this condemnation the heretics became known as the 'Albigensians'. On a pretext in 1208, Pope Innocent III (reigned 1198–1216) ordered a crusade to liberate the south of France from the Albigensians. This was to be a massive undertaking – a show of force that would establish the Catholic Church of Rome as the undisputed and sole representative of Christianity on earth. It was not to be a 'moral crusade', which would win the theological argument through debate and wit. Far from it. Within a year 30,000 armoured knights and infantry had moved south into Languedoc and began to slaughter entire populations of men, women and children, armed or not. Crops were destroyed, and towns and cities were burned to the ground. Nothing would be left to survive the Cathar heresy as town after town fell to the crusaders over a 40-year period: Béziers, Perpignan, Narbonne, Carcassonne, Toulouse .... At Béziers over 10,000 civilians died during the storming of the city. Torture, confessions of satanic worship and summary executions were carried out during the crusade, a recurrent practice of repression and one that foreshadowed the judicial methods of the Great Witch Panic.

Hatred and loathing for the heretics insulated the crusaders from the horrors of their mission. An emissary of the pope, on being asked how to identify Christians from Cathars, is said to have remarked: 'Kill them all. God will recognize His own.' One senior commander of the Catholic army in particular pursued the Cathars with fanatical zeal. He was Dominic Guzmán (c.1170–1221), a Spaniard who only seven years into the crusade was responsible for founding the strict religious order named after him: the Dominicans. His obsessive hatred of heresy became one of the fundamental precepts of the Dominican Order, and it helped to establish, within a few decades, a powerful new weapon to aid the Catholic Church in its fight against the schisms, sects and heresies that were ranged against it. This new weapon was the Inquisition, a finely honed scythe that would sweep across Europe in a never-ending search for heresy. The Inquisition would end the need for costly wars in the manner of the Albigensian Crusade, but it would not end the pain and suffering that such repression brought.

The Dominican Order was also known as the Order of Preachers, and it was hoped that its activities would preclude the need for further crusades against the heretics. Papal authority was soon secured that would enable the order to teach, preach and hear confessions anywhere in Christendom without the need to obtain any special authorization. Poverty became a key part of the Dominican message, perhaps because the Catholic Church had become, over the previous centuries, entangled in political and economic affairs. The simple and austere life of the monks was intended to counter the heretic view of the corpulent and corrupt Catholic Church.

The Catholic trust in armed might was not immediately forsaken, however. In 1220 Dominic also formed the Militia of Jesus Christ, a minor Dominican sect that committed its lay membership to defending the Church against the various heresies of the day (chiefly the Cathars) with arms and armour. A decade later the Dominican order oversaw the birth of the Inquisition, a purely judicial branch of the papacy that was charged with seeking out, trying and sentencing alleged heretics. Gregory IX (reigned 1227–41) became the first pope to wield this formidable weapon, and at its helm he placed trusted Dominican or Franciscan monks. Over time the Inquisition expanded its area of operations to encompass many of the European kingdoms and principalities.

Two inquisitors usually presided over individual tribunals, and these were assisted in their work by a small group of officials and counsellors. The jury was usually composed of a mix of both clergymen and ordinary citizens, who together helped the inquisitors come to some kind of a verdict. Wherever the name and earthly power of the Inquisition was respected, its officials were able to bring to trial any persons they wished and to imprison those they thought to be lying to them. In some cases they even had the power to excommunicate princes. From 1252 Pope Innocent IV (reigned 1243–54) gave the Inquisition the authority to use torture when it sought its confessions. This new twist would have the most awful repercussions for the would-be witches of future generations.

With the Albigensian Crusade over, it was the Waldensian sect that now began to draw much of the Inquisition's eager attention. Like the Cathars, the Waldensians (also known as the Vaudois) lived and practised their unique form of Christianity in southern France. Said to have been established by Waldo, a wealthy merchant from Lyons, the sect believed in the virtue of poverty, and its members renounced the authority of the pope and replaced it with the divine authority of the Bible. Papal displeasure was soon directed against this heresy, with wild stories of secret satanic rituals, sexual orgies, the stealing and devouring of babies and *maleficium* becoming theological fact. Waldensians incurred the wrath of the Inquisition, but amazingly weathered the persecutions to survive in tiny numbers. The sect practises its traditions in Europe and the United States today. In fact, despite the Church's concerted attempt to eradicate all traces of the sorcerous Vaudois sect, the name has more recently been linked with the word 'voodoo'.

In Germany a group of heretics calling themselves Luciferans were condemned by the pope as satanists and sexual deviants. In 1227 he dispatched a fanatical theologian, Conrad of Marburg, to root out these perpetrators and bring an end to the sect. Another group, an 'Adam and Eve' sect that predated modern naturism, also sprang up in Germany and was suppressed by the Church in 1286. It seemed as if heretical groups were springing up everywhere, and the Inquisition was seen as the answer to this rising tide. Its most famous victims were the mysterious Knights Templar. Over a period of years beginning in 1307 the Knights of the Order of the Temple of Solomon in Jerusalem (to give them their full title) were condemned as satanic heretics and persecuted to extinction. During the 1400s Waldensians and Luciferians continued their bitter fight against the savage Inquisition and were joined by new heresies, such as the orgiastic Brethren of the Cross.

The investigation and suppression of the Knights Templar pointed the way forward for the Inquisition. Throughout the medieval crusades, in order to liberate Jerusalem from the domination of the Saracens, the Templars had been thoroughly dedicated warriors. Mixing a monastic lifestyle with the daily hardships of desert warfare, the Templars were fundamental to the Christian mission in Palestine. But, unorthodox beliefs (stemming from decades of life mixing with Arabs and Jews) coupled with a lack of purpose and support following the final fall of Jerusalem meant that the Templars drew the unfavourable attentions of the pope. The Inquisition stole the Order's lands, rigged the trials and burned to death the Templars' leading knights.

Like the Waldensians and Cathars, the Templars were also accused of renouncing their Christian faith, of gathering at secret nocturnal meetings and performing acts of sexual profanity. These recurrent accusations seem to have been contrived by monks of the thirteenth and fourteenth centuries as they tried to stem the rise of the sects. The unfounded, and in most cases wholly fabricated, practices were designed to make the movements as unappealing as possible to orthodox Christians and to drum up support for their violent suppression. In effect, the medieval clerics were creating a fantastic 'anti-society', which they imagined lived just beyond their reach. The idea not only gained acceptance but also began to acquire a frightening life of its own. Applied without discrimination to almost any new variation on orthodox Catholicism, the stereotype encouraged intolerance, bigotry and hatred. Any heretical sect now became a secret satanic cult, meeting nocturnally to perform evil summonings and orgiastic and perverted sexual acts. Some (though not all) were also depicted as having a membership of skilled adepts of black magic, often involving the use of freshly abducted and killed babies. In trials across Europe these practices continually appeared in the confessions of those brought to trial.

During the fifteenth century members of the Waldensian sect and individual practitioners of *maleficium* (witches) were prosecuted side by side, and the magistrates presiding over these trials had little trouble differentiating between the two. Clearly some were of a well-defined heretical sect, while the witches were simply guilty of performing harmful magic. Yet that century saw a move away from indiscriminately tarring the heresies with all the trappings of an imagined satanic cult and instead focused more on the witches. Witches had always existed in European culture – they were the 'wise women' and the practitioners of magical spells for good, and in some cases, for ill. With the major Christian heresies on the run and rapidly dwindling in number, the stereotype of a Europe-wide satanic cult began to apply more and more to these witches. In 1435 the first ever account of a witch's pact with the Devil was printed in the book of demonology titled *Formicarius*. During this ritual the witches had to 'renounce Christ and his faith, baptism and the Catholic Church'. Later the magicians sealed the pact with Satan, each one 'drinks from the flask of liquid taken from murdered infants'.

This stereotype of a satanic cult came to be applied almost solely to witches on trial during the turbulent years of the sixteenth century. From 1517 onwards Martin Luther, John Calvin and others were responsible for a wave of opinion that split the Christian Church in two. This Reformation attacked some of the Catholic Church's long-held traditions and created a new Christian religion: Protestantism. It was a faith that abandoned the entrenched ritual and self-perpetuating dominance of Rome, shifting the main emphasis of the Christian beliefs onto the Bible and away from the pronouncements of the pope. Eternal salvation, as preached by the leading figures of the Reformation, now depended on the faith of individual believers and not on a set of requirements dictated by the Catholic Church. Protestantism provided a welcome alternative to the harsh and rigid dogma of the Catholic Church, but its leaders could be as harsh as any inquisitor – the Frenchman Calvin was quick to punish his opponents and freely burned Protestant 'heretics' at the stake. Protestant magistrates in Germany and Scotland presided over some of the harshest and most fanatical trials of the Great Witch Panic.

So widely received was Protestantism in many parts of Europe that the pope could no longer hope to stigmatize its followers with blunt and unsubstantiated claims of Devil worship and cannibalistic infanticide. Instead, it was now those individuals with some claim to *maleficium*, as well as their associates and a huge number of innocent people, who began to feel the wrath of the religious propagandists. And this low-key, yet pervasive crusade would last not decades, but centuries.

Malleus Maleficarum

Gradually, the stereotype of the witch took shape and became more clearly defined. Most of the accused were women, although men and even children could be, and were, charged with witchcraft. In many cases the profile of the witches' initiation, indoctrination and satanic life followed a distinct pattern, full of oft-repeated incidents and events. The soon-to-be witch was often in some state of distress, often isolated and alone, a woman with a grudge against her community. At this point the Devil would appear to her, either as a man or an animal, and offer her some comfort or financial reward. Sometimes the Devil intimidated her or forced her to follow him. The witch's initiation always revolved around the sex act, and mating with the Devil became one of the single most frequently repeated confessions of witches on trial. It should be noted that this was usually a painful experience for the woman (or man) involved. Pledging allegiance to her new master, the witch would renounce her Christian faith and baptism and was often physically scarred by the Devil's own hand.

Demonologist and writer Francesco-Maria Guazzo compiled a list of the elements that went to make up this initiation ceremony. In most cases the list runs like a black parody of established Catholic ritual:

1 Denial of the Christian Faith: 'I deny the creator of heaven and earth. I deny my baptism. I deny the worship I formerly paid to God. I adhere to the Devil and believe only in thee.'
2 Re-baptism by the Devil with a new name.
3 Symbolic removal of the baptismal chrism (the consecrated oil).
4 Denial of godparents and assigning of new sponsors.
5 Token surrender to the Devil of a piece of clothing.
6 Swearing allegiance to the Devil while standing within a magic circle on the ground.
7 Request to the Devil for their name to be written in the Book of Death.
8 Promise to sacrifice children to the Devil.
9 Promise to pay annual tribute to the assigned demon.
10 Marking with the Devil's mark in various parts of the body.
11 Vows of service to the Devil: never to adore the sacrament; to smash holy relics; never to use holy water or candles; and to keep silence on their traffic with Satan.

The great prize of every newly initiated witch was the granting of powers of *maleficium*, the black arts of harmful magic. With these spells the witch could create strife among her enemies in various ways, from killing cattle to causing the affliction of a sudden illness on, or the death of, a man, woman or child. She could also raise great rain or hail storms, spoil food or drink and cause impotence or mis-carriages. The power to do this derived in part from the Devil himself, who granted the ability to use *maleficium* on his initiates, and in part from the efficacious ingredients obtained from the bodies of human babies – or so the allegations ran. It was common for witches to con-fess under torture to that most appalling of all human crimes – the abduction and murder of babies. The purpose of this seemed to be two-fold. First, some magical property associated with the new-born greatly aided the casting of the witch's spells. Baby fat was often quoted as a main ingredient in the formulation of the witches' 'flying ointment' that, when smeared over the woman's body, was said to give her the power to fly through the air – usually to a night-time meeting of witches. Second, witches just loved to eat babies. This devilish craving could almost have been purposely designed to provoke the most intense loathing and anger among all upstanding medieval folk. Most wicked of all, the witch often delighted in catching and cooking those children who were not yet baptized – thus throwing their fate in the afterlife into question.

Torture not only extracted confessions of satanic crimes from the suspected witch but forced her to name her accomplices. Nocturnal flights to a witches' gathering allowed her to consort with her magical sisterhood, and interrogators always demanded a list of names of those attending these meetings. Initially called 'synagogues', the meetings later came to be known as 'sabbats', and they were attended by the witches of a neighbourhood, meeting together at a traditional spot such as a crossroads or gallows (both sites long associated with witch-craft from Greek and Roman times). Larger sabbats took place only once or twice each year, and they were attended by huge numbers of witches from across the world. Because of their size, these great sab-bats were held in some remote place, such as the summit of a high mountain. Despite the application of the magical flying ointment, a witch always travelled to a sabbat riding either an animal or an imple-ment. Of the latter, shovels, pitchforks and broomsticks proved most popular. Such was the speed and ease with which the witch could travel to and from the sabbat that a sleeping spouse would often be oblivious to such occult activities.

What was commonly imagined to take place at a sabbat is known from well-documented confessions provided by suspects under tor-ture. The Devil himself appeared at the sabbat and presided over it. Unlike his earlier incarnation, he now appeared as a monstrous black-coloured creature – that fabulous goat-man, typically associated with the appearance of the Devil in popular culture. This huge and power-ful 'black man' stood upright on goat's legs; he had the horns of a ram growing from his head; and he was bearded. His horrible appearance was often highlighted by various effects of light and flame. As the witches congregated around him, they began, one by one, to pray to their master. They affirmed their faith, repeated their renunciation of Christ and God and then proceeded to kiss the Devil, most often on his anus. As the ceremony progressed, the punishments began. Witches who had failed to perform their allotted feats of evil magic, witches who had been to church despite their new allegiance, and witches who had failed to attend the previous sabbat were all summarily whipped on the orders of the Devil. There then followed a black mass, a satanic parody of the Christian ceremony, with mock robes – all coloured black – being worn. Warnings and promises were dispensed by Satan, and gifts would sometimes be offered to him as he sat on his black throne. The bread and wine given during this ritual were always black and disgusting, for both food and liquid were supposed to be fetid, horrible-tasting substances.

The witches' sabbat always climaxed in a profane orgy of sexual abandon. Male and female witches cavorted with each other and with demons, and they assembled in a circle and danced counter-clockwise (known as 'widdershins') – the dance of the Devil. Amid the orgiastic rites there were often reported incidents of sodomy and incest. Sometimes the Devil would move among the participants, copulating with every one of his followers in turn. With the gathering of witches reaching its end, each was given a list of victims against whom they should perform *maleficium* before the next sabbat. And so at last the witches flew back to their homes and began again the life of apparent normalcy that hid a terrible secret.

Witchcraft began to be characterized in this way during the 1400s, and although it sometimes followed a variety of other patterns, it coalesced into a distinct collection of traditions and customs. By the late fifteenth and early sixteenth century a well-defined corpus of beliefs had become established. Across the length and breadth of Europe, witches were confessing to a repeated pattern of satanic crimes. They paid homage to the same Devil-figure at the same night-time orgies and performed the same horrible crimes in his name. At this point we come to a crucial question in the study of the Great Witch Panic. We must ask: how did witches confess to the same crimes and set of beliefs, although they were separated by hundreds of kilometres and bound by a well-observed tradition of secrecy? Did such a cult actually exist? Existence would certainly explain the amazing similarities between totally separate and discrete confessions. Could such diverse people as an eight-year-old child, a housewife and a wealthy prince all create the same individual fantasy when accused of witchcraft and brought to trial? Surely their accounts must have been based on a core of truth: that there *were* witches and there *was* a witch cult. Fact or fiction?

For the demonologists of the witch hunts, this would be an absurd question. Of course there was a witch cult: it threatened society, and it threatened Christendom. Although such a belief faltered and disappeared altogether as witch hunting ceased, it has more recently undergone a startling new revival. The matter is not as clear cut as it might first seem. A large body of academic opinion has been thrown behind the theory of an actual historical witch cult. These academics, once led by the famous anthropologist and Egyptologist, Dr Margaret Murray, are firm believers in the *fact* of medieval witchcraft. Murray argued quite persuasively in her book *The Witch-Cult in Western Europe* that a strong and vital thread of pagan worship survived the Christian conversion of Europe and that its adherents continued to worship its female deity into medieval times. Its ceremonies became known to witch hunters as the satanic sabbats. We shall explore the historical evidence for the witch cult later, but first, what of the alternative?

Even more disturbing than the existence of a witch society is anther explanation: that the ever-expanding and learned body of witch evidence was introduced into the confessions by the investigators themselves. Judges conducting trials undoubtedly fused elements of the accusations with their own particular dark fantasies and with reports of other cases. Overlain with a thick veneer of demonological and theological interpretation, the final results would have been a flimsy excuse for law. The presiding investigators would stop at nothing to extract confessions of activities that they believed to have been carried out. When a judge had his suspicions confirmed through torture, the case acquired a certain validity and would then be used as an example by other judges. Each case became one more link in the chain of pain stretching across Germany and into the rest of Europe.

We know that information gleaned from the confessions of witches at trial was collected and disseminated to other magistrates and inquisitors. From about 1550 to 1700 a huge library of demonic literature sprang up, and this information, based on what the writers had heard about or read in trial documents, became accepted as authoritative by the lawyers of the day. In addition, several books were written that allowed such material to be more widely read, perhaps the most influential of which was the *Malleus Maleficarum* (the infamous 'Hammer of Witches'). As more horrifying scandals came to light, each was gradually absorbed into this growing corpus of satanic literature. Witch confessions, catalogued and detailed, would help a trial judge to formulate his questions. After he had extracted the confessions of guilt, the list of satanic and heretical crimes might now be elaborated one stage further, by himself, by witnesses or by the accused themselves. This, in turn, would find its way into a new treatise on witchcraft. Printing, at the time a revolutionary new invention, speeded up this process still further. Like a beast out of control, it grew wilder and wilder, creating ever more bizarre confessions. These provided prompts, leading questions and suggestions with which the magistrates and inquisitors could bait their suspects. And once an innocent suspect had been fed the lies, crippling tortures could be used to force her to confess to each and every one of them.

The *Malleus Maleficarum* became, in effect, a handbook for witchfinders, magistrates and inquisitors. It provided a full and detailed analysis of medieval witchcraft and gave the reader carefully argued advice on how best to prosecute a witch trial. It was a terrible book, which was ultimately responsible for the torture or execution of hundreds of thousands of victims. Within 40 years it had been reprinted 14 times, a clear indication of its popularity (among academics and magistrates, at any rate). Its authors, Heinrich Krämer and Jakob Sprenger, were leading inquisitors of their day. Both Dominicans, they were obsessively caught up with the idea of the witch hunt. Krämer, in particular, had built up a reputation for himself in the Tyrol, where, from 1474, he pursued witches mercilessly. Various acts of deceit and fakery got Krämer into serious trouble with his local bishop. On one occasion, he had a female accomplice hide within an oven and, masquerading as the Devil, denounce local people as his followers. The torture of these innocent victims inevitably followed. For such acts as this, Krämer's bishop finally expelled him, and in his search for support, the unbalanced cleric appealed to the pope for help in his witch hunts. What came out of this meeting between Innocent VIII and Heinrich Krämer was the papal bull, *Summis desiderantes*, of 1484 – the pope's personal command to let the witch hunters carry out their work unhindered.

Within two years Krämer had collaborated with Sprenger to compile the 250,000-word tome: *Malleus Maleficarum*. Sprenger, too, had been an inquisitor since 1470 and had collaborated with Krämer on a number of witch trials. Both drew on past cases to support various arguments within the book. As a guide to the hunting and prosecuting of witches, the *Malleus* benefited immensely from immediate official sanction, since Krämer and Sprenger had the 1484 papal bull printed as a foreword. In this way the book, mainly derived from a collection of Tyrolean folk-tales and legends, gained a stature and acceptance it is doubtful it would ever have otherwise achieved. In addition, Krämer's collected Tyrolean folk legends now had an unprecedented audience of eager new readers. Most of these tales concerned witches and their magical activities, and Krämer seems to have embellished these legends with an obscene mix of Devil worship and ritual baby eating.

In the very first part of the book, the black and white nature of the struggle is clearly explained: 'all those who are commonly called sorcerers, and those too who are skilled in the art of divination, incur the penalty of death.' Witchcraft, says the *Malleus Maleficarum*, is high treason, and any witness may come forward to give evidence. This will usually be followed with the suspect being:

> put to the torture in order to make them confess. Any person, whatever his rank or position, upon such an accusation may be put to the torture, and he who is found guilty, even if he confesses his crime, let him be racked, let him suffer all other tortures prescribed by law in order that he may be punished in proportion to his offences.

Those individuals who denied the fact of witchcraft took a dangerous line. The *Malleus* makes it clear that such unbelievers are themselves heretics and presumably liable to the same tortures and punishments as any witch.

From these harsh and uncompromising beginnings, the book goes on to codify all manner of rules for the capture and imprisonment of a suspected witch, her stripping and shaving and then the searching of her (for evidence of any 'superstitious objects'). Finally, the inquisitor 'should have ... engines of torture brought before her' and pronounce that 'she will have to endure these if she does not confess'. The two Dominicans freely advise on the best strategies for achieving a confession, stressing that torture has a legitimate place in the interrogation of captured witches: 'let her be often and frequently exposed to torture.'

Malleus Maleficarum was an important book of its age. It did not initiate the witch-hunting frenzy, nor did it take the hunt into new directions, but it legitimized and codified the prosecutions. It was a legal tool, not a populist piece of fanatical propaganda. And it was not alone. There were many books of the same ilk, and some of those published at a much later date were able completely to encapsulate the concept of the witch and her activities. In this, the *Malleus* was in some ways deficient. It does not, for example, give any details about the witches' sabbat, a crucial part of the stereotype that indisputably links witchcraft with heretical behaviour and satanic worship. Other widely read books included the 1524 *Tractatus de Hereticis et Sortilegiis*, the 1595 book *Demonolatreiae,* the *Disquisitionum Magicarum Libri Sex* and the 1602 *Discours des Sorciers*. The German *Practica Rerum Criminalium*, published for the first time in 1635, became notorious as a *Malleus Maleficarum* for the Protestants, who were just as eager as the Catholics to pursue and punish witchcraft in their lands. If one work in particular illustrated the way in which case histories, testimonies and confessions were used and reused, ready for a new generation of inquisitors, then the Italian *Compendium Maleficarum* was it. Written in 1608 by a friar, Francesco-Maria Guazzo, it borrowed heavily not only from the *Malleus* , but also from several of the books mentioned above. It also merged elements of a whole host of different sources. Demonologists, those academics who specialized in the study of witches and their satanic rites, were scrupulous collectors of additional 'evidence'. Information, gained from trials and books on witchcraft, was constantly added to the growing wealth of 'witch lore'. Hardly anything was consciously subtracted from this pregnant body of knowledge; nothing was satisfactorily disproved or found to be false.

What did this mass of demoniacal literature mean to the common men and women, living their lives amid the communities of illiterate peasant farmers of Europe? Very little. Minimal effort was expended by the Inquisition, by magistrates or by the Church to convince the peasantry of the existence of witches. For rural folk, local magicians and wise women were already a well-accepted fact, along with a complex array of supernatural beings and beliefs. Boggarts, brownies, imps, incubi and succubi, goblins and other bugbears all existed on the fantastical fringe of medieval village life. What these books helped the authorities to do was link together these magical traditions with satanism. The supernatural beings became the demonic servants of the Devil, while the neighbourhood witches became his priests and priestesses. And this link was a difficult one to forge, taking decades, even centuries to create. In many locales, of course, the rural folk continued to see *maleficium* simply as evil magic and witches simply as practitioners of that magic. It required a concerted campaign to convince the community of the frightening satanic nature of these phenomena. Church sermons and the reading out of charges at public executions were the two main ways in which the hierarchy 'educated' the lower classes in the ways of witches and demons.

Pursuing the Enemy

The popular image of the witch is almost certainly that of an old hag, dressed in black robes with a tall, black hat riding to a sabbat on her broomstick. Invariably, she is a woman with a black cat and a propensity to create sinister brews in a large, black cauldron. When we look at what the investigators of the fifteenth, sixteenth and seventeenth centuries believed and pursued, we discover a different image. The witch could be a man, or even a child. It could be someone old and ugly, or it could just as easily be a willowy young maiden. The inquisitors were so diligent – and so paranoid – that they suspected anyone of witchcraft. No one, from the richest nobleman to the lowliest swineherd, was automatically free from suspicion. It must be remembered that witchcraft was seen not as the profession of misguided old women but as the membership of a satanic cult, a secret society of Devil-worshippers and deviants. Brooms, pitchforks and other paraphernalia were said to be used by witches in order to fly to the sabbat. Black cats (as well as all manner of other creatures) *were* often found to be the personal demons (or 'familiars') of witches, but familiars could also be dogs, rats, birds and insects – or any other kind of creature for that matter.

Women, often impoverished and lonely, did indeed, however, seem to have made up a significant portion of the witches brought to trial by the authorities. Why? One has only to turn to the bigoted and misogynist pages of the *Malleus Maleficarum*, and in particular to one section entitled, 'Why Superstition is Chiefly Found in Women'. The

book continually degrades women, their weaknesses, their wicked-
ness, their foolishness and their lustfulness. 'Since they are feebler
both in mind and body,' declare the writers, 'it is not surprising that
they should come under the spell of witchcraft.' Sexuality became a
driving force in the witch hunts, with celibate Church officials often
prosecuting women whom they thought were obsessed with satanism
and sexual abandon. The *Malleus* makes it clear: 'All witchcraft comes
from carnal lust.' It was a preoccupation with sex and its inherent evil
that shot through many of the trial confessions. Women were considered weak, lustful and conniving – the very attributes sought by the
Devil for his disciples.

In identifying a witch, the witch hunters first sought a 'devil mark'
on his or her body. This was a secret and well-hidden mark made on
the witch's body by the Devil during the initiation rites. It varied in
shape but was commonly found to be in the shape of a cloven hoof.
Investigators sought such a mark under men's eyelids, in the armpits
and on the lips or the anus. On women they looked for the mark of the
Devil on the breasts or the groin. Shaving a witch helped in this
process. Existence of such a mark (a mole, birthmark or other skin
imperfection) was, of course, proof of a satanic compact. Even without
a 'devil mark', the investigator could still prove his point (quite literally). An invisible mark could still exist on the woman, and this was
found by 'pricking' the witch's skin with a small pin-like implement.
An invisible mark was painless and did not bleed. Some torturers
were not above using retractable-bladed 'witch prickers', which
allowed them to implicate any prisoner that they chose.

Torture was universally thought to be the only method of obtaining
a true confession from a witch, for the demons possessing her gave her
considerable mental resilience against them. And so torture till confession was commonly practised. A cruel 'no-win' situation existed
anywhere torture was practised. It forced an innocent person, accused
by people whose identity she would never learn, to confess to crimes
put to her by the judge. She would be tortured until she confessed to
these charges – or died resisting the pain. It was common practice to
force from her the names of her fellow witches and co-conspirators,
and to avoid even more crippling tortures, the poor woman would reel
off a list of names at random. Sometimes these people would be apprehended by the authorities and be subjected to torture and forced to
confess.

One particularly brutal trial around 1590 depended on the accusations of five children from the village of Warboys in Cambridgeshire.
Nine-year-old Jane Throckmorton and her sisters accused an elderly
neighbour, Alice Samuel, of casting spells that caused Jane to have
fits. According to the girl, Alice was able to bring an end to the fits by
reciting a spell that included some reference to witchcraft. They even

pretended that they could see invisible imps at the old woman's feet. After several years Alice Samuels was forced to confess to practising witchcraft, and by that time both her husband and daughter were being accused of witchcraft by the Throckmorton children. In 1593 all three members of the family were hanged.

Reliance on the testimony of children was not used at all times and in all places, but it does indicate to what lengths the ecclesiastical authorities would go to pursue their imagined enemies. Following the Samuels's trial, there were outbreaks of children-inspired trials in other parts of England and across Europe. Although the Warboys trial had been held in England, relatively few convicted witches were actually executed there, at least compared with the numbers reached on the continent. Of perhaps 100,000 executions carried out for witchcraft up to about 1700, only 5000 were executed in England and Scotland. Burning at the stake became the preferred method of execution on the continent, while in England death by hanging was the norm.

In order to gain a confession, conviction and ultimately an execution, the Catholic Inquisition applied itself almost mercilessly to the task. It gave little quarter and stacked the odds unashamedly in its own favour. Of all the miscarriages perpetrated, one of the greatest was the fact that any person accused of witchcraft was automatically assumed to be guilty – until such time as she could prove her innocence. Gossip and hearsay became the most common way in which a suspect could find herself on trial. A suspect would never know who had accused her or who was giving testimony against her. It had been Pope Innocent IV who, in 1254, had granted witnesses and accusers the privilege of anonymity. Those witnesses who later retracted their testimony, for whatever reason, were liable for prosecution for perjury, yet the words that he or she had submitted for the Inquisition were allowed to remain as evidence. Every one of these witnesses was hostile to the accused witch, because local people wishing to testify on her behalf were not allowed to do so. Nor would they, for fear of being tarred with the same brush. Witchcraft was contagious. Because of this, even lawyers would shun witchcraft cases and would risk being charged with heresy if they attempted to defend a suspect. The victim had to defend herself – yet the only admissible testimony she could give was proof of her own guilt. This was dark justice indeed.

In all, the papal Inquisition was a systematized and regularized machine of death. Once accused of some *maleficium* by neighbours or local gossip, an innocent victim would be set on a painful and long-drawn-out procedure that would inevitably result in his or her execution. Organized by well-educated and intelligent professionals, the Inquisition chewed up and spat out countless poverty-stricken, ill-informed and uneducated rural peasants. Many had little chance to counter seriously any of the charges put to them, and in any case, the threat and use of torture would quickly bring argued debate and protestations to an abrupt end. As the mayor of Bamberg, Johannes Junius, wrote in a letter to his daughter just before his execution: 'Innocent I came into prison, innocent I was tortured, innocent I must die. For whoever comes into the witch prison must become a witch – or be tortured until he invents something out of his head and, God pity him, thinks something up.'

Officially, torture was to be used only as a last resort, but it was frequently used at a much earlier stage in most trials. Many courts employed it, but the Inquisition actually extended and regularized its use. As a means to root out heresy, Pope Innocent IV had sanctioned the use of torture by his agents in 1257. The official decree, or papal bull, that legitimized the use of torture was entitled *Ad extirpanda*, and it continued to be legally binding until its abolition in 1816. Although the bull allowed torture to be used in extracting confessions from suspect witches, it was technically unlawful to repeat a torture if it did not produce the desired results. Inventive inquisitors were able, however, to 'continue' torture at some later period, without breaking any law. Three sessions of torture were typically held, during which time the prisoner usually confessed to the heresy of witchcraft. In order to secure this confession, many judges forced the witch to confess a second time in sight of the torture chamber and its implements. Thus the inquisitor was able to declare a 'confession without torture', not only a misleading statement but a wholly inaccurate one.

Torture already had a place in the traditional legal system. It was, however, the widespread and regular use of this legal mechanism that has since given the name of the Inquisition such a chilling air. Three centuries of torture allowed several refinements in procedure that greatly enhanced the persuasiveness of the techniques but that spared nothing for its innocent (and even its guilty) victims. The *Malleus Maleficarum* set out all the procedures – the stripping of the prisoner, the emotional attempt to have her confess in front of the torture equipment, which stood prepared and ready, and the feigned initiation of the tortures, with a sudden halt in the proceedings – and a final plea for a confession. When all failed, the torture was begun with continued requests for a confession, beginning with the lighter charges and progressing to the more serious charges as time went on.

The tortures varied, from the seemingly innocuous 'cold water baths' to the most horrifying physical tortures imaginable, including the 'rack'. As the Inquisition could make little headway in England, the tortures employed there were less severe than elsewhere. Among the German principalities, where the Great Witch Panic had firm hold of both the state and people, the Inquisition reigned supreme. It inflicted a wide range of tortures on its victims in order to secure confessions of witchcraft. At the lower end of the range of practices were the tortures designed specifically to discomfort the suspect witch, including continued sleep deprivation and immersion in ice-cold water.

More physical tortures included the thumbscrews (charmingly known in England as the 'pilliwinks'), which crushed and deformed a victim's fingers, whippings, painful leg vices, stocks fitted with iron spikes and baths of scalding water (to which burning lime could be added). A simple and effective torture involved the stacking of weighty stones or iron bars onto a board that lay across a victim, crushing her ribs and causing asphyxiation. Everyone has heard of the 'ducking stool', the simple wooden mechanism used throughout the panic to immerse bound witch suspects into a river or pond. King James I of England (reigned 1603–25) also sanctioned the practice of witch 'swimming' whereby a bound suspect was thrown into a river. If she floated, she was guilty of witchcraft; if she sank to the bottom, she was innocent – and would usually drown unless the villagers quickly hauled her back to the riverbank. In his book *Demonologie* (1597) King James justified this practice by stating: 'God has appointed, for a supernatural sign of the monstrous impiety of the witches, that the water shall refuse to receive in her bosom those who have shaken off the sacred water of baptism and wilfully refused its benefit.' And thus they were forced up and to the surface by the waters of the river or pond – into the waiting arms of the gallows.

At the extreme end of the painful tortures were the twin practices of strappado and squassation. Strappado involved hoisting the victim off the ground by ropes after heavy weights had been tied to her feet. Muscles, tendons, joints – all would be stretched to excruciating limits. Left for hours on end to endure this agony, the prisoner would confess to anything. The fiendish imaginations of the torturers were able to refine this technique to create the technique called squassation. After long periods of suspension from the chamber's ceiling, the victim would be hoisted right up to the wheel of the pulley and then suddenly let down, almost to the floor. After hours of stretching, this sudden jerk would violently dislocate the prisoner's joints. The ladder, or rack, which similarly stretched the unfortunate victim and dislocated arms and legs, is today popularly regarded as one of the most common medieval tortures.

The ingenuity of the Inquisition developed ever more bizarre, inhuman and effective tortures that were commonly inflicted on innocent victims of the Great Witch Panic. They included using a rope to cause friction burns around the neck, so deep as to cut to the bone; the burning of tarred feathers stuck into the armpits and groin; force feeding on a diet of salted herring and the denial of water; and the 'prayer stool', a kneeling board mounted with rows of painfully sharp wooden pegs.

All of the tortures mentioned here were employed by the Inquisition in Bamberg, as well as in towns and cities across Europe.

Away from the Inquisition

The brutality and inhumanity of the tortures and the diligence and obsessive behaviour of those seeking to carry them out, climaxed in Germany in the early 1600s. France, too, was caught up within the panic, but the other kingdoms of the continent less so. In comparison, the English witch trials were a comparatively minor affair. This fact can help us understand what really motivated the witch hunters, why they flourished in one place and not another. Of overriding importance was the fact that the pope's Inquisition had little power across the Channel. Before the craze took a firm hold, King Henry VIII had split from the Catholic Church and declared himself independent from any decisions the pope cared to make. Thus Innocent VIII's 1484 bull had little influence among the courts of England, and the *Malleus* did not receive an English translation until modern times. This had some bearing not only on the scale of the witch hunts in England but also on the nature of English witchcraft.

Three main components can be recognized in European witchcraft; first, as we have already seen, there was *maleficium*, the casting of evil magic; second, there was a satanic pact; and third, there was a grand gathering of diabolists, at which black mass was celebrated – the sabbat. All three aspects are found in many different combinations on the continent during the climax of the witch craze. In England, however, *maleficium* seemed to dominate and witchcraft had little connection with the Devil or with an 'anti-society' practising satanism. On the continent, confessions of diabolism and attendance at sabbats were often made only after torture had begun. This would explain the very low incidence of satanic confessions in England, since tortures in that country were, if they were used at all, usually of a much milder form. It also helps to support the idea that any evidence of a satanic witch cult was introduced by the European judges who presided over torture. Three witches tried for witchcraft on the Channel Island of Guernsey in 1617 were found guilty of performing *maleficium* and faced execution. Following the pronouncement of sentence, however, one of the women, Colette Du Mont, announced that she was a witch. The judge could not get any more from her and had the woman tortured. This produced a confession that included her relationship with the Devil and her attendance at the local sabbats. Torture at the very last minute had produced an utterly fantastic confession.

Unlike the rest of Europe, which was pitched headlong into the Catholic frenzy of fear, English witchcraft was usually seen as a secular offence rather than as a religious heresy. Witches, sorcerers and other magic users had existed on the fringes of English society for many years, and they suffered from both the bad press of their fellows on the continent and from an international paranoia that pervaded towns, villages, courtrooms and palaces from Sweden to Scotland, from Germany to Spain. The first great English witch trial was held in Chelmsford in 1566, only three years after Queen Elizabeth I had put forward legislation to curb witchcraft. The three female suspects were Agnes Waterhouse, her daughter, Joan, and Elizabeth Francis. Their confessions were gained through close questioning by several important officials, notably Sir Gilbert Gerard, the Attorney General, and John Southcote, one of the Queen's judges. The court was able to discover all about Elizabeth Francis's feats of magic, her curses, her ability to cause lameness and death and the relationship that she enjoyed with her cat familiar, which was called Satan. Initially imprisoned for 12 months, Elizabeth Francis was brought before the court 13 years later and hanged. Her crimes then, as before, were the use of evil magic to bring harm to others – *maleficium*.

Chelmsford gained an unenviable reputation for witch hunting for the 1566 trial, and two more famous trials were to follow, in 1579 and in 1589. The St Osyth witches of Essex were also tried in Chelmsford in 1582. England's witch hunting climaxed in Essex with the rise to prominence of the 'witch-finder general', Matthew Hopkins, in 1645. Witchcraft was taken seriously in other parts of the kingdom, but without the driving power of the terrible Inquisition, these witch hunts were local affairs that would cause a stir when only half a dozen witches were tried together. Compare the largest English execution of 19 women in 1645 with the mass-burnings of a hundred or more witches at a time in parts of Germany. Nevertheless, around one thousand men and women were hanged as witches across the country, many hundreds of them in Essex.

Following the return of the English monarchy under Charles II in 1660, the hangings slackened in pace and, after 1684, stopped altogether. It was not until 1723 that the execution of witches stopped in Scotland, however. Unlike the authorities in England, the Scottish courts proved more than willing to search out and execute suspects. Upwards of 4000 men, women and children were tied to the stake (witches were burned in Scotland, not hanged) for witch crimes. The ferocity of Scottish torture could be compared with some of the worst depravities of the German cities, and the persecution burned brighter and for longer than that south of the border. The difference in approach was again due to the difference in religion. The Scottish Church was Presbyterian, an outgrowth of the Protestant Reformation of the sixteenth century. Like the English Church, it had no connection with the Roman Catholic Inquisition, yet its Presbyterian clerics took it upon themselves to pursue witches in the same manner. They could also work in concert with the secular courts to prosecute their suspects.

Eventually, after three hundred years, the madness stopped. A reappraisal of the witch hunts confirmed the horrible truth: there was no satanic conspiracy and no international witch cult. The Bible had never mentioned one; nor did the early Christian writers. At last, the Age of Reason, the Enlightenment, swept any notion of sorcery, witchcraft and satanic sabbats away. The cost had been between 100,000 and 200,000 lives and the psychological well-being of a continent. No one had been truly free of the persecutions or their ominous shadow. Fear and terror had become an established part of life throughout the fifteenth, sixteenth and seventeenth centuries. But if the witch hunts had been initiated all those generations ago by the ecclesiastical authority of the Inquisition to crush heresy, why were they then allowed suddenly to slacken and die?

During the thriving years of the witch hunt a new intellectual and cultural tide, the Renaissance, was rising. Renaissance thought revived aspects of Greek and Roman culture to challenge established medieval learning and thought. Witchcraft was part of that medieval learning. Key figures in the humanist movement did voice some opposition to the horrors of the witch trials. But the rationalist voices of people like Agrippa of Nettesheim (also known as Cornelius Agrippa; 1486–1535) and Desiderius Erasmus (c.1466–1536) were not heard over the clamour for more victims. Renaissance philosophy, called neo-Platonism, did not discount the existence of either the Devil or workable magic, and so any argument that tried to prove that witchcraft did not exist was doomed to failure. By the mid-seventeenth century the intellectual revolution had gained many followers who were far more sceptical about the power of the Devil to intervene in earthly affairs. This, combined with tougher rules on court procedures – such as the need for tangible evidence of *maleficium*, restrictions on the use of torture and the abandonment of the Devil's mark as evidence – gradually brought the Great Witch Panic to a halt. Scepticism had grown significantly by the end of the seventeenth century, spurred by a philosophical system that required the educated man to question everything, including authority. A rational outlook was sought, one that saw the universe as ordered and stable and operating according to natural laws. Supernatural activities were beginning to be dismissed or explained with these laws.

Of course, the peasant communities continued to believe in the existence of magic, of *maleficium*, but once the magistrates, judges and, to some extent, the Church were exposed to this less claustrophobic climate of belief, witch hunting rapidly declined.

The Witch Cult

For the people of the witch-hunting era, magic was a reality. This cannot be denied. It was a legacy that had been inherited from the Romanized Gauls and Britons. At the Roman baths in the English city of Bath, small lead curses have been discovered in great profusion, each scrawled with an individual curse to an enemy. These *defixio* were thought to be an effective way to harm a thief or a hated neighbour, and they were a simple method of casting magic. The curse retained its mystic potency into the medieval period, often merging inextricably with traditional prayer. When Margery Bluck from Hereford cursed Mary Davies in 1630 by 'praying to God that an evil end might come of her', was this a prayer or magical curse? Calling the Devil to curse one's enemies was also a common enough occurrence, as was the use of local magical stones or wells, which almost guaranteed that a curse would never fail to take effect. One particularly perverted kind of curse was the 'black fast', carried out by an injured party to harm another. Elizabeth Parker of Bowland had publicly declared her intention to carry out a fast, which had the power to harm another person, against her victim, Edmund Parker, in 1519, and she was hauled up in front of the ecclesiastical court of Whalley as a result. Black fasts were banned by the Bishop of Durham later that century.

Wax dolls, made in the likeness of an enemy and skewered with pins in the hope of causing harm to that person, were also popular. The authorities often searched out such images for fear that they represented a member of the royal family. Such dolls and the fear of their effectiveness did exist. *Maleficium*, then, was a reality for those who practised it, for its victims and for those who sought to bring it to an end. These witches carried out their black craft across the continent, but were they alone, dabbling in primitive magic without the help of others? Or were they far more organized, forming a witch cult?

For Greek and Roman writers, witchcraft was likewise a dark reality, and witches were known to gather at crossroads during the night. They called on Hecate, goddess of magic, to blight crops, wound people and summon storms. Hecate, the black sheep of the Olympian pantheon, became the embodiment of dark magic and evil rituals for the ancients. At night she would stalk the land accompanied by a legion of undead corpses, and she was often associated with *empusae*, demons who appeared as beautiful women and waylaid travellers in order that they could feast on their warm blood. Hecate was a triple goddess, reigning on earth as Diana, goddess of the hunt; in heaven as Luna, goddess of the moon; and as Proserpine, goddess of the underworld. Embracing all three aspects of the universe she became the symbol of nature's never-ending cycle. Her triple identity was represented by either three bodies or three heads (images vary) and by the three phases of the moon.

Hecate's priestesses were witches, the adepts of harmful magic, of curses, poisons and the control of spirits. Whether a witch or not, any Greek or Roman citizen who wished to curse his neighbour invoked Hecate's name to do so. According to classical writers, the witches of Hecate did gather together for the worship of their macabre goddess, although the satanic overtones were obviously absent from their ceremonies. Even at this early date, before the Christian witch hunts and the rise of the hated heresies, popular folklore recognized that a cult of darkness and death existed just out of sight. Later, in the Frankish kingdoms and among the Vikings, witches were also thought to meet at secret nocturnal gatherings. The priestesses favoured locations considered holy or 'magic-rich', including crossroads, tombs and the scenes of murders.

Memory of Hecate survived the fall of Rome, and under the name Diana, she is believed by some academics to have re-emerged as a pagan goddess during the Middle Ages. Witches at this early period were also referred to as 'night-riders' and were considered to be blood-sucking demons flying through the night sky on their way to cult ceremonies. Witchcraft beliefs mixed elements of the *empusae* myth and aspects of the religion of Diana to create a new kind of pagan cult. Little proof exists of this clandestine religion apart from scattered words and phrases in the early Church literature. For example, St Caesarius exorcized a young French girl in the sixth century, naming 'the demon whom the peasants call Diana'. In one case in 1318, the night-riders were referred to as 'Dianae', and they were supposed to have slept with magicians at the court of Pope John XXII.

The Catholic Church was deeply affected by stories of Diana, or Hecate, and her train of seductive, vampire demonesses. It transferred the Roman concept of Diana and the nocturnal meetings and horrible rituals to the paranoid mind-set of early medieval Europe. Women, of course, were prime suspects for this kind of activity, since they traditionally made up the largest part of Hecate's followers. Every awful power originally ascribed to the demonesses of classical mythology was now being associated with Diana's witches. They fed on babies, they flew to night-time meetings, they cast evil magic, and they seduced morally upstanding men. How much of this actually happened is unknown; how much of it the rural peasantry believed is also unknown. All that we do know is that the cult is mentioned briefly here and there in religious literature. During the rise of the European heresies, the cult of Diana, real or imagined, faded from view, to be replaced in the fifteenth century by the satanic conspiracy already described. Now the Devil, not Diana, was alleged to preside over the witches' coven.

The devotees of Diana did not completely disappear. Margaret Murray saw in these early myths and Church beliefs the bare bones of a religion that she believed actually existed. In addition, the religion continued through into the nightmare years of the Great Witch Panic, to be persecuted as the 'witch cult'. Murray examined evidence from selected witch trials and was able to build up a picture of this secret fertility cult.

If there was a modern book that had as much impact on witchcraft as did the *Malleus Maleficarum*, then that book would be Margaret Murray's *The Witch-Cult in Western Europe*. This overturned centuries of uncompromising religious propaganda and replaced it with something different again. Not only did the book take the academic world by storm on its publication in 1921, but it led eventually to the 'legitimization' of witchcraft and the formation of an entirely new Western religion: Wicca. However, a book is a milestone only if it is preceded by others, cautiously marking the way. Margaret Murray's central influence seems to have been the ground-breaking anthropological work of Sir James Frazer, *The Golden Bough*. Published initially in 1890, Frazer's work had grown to 12 volumes by 1915, and it changed the way in which magic and ritual were perceived by Western minds. *The Golden Bough* looked at magic in ancient history as well as the tribal magic being practised around the world and linked much of the ritual and ceremony of magic with the fertility of sacred plants. The fertility god and the universal myths that accompanied him were seen under the guise of gods from many different mythologies. Essentially, Frazer had postulated a worldwide 'fertility cult'. Margaret Murray linked the oft-theorized witch cult with the fertility religion and produced her famous book.

The Witch-Cult in Western Europe sketched out the history of this ancient fertility cult. Based around the personality of Diana and led by priestesses not male priests, it was a cult dominated by the participation of women. It had nothing whatsoever to do with satanism. For Murray, the witchcraft cult of western Europe was the true religion of the population while the Catholic Church was struggling to hold on to its congregations. She theorized that the witch hunts began in earnest once the Protestant Church became popular with the people of Europe. Her sabbats were well-organized congregations, called covens, each made up of 12 initiates and one leader. The size of the cult was breathtaking. Murray wrote:

> The only explanation of the immense numbers of witches who were legally tried and put to death in western Europe is that we are dealing with a religion which was spread over the whole continent and counted its members in every rank of society, from the highest to the lowest.

The theory was widely read and found academic as well as popular support. Margaret Murray was invited to write the 'witchcraft' entry for the *Encyclopaedia Britannica* until well into the 1960s. And this entry simply encapsulated her theory as if it had been proven beyond doubt. It was an attractive theory to many, most especially because it created some sense of action and reaction in the story of the Great Witch Panic. It provided an easily understandable rationale to explain an incredibly complex issue. But Murray read little of the histories of the witchcraft trials, and of medieval history in particular, and she saw everything through the distorting lens of Sir James Frazer's fertility cult theory. The accounts of the trials with which she illustrated her theories were highly selective and edited to exclude any fantastic and magical imagery. These trials – for example, that of alleged witch Isobel Gowdie in 1662 – seem on the surface to be no more than accounts of licentious ceremonies of drinking and feasting, presided over by 'the Devil'. Such boisterous meetings do indeed tally with what we know of early fertility religions and could be taken as honest and reputable reports of such. But from Isobel Gowdie's confession we find this passage selectively removed from Margaret Murray's quotation: 'All the coven did fly like cats, jackdaws, hares and rooks, etc., but Barbara Ronald, in Brightmanney, and I always rode on a horse, which we would make of a straw or a beanstalk.'

Critics of Murray and *The Witch-Cult in Western Europe* have pointed out these deficiencies in her arguments and have made great headway in re-establishing a more level-headed approach to the study of medieval witchcraft. Their established view recognizes the overpowering importance of books like the *Malleus Maleficarum* and the judges who used them, rather than any sort of organized witch cult. The concept of a historical witch cult predated Margaret Murray by almost one hundred years. She did not invent the idea but merely developed an argument that first began to circulate in the 1830s. One of the influential scholars of the day was Karl Jarcke of the University of Berlin. Jarcke, like Murray, thought that witches were the followers of an ancient pagan religion that had survived the official adoption of Christianity. As a nature cult, it employed magical spells for the influencing of the weather and the rhythms of the seasons, and these powers depended for their efficacy on the Devil. Church leaders in Germany began pursuing this nature cult in order to halt the growing intervention of the Devil in the affairs of man. It became recognized as Devil worship by both witch hunters and witches, and (according to Jarcke) the witch cult evolved to become a Devil-worshipping secret society.

It was a sign of the times when, 30 years later, a French writer, Jules Michelet (1798–1874), depicted witchcraft as a revolutionary conspiracy in his book *La Sorcière*. He saw the poor and wretched serfs, caught up in a crushing feudal society, turning to clandestine meetings in secluded spots in order to conspire. Mixing earthy pagan ritual with comedic lampoons on local dignitaries and officials, the night-time ceremonies were seen as parodies. The black mass, with its reversal of the staid and revered Christian service, was the peasants' crude and symbolic defiance of the hated establishment. At the centre of the meeting, Michelet introduces a priestess who dominates the entire sabbat. It is she who has organized and staged the affair and who is the peasants' spiritual leader. On her prostrate body corn was offered to Satan, and a cake was cooked for distribution in the black mass.

Michelet, just as Murray after him, chose his texts carefully, and he had to explain away the fact that no account of a sabbat bares any resemblance to his fictional romanticizing. But the power of his writing gave *La Sorcière* a standing and authority that it barely deserved. What Michelet handed down to those who would later pick up the story of the witch cult was the concept of a fertility religion. Corn and cakes were agricultural offerings, and at a crucial stage of the sabbat the nubile priestess mounts a large wooden figure of Satan, complete with erect phallus, as if to mate with it. This is powerful fertility imagery. Both James Frazer and Margaret Murray were able to take this romantic imagery to new heights and into new academic territories.

Today witchcraft (occasionally referred to as 'the Craft') is alive and well. However it is not witchcraft in the sense that a medieval caster of *maleficium* would recognize it. Wicca is a modern-day religion that carefully picks out the most inoffensive aspects of witchcraft and presents it as a neo-pagan 'folk religion'. Wicca is a gentle, environmentally friendly, feminist-dominated belief system that has no established connection with either the witches of old or the Celtic pagan religion from which it claims descent. Margaret Murray provided the central thesis of work around which much of Wicca is based, yet the Dianic cult, with its priestesses and its fertility rituals, is a fabrication. It was supported, in 1931 by her follow-up work *The God of the Witches* and also by *The White Goddess*, Robert Graves's monumental yet esoteric, Frazer-influenced study of the Moon Goddess in Western religions.

Modern witches have accepted the validity of Murray's arguments and built a religion around them. One of the most influential of the modern neo-pagans was the Freemason Gerald Gardner, who first brought modern witchcraft into the public consciousness. He broke new ground in the 1950s with his book *Witchcraft Today*. As a member of an established secret society and an associate of the famous real-life sorcerer Aleister Crowley, Gardner wove both masonic and magical ritual together with aspects of folklore and naturism.

The religion that has developed is very loosely organized, democratic and easy-going. It is, however, wholly a product of the twentieth century (notwithstanding a hint of earlier occult practice), and whether it deserves to have any connection with the word 'witchcraft' is debatable. Attempts to place the origins of the word 'Wicca' usually lead to a Saxon root word meaning 'to bend' or to the Saxon word 'wit'. Whatever its actual derivation, the unfavourable connotations of the phrase 'witchcraft' are being left behind. Practitioners of Wicca have themselves gone to great lengths in the past to disassociate this word from their religion.

The single defining characteristic of witches in the fifteenth, sixteenth and seventeenth centuries was their ability to cast *maleficium*. Their links with Satan and the sabbat brought down the wrath of the Inquisition, but in the end it was their evil magic that identified the witches as such. Modern witches practise only 'white' magic, if they practise it at all – which raises the question: are they witches or pagan reformers?

In 1928 the Reverend Montague Summers translated the *Malleus Maleficarum* into English – like all legalistic documents of the medieval period the original text was written in Latin. He was quite willing to believe in the witch cult, as he says in his introduction to the book:

> It seems plain that the witches were a vast political movement, an organized society which was anti-social and anarchical, a worldwide plot against civilization.

This description smacks more than a little of another 'worldwide plot against civilization' that existed in Summers' time – the Bolsheviks, the communist revolutionaries in Russia. His portrayal of the witch cult as an immense spider's web of ranks and branches and covens, rates it alongside some of the most sophisticated secret societies, and Summers does, in fact, weave the name of Adam Weishaupt into his witch narrative. We will meet Adam Weishaupt in a later chapter as the 'profoundest conspirator that has ever existed', the founder of the infamous but short-lived sect known as the Illuminati.

We have, then, a number of diverse and mutually exclusive theories to explain the nature of witchcraft. Modern academic study dismisses most of these theories as unsubstantiated fantasy. In order properly to weigh the information gleaned from trial confessions taken under torture, one must ask: Who is recording this information? We speak today of the 'power of the press' and are intimately familiar with the power of the written (and spoken) word. For the majority of people in the fifteenth, sixteenth and seventeenth centuries the written word was an unfathomable code known only to an educated élite. What was more, many of the books on demonology were written in Latin, rendering them doubly distant to the ignorant peasant.

The judge oversaw all confessions and all tortures, and often considered the evidence himself to produce a verdict. But did torture really force victims to tell the truth or did it force them to confess to whatever the judge told them to? Torture is, to the modern mind, the most repugnant and most horrifying aspect of the Great Witch Panic, and it is perhaps one of the most powerful arguments for dismissing any accusations of a real witch cult as nonsense. For the inquisitors and magistrates of the day quite the opposite was true. Torture had its place and was central to the fight against demons of possession. The *Malleus Maleficarum* was the casebook on every magistrate's desk and was the companion of inquisitors and witch-finders everywhere. After translating the book, Summers called it 'admirable' and found little within the legalistic text to disturb him. Yet, despite there being one section entitled 'Setting Forth of Various Means of Overcoming their Obstinacy in Keeping Silence and Refusal to Confess', Summers declared: 'We must be prepared to discount certain plain faults, certain awkwardnesses, certain roughnesses and even severities.'

Montague Summers was firmly convinced of the cult's reality, and in some cases where the intent of the witches was believed to be undeniably anti-social and evil, such abominable tortures were considered justified and fruitful. But the modern reader must face the startling prospect that the cult existed only in the minds of those who pursued it. Many hundreds of thousands of innocent people were tortured, and a huge number of these were cruelly executed. The early writers who tried to discover some reality behind the panic were seeking order behind the chaos, reason behind the madness.

A stark analysis of the Great Witch Panic must abandon any notion of a cult (fertility or otherwise) and face the fact that the Inquisition, and the judges and magistrates who served its purpose, were the active members of a sinister brotherhood, an élite and loose organization devoted to torture and murder. With their activities legitimized by papal decree and as a divine mission to make war on the Devil, these educated men pursued an invisible, intangible, non-existent enemy. With ruthless abandon they imprisoned, tortured and killed. Panic is defined as 'a sudden overwhelming feeling of terror or anxiety, especially one affecting a whole group of people'. We can barely understand the scale of the panic that gripped Europe during those dark centuries, not just the panic of the suspects (which is readily understandable), but of the inquisitors themselves.

As we look at some of history's equally violent cults in this book, we may see in their fear and paranoia, their willingness to be a party to the most abominable crimes and their unshakeable faith and devotion something of Europe during the Great Witch Panic. Despite the pain and paranoia suffered by the people and the driving ideology of the inquisitors who carried out the atrocities, we shall find strange parallels with the high-tech cults of the 1990s. The Great Witch Panic may even help us to understand the modern cult phenomenon, which we look at in a later chapter.

CHAPTER TWO

Race Hate and Religion

As dusk settles over the city, a vast crowd assembles for the religious ceremony. A dazzling array of cult flags, pennants, banners and emblems adorns the arena. Official members line up, row upon row, huge blocks of colour and spectacle, their ranks and responsibilities marked by insignia and costume. The messianic figure who stands to address the huge and devoted crowd speaks with an electrifying energy, an energy that inspires the watching congregation. With boundless emotion and an almost hypnotic devotion to the tenets of the creed, the crowd rhythmically chants the words of the religion and then begins to make the special cult sign, as a mass in unison, a single devoted following. Their messiah is saviour, leader, god. He is Adolf Hitler.

Nazi Germany was far more than a ruthless totalitarian state with harsh anti-Semitic laws and a lust for European domination. The nation had adopted all the trappings of a religious cult, and its citizens became its members. Nazism was not just an economic, political and social movement – it also incorporated belief, faith and devotion. Unquestioning loyalty, even love, was demanded by Adolf Hitler, and total self-sacrifice for the tenets of the cult was expected. At its height during the Second World War, Nazi Germany became almost a 'super-cult'. Not a nation, a people or a race, but a religious movement carried forward by an élite membership. Those Germans not able to qualify for membership of this 'super-cult' were treated worse than animals.

National Socialism (Nazism) was a political movement that flourished under the leadership of a young Adolf Hitler during those dark days of the 1930s. It was perhaps the most important movement of the twentieth century. The power politics of the early years of the century and the Great War that they created led inexorably to the formation of the Nazi Party. And ever since Hitler's death at the end of the Second World War, the Western world has lived in the shadow of a German nationalist movement. With the impending millennium, it seems that the Nazi legacy is still strong in some quarters, attracting the weak-willed and easily led with its bold and simple ethos: right and wrong, pure and impure.

Although Nazism itself was almost pre-destined to rise from the battered German nation from the day of the 1918 armistice, the fact that it took on so many cult trappings was in part due to the strange and murky occult underworld that existed in Germany at the time. This, combined with a rabid racial doctrine that drove the movement onwards, produced a nightmarish society that totally overturned twentieth-century norms. The rise to power of the Nazi Party is a tragic story, influenced by mystical forces, secret societies, folklore and the popular revival of a pagan religion.

The Aryan Movement

At the end of the hostilities of the First World War, the Allies demanded that Germany pay huge reparations to the nations against which she had fought so bitterly. Germany, already economically crippled by the immense cost of fighting the war, struggled to meet the harsh payments. Not only that, but her industrial heartland in the west had been occupied by a French garrison. Morale in Germany reached an unprecedented low. Old wounds and rivalries that had initially led to the war, were not addressed but were left to fester. Bitterness and hatred towards the other European nations grew ever stronger. The Treaty of Versailles included an agreement that Germany should not attempt to rearm with an army, navy or air force. Post-war Germans considered themselves the wronged victims of an evil and greedy European alliance.

The economic catastrophe of post-war Germany created the perfect climate for the rise of a radical new party, but Nazism's unique 'racial' slant had its origins in a long-standing German tradition of 'Aryan' societies. In the previous century a philosophical and artistic movement had flourished that glorified Germany's wealth of folklore, history and mythology. The composer Richard Wagner had celebrated the past of the German people in his music, which reflected his belief in the unique and superior nature of the German character. By the turn of the century, a number of societies had sprung up that also adhered to these principles. They referred to themselves as *Völkischen* cults (from the German word *Volk*, meaning 'the people'). Leading lights among this clique included the Thule Society (*Thulegesellschaft*), the Vril Society (*Vrilgesellschaft*) and the Germanic Order (*Germanenorden*). National Socialism eventually proved to be the pure political expression of these groups, and several Nazis were deeply involved in them.

The rise and fall of these tiny cultural societies, while fascinating, cannot alone explain the rise and fall of the Third Reich. One of the most horrific and alarming of all socio-political systems, Nazi Germany had many roots and many diverse influences. The reparations demanded by the victorious Allies, the philosophy of intellectuals such as Friedrich Nietzsche and Oswald Spengler, the pre-war German obsession with expansion combined with the demilitarization and occupation of the Rhineland, the fear of communism and the legacy of Prussian militarism all had an impact. The racist cults, the *Völkischen*, added one more layer to the complex social, economic and political problems confronting Germany in 1918, and they help to explain, in part at least, the ritual and the racist dogma.

A common theme of the *Völkischen* was the revival of pagan festivals and rituals from the long-dead Teutonic pantheon, including the gods Wotan and Thor. Christian ceremonies were abandoned by members of the groups, and pagan ritual reconstructed to take their place. Baptisms, marriages and funerals were all coloured with this neo-paganism. The racial heritage that the cult members were sharing and celebrating was essential to the ethos of such groups. Ensuring the purity of the German heritage and race was regarded as of the utmost importance by the *Völkischen*. Several labels identifying this common racial heritage were current among the leading writers of the movement, including Germanic, Teutonic and Aryan. This last word became the pivot around which the *Völkischen* and Nazi movement revolved. Used by the cult writers to denote someone of north European extraction, the word became a title, a definition and an ideal. For the Jews, who made up the greatest non-Aryan minority in Germany at that time, the rise of the movement proved to be disastrous. The philosophical ramblings of those purporting to be celebrating and defending the purity of the Aryan – that is, Germanic – peoples were inevitably anti-Semitic. Dominating the pre-Nazi scene were three influential organizations: the Vril Society, the Order of New Templars and the Thule Society.

The Vril Society had its origins in Edward Bulwer-Lytton's 1871 novel *The Coming Race*, in which a race of people was able to manipulate and wield *vril* or the 'life force'. Within only a few years, the trend towards establishing mystical secret societies led to the establishment of a Vril Society in Germany. Like most mystical cults, it merged previous traditions to form a secret agenda of its own. Elements taken from the Jewish Kabbalah, Hindu mysticism, the eighteenth-century Illuminati and the Theosophical Society were incorporated into the Vril Society's teachings.

Perhaps the most influential of the pre-war cults was the Order of New Templars, which was founded in 1907 by a former Cistercian cleric named Adolf Lanz. Lanz was a fanatic, who wrote voluminously on the Aryan movement. He even created Aryosophy, a religion that defined the entire world in terms of non-Aryan and Aryan. Lanz believed that the priceless blood of the German people was in grave danger from a malign group of sub-humans: the *chandalas*. *Chandalas* were animal-humans – non-Aryans – who were led by their baser instincts. Jews, Arabs, Negroes, Gypsies, Hispanics – all were *chandalas*, fit for only non-human work in Germany's mines.

Lanz preached his twisted philosophy through the medium of the Order of New Templars (*Ordo Novi Templi*) and through the Aryan magazine, *Ostara*. The Order of New Templars was a revivalist society that modelled itself on the medieval Knights Templars, the famous warrior-monks who donned armour and the splayed red cross of Christ and took to the crusades. The Templars were famed for their fighting prowess, for their piety and devotion to God and for the diabolical occult rituals that they were rumoured to perform. Lanz's modern order also based itself on another élite band of holy warriors, the Teutonic Knights, who were crusaders on Germany's northern frontier in the Middle Ages.

Established initially on the Danube in Austria and later at other sites in Austria, Germany and Hungary, the Order of New Templars attracted rich and well-respected gentlemen who wanted their racist ideas to be reinforced by those around them. Writers, businessmen and officers from the army and navy were involved, and one of its members, August Strindberg, was to have almost as much impact on the development of the Aryan philosophy as Lanz. Cult members modelled themselves on the 'Aryo-heroics' who peppered world history, great characters who fought *chandalas* and stood up for the blond, blue-eyed race. Lanz even identified Jesus Christ as one of his Aryo-heroics, claiming that as a true Aryan he battled the dark forces of the *chandala* Jews! The absurd notion of Christ actually representing the northern European peoples in their fight against the Jewish people is still preached as doctrine by some modern fascist neo-Nazi cults.

New Templars, clad in white robes and with their faces hidden by white hoods, conducted torch-lit pagan ceremonies. Ku Klux Klan imagery was strong, but the New Templars did not parade beneath a burning cross – they had their own flag, emblazoned with the symbol of a swastika. The red swastika lay on a gold background and was flanked by blue lilies. The swastika was not another of Lanz's wild inventions, but an established religious design, a symbol of good luck found in pagan Teutonic carvings and throughout the ancient world. Mosaics surviving at the fourth-century AD Roman villa at Lullingstone, Kent, in England show swastikas on either side of a mythological illustration of Jupiter disguised as a bull. Attempts were made to link the pagan swastika with the Christian cross in the same way that Christ was being identified with the Aryan movement.

Writing in the New Templar magazine *Ostara*, Lanz pushed his racial theories, claiming that the Aryan people formed a racial aristocracy. He truly believed that 'blonds possess secret knowledge'. As far as he was concerned, the German people were the only true humans alive, and they represented science, advancement, morality and God. Among others, Lanz deeply admired the British general Lord Kitchener, who had organized colonial troops to fight hostile tribes – *chandala* versus *chandala* for the goals of the Aryan people. He also claimed that Kitchener was a subscriber to *Ostara* and that the general had corresponded with him.

Typical *Ostara* advertising ran: 'Are you blond? Are you a Man? Then read *Ostara!*' The magazine was published from 1905 until 1931, and many a German soldier in the trenches of the First World War had a copy in his kit-bag. The publication had an immense impact on one German veteran in particular: Adolf Hitler. Hitler had read *Ostara* before the war, and once personally met Lanz in order to acquire two issues he had missed, numbers 30 and 31. Lanz made a gift of them. Hitler was a poorly paid house-painter at that time, and he treasured his copies of the New Templar magazine at the hostel where he was living. Aged 20, he was open and responsive to such theories and ideas, and the copies Lanz had given him contained most of the cult leader's radical racial theory. The back issues were to fuel his own passions and have a lasting impression on the young man.

In fact, Adolf Hitler plagiarized much of Lanz's work, plundering the basic elements of his Aryan ideology and putting it into macabre practice, but as he rose to power in the early 1930s the newly appointed Führer failed to acknowledge either Lanz, the New Templars or *Ostara*. In 1938, after stealing Lanz's 'philosophy' of racial hatred, the Nazi regime banned Lanz's work completely. Hitler had been deeply affected by what he had read and had absorbed much of the Aryan thinking, yet he felt only contempt for these powerless and elitist men's clubs. They debated, published and conducted religious ritual, but they could not hope to come any closer to their dream of an Aryan-dominated world. This mission was Adolf Hitler's. His manifesto, *Mein Kampf* ('My Struggle') was written in 1923 and contained several arguments stolen from *Ostara*.

Lanz, as might be expected, felt betrayed by Hitler and always regretted giving him those two fateful issues of the magazine. He was never critical of the Aryan ideology that he had helped Hitler formulate, only of Hitler himself. Even after the end of the war, Lanz continued to affirm his earlier beliefs. In the opinion – and words – of the leader of the New Templars, Hitler was a rough and uncouth *chandala,* while the Nazi's themselves were ignorant and vulgar, utterly beneath contempt.

Famous Nazi politicians Rudolf Hess, Wilhelm Frick and Alfred Rosenberg are all known to have been involved with the Thule Society, the third of the main *Völkischen* groups. One of the cult's most influential members, Dietrich Eckhart, who had become involved in a number of other *Völkischen* cults too, even received a dedication in

Hitler's *Mein Kampf*. Like most *Völkischen* cults, the Thule Society was an intellectual secret society, and it had a profound influence on the development of the Nazi Party. It was first established in Munich at the end of the First World War by a steamship stoker called Sebottendorf. During his life he had travelled throughout the eastern Mediterranean, and it was there that he claimed he had been initiated into a lodge of Freemasonry. His 'eastern travels' and 'masonic initiation' thus conferred on him a mystical authority, which his followers were eager to recognize. Into the fabric of his society, Sebottendorf wove various mystical traditions, ranging from alchemy, Freemasonry and Islamic Sufism, as well as the knee-jerk, right-wing promotion of anti-Semitism and anti-Bolshevism (the Bolsheviks were the Russian communists who had so recently brought down the tsarist government).

As Hitler's National Socialism rose to prominence in the late 1920s, it received support from the Thule Society. But the Nazi monopoly on right-wing thought soon eclipsed the Thule Society and other, similar groups. The society was broken up, and Sebottendorf was arrested in 1934. Only Nazi-sanctioned societies would be tolerated by the new regime, for Hitler realized only too well how the seed-bed of fringe politics and secret societies had given rise to his brand of anti-Semitic rule. To seal his victory, it was imperative that he destroy that seed-bed, before another extremist faction rose to challenge him. In this way, Hitler's method resembled that of the Chinese secret societies, most famously represented by the Triads. For hundreds of years the secret societies plotted and planned to overthrow the current Chinese emperor. When one or another cult actually found an opportunity to do so, the emperor that it installed on the Dragon Throne turned on the secret societies that had put him there and ruthlessly persecuted them to destruction. Sebottendorf was soon released and moved to Istanbul, where he claimed to be working for the Nazi secret service, the SD (*Sicherheitdienst*).

The greatest influence that the Thule Society had on Nazi policy was its translation into German of the *Protocols of the Elders of Zion*. These documents had a profound effect on Hitler before he wrote *Mein Kampf*, and they provided a macabre legitimization for the execution of millions of Jewish people during the Second World War. Probably originating in Russia a century earlier, the *Protocols* were purportedly the master-plans of an international Jewish conspiracy that was trying to bring about a worldwide Jewish government. Like the very worst demonological tracts of the Great Witch Panic, the *Protocols* sketched out the existence of an evil international secret society, hell-bent on domination of the Western world at any cost. Did it actually exist? And if it did not, why were the falsified documents so convincing?

The *Protocols* first appeared on the scene in Russia around 1903, when they were presented to Tsar Nicholas II as evidence of a grand Jewish conspiracy. Behind this presentation was one Sergei Nilus, who claimed that the documents had actually been written at the International Judaic Conference held in Basle six years earlier. We know nothing of this Nilus, but his plan to enflame the Russian government against the Jewish population failed. The tsar had all copies of the *Protocols* burned, and Nilus was duly banished. Copies did survive, however, and printings took place in 1903 and 1905. After the First World War they began to achieve a certain notoriety and were held up by soon-to-be Nazi Alfred Rosenberg as the legitimate blueprint for a Jewish secret cabal. By the early 1920s they even began to be discussed in British newspapers. On 8 May 1921 *The Times* printed the following:

> What do they mean, those Protocols? Are they Genuine? Has a gang of criminals really drawn up such plans and is triumphing over their fulfilment? Are they a forgery? But how can one explain then this terrible prophetic gift that foretold all this before hand? Did we fight all these years to destroy the world power of Germany only to find ourselves now facing a much more dangerous enemy? Have we saved ourselves through enormous efforts from PAX GERMANICA only to fall a victim to PAX JUDAICA?

As it became clear that the *Protocols* were, in fact, a forgery, *The Times* soon admitted that it had made an error in printing such a piece. In August that year the newspaper ran an article comparing the *Protocols* with a book published in Brussels in 1865 titled *Dialogues in Hell*. But the damage had been done, and an endless debate over the authenticity of the *Protocols* began that continues to this day (albeit by neo-Nazi groups in the US and western Europe). The words of the manufactured documents hammered themselves into the psyche of the anti-Semitic *Völkischen* cults and were repeated as truth by Nazi propagandists throughout the 1930s and 1940s. One English translation carries the full force of the conspiracy:

> Out of the temporary evil we are now compelled to commit will emerge the good of an unshakeable rule ... The result justifies the means ... Before us is a plan in which is laid down strategically the line from which we cannot deviate without running the risk of seeing the labour of many centuries brought to naught.
>
> *extract from* PROTOCOL ONE

Every possible social ill, from socialist revolution to alcoholism was mentioned among the weapons of the Jewish conspirators. In Protocol Nine, the fanaticism ascribed to the Jewish 'Elders' reaches dizzy heights:

The weapons in our hands are limitless ambitions, burning greediness, merciless vengeance, hatreds and malice. It is from us that all-engulfing terror proceeds. We have in our service persons of all opinions, of all doctrines; restorating monarchists, demagogues, socialists, communists and utopian dreamers of every kind. We have harnessed them all to the task.

extract from PROTOCOL NINE

Just as the Inquisition invented the satanic conspiracy of witchcraft so that it could pursue and destroy it, so, too, the Nazi propaganda machine promoted a belief in a fictional Jewish international conspiracy so that it could destroy its alleged membership. Fear drove not only the persecutors but also the German public, which watched and assisted. But far more than 100,000 died in this 'panic' – estimates put the number of Jewish dead at 6 million. Added to that macabre total are hundreds of thousands of others including Poles, Russians, Gypsies and communists.

The Holocaust and the anti-Semitism that spawned it were complex creations, with very diverse origins. First, there is no need, in a pragmatic universe, to ascribe the extermination of 6 million people wholly to a fabricated tract that pretends to be the boardroom minutes of an international secret society. The *Protocols* did nothing more than provide the Nazis with a piece of literary evidence with which to back up a policy of race hate that had no justification whatsoever. Second, Lanz's ravings about *chandalas* and the Aryan struggle against the Jewish race similarly had no religious justification, but merely added to the ground-swell of German elitist thought. The New Templars, the Vril or the Thule Society were the symptoms of the German mass-delusion, not its cause. Finally, racial theories that classified the Jewish people as a separate species with definite sub-human traits were current in the 1920s, and were propounded by Adolf Lanz and the German Professor Günther. These anthropological theories again were not themselves motivation for the mass-extermination, but merely vapid attempts at its justification.

What then, motivated the German state to persecute and execute millions of its own innocent citizens? As we have already noted, the reasons are many and complex. In part, a scapegoat was needed for the severe government measures that were being formulated. The Nazi shake-up of the collapsed German government, meant that something had to give. The Jewish minority had been a scapegoat for local disasters in Germany since the Middle Ages, but to a limited degree and for only limited periods.

The start of the Depression in the late 1920s, coupled with the crippling payments to the victorious Allies after the First World War, left Germany in social and economic ruin. The world as most Germans knew it had collapsed, traditional social structures were in decline, and inflation and uncertainty spiralled out of control. What the desperate populace needed was stability and order. With this they had a future – and a life. What they would get was an institution that provided three essential things: certainties, excuses and order. It would perform all the duties of a government and a religious body. It found the Jews guilty of causing the economic nightmare – and a method for purging Germany of them. It promised what seemed impossible: that the weakest, poorest and most down-trodden of nations could aspire to be the leader of the West, not for a decade or two, but for a thousand years. National Socialism was an institution that inspired a dream. In Hitler, the Germans would get their messiah.

Nazi Mysticism

Adolf Hitler certainly considered himself to be the saviour of the Aryan race. Obsessed with the myths and legends of the German people – he was himself born in Austria – the veteran trench-soldier became engulfed by hatred, and was indignant that the Germans could have fallen so low. His ideal of a 'glorious past' was shared by members of the various *Völkischen* cults and harked back to the operas of the anti-Semitic Richard Wagner. Adolf Hitler made the rounds of various right-wing meetings in post-war Germany, and stumbled on a small meeting of nationalists, the German Workers' Party. Interrupting the meeting with an impromptu speech from the floor, Hitler showed himself to be the fanatical and mesmerizing speaker who would one day enrapture the nation, and he was snapped up as the main speaker for the tiny movement. Soon, he came to dominate the organization, which he renamed National Socialism.

The philosophy underpinning Hitler's National Socialism was the acknowledgement of German pride and a recognition that its Aryan people were the unquestioned masters of the human race. Everything Aryan was good, everything good was Aryan. Just beyond the present, Hitler and others saw a human ideal that became known as the *Übermenschen* (supermen), who were especially bred and educated to dominate humanity. This concept owed much to the cold logic of the German philosopher Friedrich Nietzsche. Hermann Rauschning wrote in the 1940s: 'Nazism is more than a religion; it is the will to create the superman.' Such a superman would be partly sturdy peasant, partly Germanic warrior, partly god. Nazism initiated every German into the Aryan 'cult', and membership of this cult of the future was dependent on German citizenship. The German nation – its ambitions, fears and difficulties – was hijacked by Adolf Hitler and became for him the basis for what we could perhaps describe as a 'mind-control' or 'doomsday' cult. One working definition of such an organization is a religious group that engages in extreme spiritual, physical, mental and emotional control of its members in order to control their beliefs, thoughts, emotions and behaviour. The word 'extreme' is crucial here. All religions encourage their members to hold certain beliefs and to act in certain ways, but it is the systematic and sustained methods of mind control used by a group that identify it as radical and dangerous. Conformity and loyalty are enforced by a number of methods:

1 Access to outside information is restricted;
2 Thoughts and beliefs are controlled by generating fear and paranoia, and by punishing any criticism of the group's policies or leadership;
3 Behaviour is controlled by the use of confessions and informers, by the public humiliation of uncooperative individuals and by isolating members from any external family contacts.

Characterizing almost all of these doomsday cults is the powerful role of a single, charismatic, male leader who claims divine appointment and who often demands unconditional obedience. In addition, such cults frequently consist of a relatively small religious community living in isolation from the rest of society. The theology of the doomsday cult focuses on prophesies of a great forthcoming struggle against the forces of evil, after which there will be a paradise for the loyal initiates. Such groups amass a vast stockpile of weaponry with which to wage this war. Day-to-day life within the cult is coloured by intense paranoia, as members believe that they are in danger from non-members working against them.

At the peak of his career, Hitler's Nazi-organized rallies were quite unambiguously religious events. His audiences were not potential voters, but a massed congregation, hanging on his every word, every verbal crescendo. Under the organizational flair of Albert Speer, each rally became a rich spectacle, a pageant of colour, sound and light that dazzled and bewitched. The most breathtaking image created at such a ceremony was the blazing skyward of powerful searchlights ringing the arena. Columns of light, half a kilometre high, turned a secular stadium into a glorious ancient temple. A shrine of light and dark that signalled the brilliance of a thousand-year reign taking its first steps forwards. Hitler believed in certain biblical prophesies made by St John that predicted his thousand-year Reich could never come to pass until Satan and his followers were destroyed. For Hitler and the Nazis, this meant the Jewish people.

The Jewish people became the victims in Hitler's great purge of German society. His death camps were machines for mass-murder. Train-loads of dissidents and Jews arrived from all over occupied Europe. Those who were fit for work in the armaments factories worked; those who could not work waited their turn to be stripped naked, forced into airtight chambers with a group of others and gassed with hydrogen cyanide. In the name of medical research, Dr Josef

Mengele oversaw a catalogue of inhuman tortures on the most unfortunate victims of all. Pointless explorative surgery was carried out without anaesthetic, and some prisoners were locked into chambers that simulated altitudes of 3000 metres (10,000 feet). Two prisoners screamed for mercy, pleading to be shot, rather than to continue to suffer the pain of sub-zero temperatures in another chamber. Experiments to sterilize Jewish inmates ranged from surgery to the injection of crippling chemicals and even the bombardment of the groin with X-rays. The nightmarish list of atrocities carried out by the Nazis against their fellow man is a long and disturbing one.

Murder carried out in the heat of an argument or out of savage desperation can, to some extent, be understood, even though it may not be forgiven. The construction of huge death camps, the planning of train timetables to ferry millions of prisoners to them and the commissioning of a company, I.G. Farben, to design and manufacture an efficient gas chamber defy comprehension. Those planning and executing the death-camp system and the ruthless and evil warders who ran it divorced themselves from the inmates as a worker in a slaughterhouse divorces himself from the cattle he is about to kill. Considered to be much lower in the scheme of things than animals, however, the Jewish prisoners were humiliated, abused and tortured by the fanatical guards.

Every saviour needs his devoted priesthood, and Adolf Hitler had the *Schutzstaffel* (defence or protection squads), more commonly known as the SS. The organization was manned by the loyal devotees of Hitler's new religion, men and women who revelled in its inhumanity and cruelty. More than one Jewish inmate noticed, when SS staff were occasionally replaced by soldiers of the Wehrmacht, how far less terrible and cruel the regular troops were.

Before the war the SS did indeed possess several remarkable features that differentiated it from a mundane intelligence and paramilitary organization and propelled it deep into the realm of the mystical. Any similarities between the SS and the ancient Teutonic Knights was not entirely coincidental. The initiation rituals had all of the trappings of a medieval order, and those wishing to gain admittance to the order at that time had to trace back their family histories to prove that their Aryan bloodlines had been pure for 250 years! That was for enlisted men and for non-commissioned officers. Candidates wishing to be officers had to trace back a pure bloodline for 300 years. Prospective initiates were obliged to enter the order as novices rather than full members, a tradition that mirrored that of various religious orders. Other aspects drew inspiration from a variety of different sources: emblems from ancient Germanic religion, a high-priesthood of 13 members from the occult 'covens' and a rich hierarchy of rank and insignia from Freemasonry.

Most surprising in any discussion of Hitler's SS is the continual appearance of occult meaning and interpretation. Heinrich Himmler, the commander of the unit, was himself utterly obsessed with occult forces and, like all the top SS *Obengruppenführer* (lieutenant-generals), believed himself to be the reincarnation of some important historical personage. At the SS headquarters, a castle in the German town of Wewelsburg, each of the 13 'high priests' who made up the black coven in charge of the SS machine had a room of his own. Each of these rooms was furnished in a historical style that corresponded with the historical era during which that SS officer was supposed to have lived in his previous life. Himmler and his 12 generals, who styled themselves as Germanic 'Knights of the Round Table', met ritually in the castle's north tower. Far below the meeting hall, a crypt held a symbolic flame, and this was itself surrounded by ritualistic pedestals. In true masonic style, the SS strategy was to create an entire town, carefully planned and constructed to surround and complement the castle at Wewelsburg. The triangular castle would become the tip of an architectural spearhead, with a long, dead-straight road leading up to the complex, in effect forming a perfectly proportioned spear shaft. The town was to radiate concentrically from this tip.

Himmler considered the location of the SS headquarters of great occult significance, and at various times the study of ley lines and earth powers were brought in to qualify this idea. Wewelsburg was compared with such spiritually uplifting sites as Stonehenge, and articles were published to advance such theories. The final master-plan for the area was the creation of a supreme ritual centre, an SS capital that would represent the very centre of Nazi spirituality. Wewelsburg was to become the *Mittelpunkt der Welt* (mid-point of the world). This, and other occult mystical connections, did little in the end to extend the Nazi regime beyond more than a decade and a half.

Was Hitler the mystical prophet of a vast mind-control cult? We can see in the devotion, the ritual and the delusion of the German people, that some aspects of this kind of organization can actually be identified. But the Nazis were not, in truth, the antecedents of the People's Temple or Waco. The trappings of 'cult' existed at every turn, but ultimately that vital ingredient seems to have been missing. While the modern cult leader controls his followers personally, in an intimate one-to-one relationship, Hitler became utterly divorced from the people. His government ran itself, and the upper echelon of Nazis tripped over themselves to win his favour. Hitler, unlike the true cult messiah, ruled by proxy as well as by fear. His unwillingness to become personally involved in matters that affected, and even ended, millions of lives perpetuated a state that rushed headlong towards some undefined 'vision'. How and why the German people followed an uneducated and ignorant Austrian corporal are questions with which historians will be wrestling for many years. Perhaps both the *Völkischen* societies and the phenomenon of modern doomsday cults can provide two more pieces of this complex jigsaw.

Hitler's armies fought savage wars against the people of Europe and against the long-standing enemy of Germany, Russia. Eventually, however, the Allies prevailed. The German Luftwaffe was systematically destroyed, and Allied troops battled across France and Italy and deep into Germany. Finally, in 1945, Russian troops entered a devastated Berlin, still defended by young boys and old men. In the bunker that served as his headquarters, Hitler and his generals had sought to win an unwinnable war, a war of absolute destruction that he had wrought on himself. His fear of capture was so great that he shot himself. His body was partially burnt in a pit outside the bunker. Hitler's crusade against the Jews, the Russians and the nations of western Europe had ended.

The Klan

It was Nazism that had been defeated by the Allies in 1945, however, not racism. The United States, that great nation that had championed the cause of anti-fascism, was itself plagued with a race problem. It was a problem with a savage past and a violent future, embodied in the Ku Klux Klan. In the post-war period the Klan was poised on the brink of a national resurgence that would take the authorities by surprise. Actually predating many of the *Völkischen* cults and Lanz's twisted Aryosophy, the Ku Klux Klan has carved a deep and ugly name for itself in American history.

It had all started so innocently. A group of army officers from the defeated Confederate Army had returned to the little town of Pulaski, Tennessee, after the Civil War. Bored with civilian life, the six young men dreamed up the idea of a secret club, entitled mysteriously 'the Circle' or, in Greek, *kuklos*. From this, and adding a touch of the townsfolk's fondly remembered Scottish ancestry, the veterans' little club soon became known as the *kuklux klan*. Full of false occult suggestion, the name inspired the members to dress up in ridiculous costumes made from white sheets and pillowcases. With conical hats and plenty of occult-looking emblems sewn onto their costumes, the klan members rode their horses through the quiet town, whooping and screaming. Local townsfolk were surprised and shocked, much to the hilarity of the six klan members.

One of these men, James Crowe, stated that the aim of the group was 'purely social and for our amusement'. Nothing of the terrible deeds that occurred in the century following could be glimpsed in this gang of good-natured young men, who found amusement in playing harmless pranks on local residents. They often gate-crashed open-air parties, picnics and barbecues held in the evening, riding in on horse-back, dancing and generally acting the fool. Initiation rituals were used simply to raise a laugh at the poor candidates' expense, but this did not stop people from joining. Young men from the surrounding counties in Tennessee soon heard of the exploits of this Ku Klux Klan, and wanted to join in the fun. There was little other fun to be had in the unsettled and troubled period following the Civil War.

Fought from 1861 to 1865, the war was essentially a struggle for dominance between the slave-owning south and the industrialized (and non-slave) north. Slavery was only one part of a complex issue, and it is wrong to say simply that the American Civil War was fought by the northern states to prevent the practice of slavery in the south-ern states. The United States split in February 1861; those in the north continued to uphold the Union under President Lincoln, while those in the south formed their own 'Confederate' government. Within months war had broken out. Four years, and over half a million casu-alties later, the Civil War came to a halt. Industrial might had tri-umphed over near-feudal, slave-owning plantation owners in the south. Perhaps the greatest effect of a northern victory was the libera-tion of slaves throughout the now-defunct Confederacy. These slaves were all of African descent – blacks who had been shipped in their millions across the Atlantic to work on the cotton plantations of wealthy southern landowners.

As a new government began 'reconstructing' the United States, a frightening period of lawlessness gripped the south. White masters were horrified to find their loyal black slaves deserting almost to a man. Trouble flared daily, as black freedmen mixed more freely and became on 'familiar' terms with white men and women. The lot of the freed slave was far from the long-hoped-for utopia, however, for many southern whites angrily resented the new state of affairs. Black men were lynched for greeting white women, for pulling out of labour con-tracts when they discovered they were not going to be paid and for a host of equally senseless and cruel reasons. Vigilantism became ram-pant, and the bodies of black freedmen littered the countryside, as General George Custer reported from Texas. Commonly, these white vigilantes acted sporadically and anonymously in disorganized bands of Confederate war veterans and ex-slave masters. Roaming around Mississippi and South Carolina, however, were more ordered bands, who called themselves Regulators, and these fanatical killers took ter-rible revenge on black freedmen and their families. Tennessee had its own vigilantes, the Red Caps, and others were called the Yellow Jackets. Although still disorganized, the Regulators were usually formed of combat-hardened veterans, now jobless and embittered, who were prepared to hire out their murderous services to plantation owners. They routinely harassed, persecuted and murdered freedmen who refused to work on a plantation on the strict terms laid down by its owner.

Politically, things were just as chaotic. The southern states were fighting tooth-and-nail against Washington's attempts to restore the Union. Because of this political opposition, from March 1867 a series of laws was enacted that marked the start of Radical Reconstruction. The more the south resisted, the more it was forced to yield. By the end of 1866, only months after it had been established, the Ku Klux Klan began to get caught up in the grand political and social currents that were swirling about it.

The butt of the Klan-members' jokes was often the local black population. A favourite trick was for a group of Klansmen to pretend to be the avenging ghosts of Confederate cavalrymen. Several news stories reported the terrified encounters, although critics have wondered since whether the freedmen recognized ex-masters in these parodies and fled for fear of retribution. Actual belief in the reincarnation of Confederate soldiers seems highly unlikely. The swelling numbers of the Klan quickly picked up pace, and it began to turn its attention to more serious matters. As men with a real grievance against the impositions of the north and the hated Reconstruction government joined the Klan, its demeanour became ever more sinister. Within only a year or two of its foundation it became an illegal organization, with members drawn from all the southern states in whole-hearted opposition to the Reconstruction government and the freedoms given to former slaves. Blacks were harassed on a more widespread basis – their firearms were seized, and gatherings and prayer meetings were routinely disrupted. Those seeking to hold some office were terrorized, and the voting rights of blacks in general were disrupted by violence and intimidation.

Nashville, Tennessee, became the venue for a secret convention of Klansmen in 1867. At that convention, a prominent member named George Gordon, a former brigadier-general in the Confederate army, unveiled a 'Prescript' or pamphlet of rules, which became the basis for the Klan's activities. It gave a real purpose to the Ku Klux Klan and expanded on those first occult cues with an entire hierarchy of mystical ranks. Local dens led by a Grand Cyclops, formed the smallest unit of Klansmen in towns throughout the south. Dens within a county (Province) were controlled by a Grand Giant and four assistants, who were known as Goblins. Counties within a district (Dominion) were controlled by a Grand Titan and six assistants, who were called Furies. At the state (Realm) level, Grand Dragons represented all the Klansmen therein and were assisted by eight Hydras. At the very head of this so-called 'Invisible Empire' stood the Grand Wizard, who, with his ten Genii became the spokesman of the Ku Klux Klan as well as an autocratic leader. The aims of the Klan were vague, unspecified and thus perfectly in-keeping with those of other secret societies. Crosses were often worn on the Klansmen's bizarre costumes; the members were defending not just white rights, but Christianity and the 'American way'. A dedication ended Gordon's Prescript:

> To the lovers of Law and Order, Peace and Justice, we send greeting; and to the shades of the venerated Dead, we affectionately dedicate the * *.

The twin asterisks are all that stood for the words 'Kuklux Klan' throughout the entire document – nowhere is that title officially mentioned. This is truly a secret society! In fact, the Ku Klux Klan owed much to a secret society that operated for some years before the Civil War. This society, which called itself the Order of the Star Spangled Banner, was established in Boston in 1849. Although it used much masonic ritual, in particular handshakes, secret codes and mystical ceremonies, the order represented the anti-immigrant and anti-Catholic movement in the country at that time.

Six years later the order was reorganized as the Know-Nothings, and it adopted a complex hierarchy that would greatly influence the Ku Klux Klan after the war. One of its members went on to form his own secret society, which became popular throughout the southern states during the 1850s. Called the Knights of the Golden Circle, it vowed to raise its own army that would march south into Central America to capture lands and set up new slave states, thereby strengthening the southern cause. The Knights were motivated by a desire to defend the slave-owning southern whites against the depredations of the north, and this foreshadowed much of what the Ku Klux Klan came to represent. When Gordon put forward his Prescript at the Nashville convention, he was reusing much of the elaborate ritual and purpose of the Golden Circle, the Know-Nothings and their forebears, the Star Spangled Banner. Perhaps the most crucial carry-over was to be the statement of intent of the Golden Circle, to give the south an 'organization capable of defending her rights'. It was this statement that turned the Ku Klux Klan from a midnight meeting of pranksters into what became a secret self-defence militia.

Self-defence meant violence, and incidents of violence against blacks, Republican politicians and northern reformers ('carpet-baggers') intensified as the Ku Klux Klan itself went public. Marches were conducted through towns, and an interview was given for the newspapers. In this crucial interview, Nathan Forrest, the Grand Wizard of the Klan, described the society as a 'protective, political, military organization'. It was Forrest who decided to disband the Klan in 1869, only three years after its inception. Local Klansmen had become so violent and uncontrollable, revelling in a new-found popularity and acceptance, that Forrest felt its members had abandoned the Klan's patriotic goal. Many Dens did as Forrest asked and abandoned the

Klan; others did not. Those members who continued to run riot, maiming and murdering blacks and pro-Reconstruction whites, were the very people Forrest had hoped to target. They were the roughest and lowest of men, impossible to control and after blood.

The continuing reign of terror across the southern states lasted until April 1871, when Congress implemented the Fourteenth Amendment to the Constitution, guaranteeing the rights of all US citizens. President Ulysses S. Grant called on the members of all illegal societies to disband, and from that time remaining Klan members were forcibly rounded up and arrested. It seemed that the Ku Klux Klan was being hit hard and was rapidly losing its membership, its power and its aims. Congress legislated on behalf of black citizens of the south in a way it would never have done if the Klan had not created such a furore.

By 1877 practically all the Federal army that had aided in the suppression of the Klan had returned to the north. With the south back in the hands of southern Democrats, the Klan – and the need for the Klan – waned. Terrible atrocities did still occur, isolated and improvised affairs that brought misery and death to a black or white family somewhere, but the evil perpetrators were not Klansmen, but disorganized and violent white malcontents.

It seemed, for a generation, as if the dark forces of the Ku Klux Klan were gone for good. The twentieth century arrived, and with it all the technological marvels of a new age – motor cars, aeroplanes, telephones and cinema. And it was cinema, in fact, that was responsible for the unfortunate resurrection of the Ku Klux Klan. While the First World War raged in Europe, in 1915 a block-busting new motion picture, *The Birth of a Nation*, was previewed in Los Angeles. The film was typical of others of the period in that it was silent and shot in black and white. In all other respects it was ground breaking. *The Birth of a Nation*, the brain-child of its innovative producer D.W. Griffith, was a three-hour extravaganza whose like the movie-going public had never before seen. Accompanying the screenings of the film was a full orchestra, which provided an incredible atmosphere, unrivalled in the movie business at that time. Epic in scope, the movie told the story of the Reconstruction era following the Civil War, and it painted a lurid picture of the role of both the black freedmen and the black soldiers of the Union army. At the end of the movie, the Ku Klux Klan arrived in a spectacular cavalry charge to the music of Richard Wagner's 'Ride of the Valkyries'. The Klansmen were depicted as the righters of wrongs and as the saviours of the poor, oppressed white heroes of the south.

Griffith's movie was an instant and outrageous success. Based on the insulting and highly racist best-selling novel, *The Clansmen* by Thomas Dixon, a Baptist minister, *The Birth of a Nation* fuelled a popular mood that should really have been suppressed. In the 1910s America still suffered from a pessimistic view of the place of blacks in society. In the days of Reconstruction the freed slave found friends among the northern educators and politicians, but in the course of a single generation the balance had swung. By the end of the nineteenth century the black population had become the victim of discrimination. Southern-born president, Woodrow Wilson, had begun to pass various anti-black legislation, and fears of black migration in the north were growing.

President Wilson was one of the first Americans to see the finished movie. Griffith arranged for a private showing before its public release, and Wilson was deeply impressed by what he saw. 'It is like history with lightning,' he said to Griffith, 'and my only regret is that it is all so terribly true.' With official sanction, the passage of the movie through the censors and into the movie houses was secure. Its popularity, and that of the novel that inspired it, suggested to many people that the Ku Klux Klan be revived. At a generation's distance, the Klansmen were romantically remembered as 'white knights', and Thomas Dixon found himself corresponding with numerous interested parties. Suggestions for the name of this Klan-like organization included the Aryan League of America and the Sons of the Clansmen. Dixon declined the invitations to head one of these new organizations, but unfortunately, another racist preacher had been contemplating reactivating the Klan and saw in the media furore generated by *The Birth of a Nation* the perfect springboard for a new society.

This preacher was Colonel William Simmons. Responsible for establishing the modern-day Ku Klux Klan, Simmons brought the organization out of the Deep South and into the bustling industrial cities of both north and south. For several years it resembled the benevolent and socially orientated clubs that were already familiar to the urban middle classes. This particular fraternal society, however, stressed Protestant white supremacy above all else. During an all too conscious attempt to expand the Klan, its popularity and its activities and interests, Simmons embraced the idea of defending 'Americanism'. This decision was to cause decades of misery for those who did not meet the impossible standards set by the Klan. New Klan Dens were frequently told to 'clean up the town' by the headquarters in Atlanta. To do this, its members had to impose a radical and strict doctrine on the neighbourhood – not only did they hate blacks, but also Jews, orientals, Catholics, drugs of any sort, bootlegging, corruption, assorted scandalous behaviour, un-Christian attitudes and unfair business practices. The vast immigration programme that encouraged almost 15 million people to enter America between 1900 to 1920 also caused tremendous concern.

Prohibition, labour unrest following the First World War, and the

war itself accentuated all these obsessions, turning a 'benevolent' fraternal society into a secret hate cult. From the 1920s onwards the Ku
Klux Klan as depicted in books and movies flourished. That decade
provided Americans with many opportunities to join the Klan, and
with many opportunities to hate and to commit violence. Secrecy,
treachery and fear existed everywhere in all walks of life. Did the
'non-native Americans' support the war effort? Did the unions have
America's real interests at heart or were they part of the Bolshevik
conspiracy? Prohibition, the US amendment enacted in 1920 that
made the sale and consumption of alcohol illegal, spawned the secretive, violent (and highly un-American) bootleg gangs. Many of the
gang leaders were immigrants, with Jews, Irishmen and Italians pre-
dominating.

At the war's end, an economic slump had hit the northern cities
hard, and black workers who had migrated there during the boom
years suffered from the resulting frustration. In the latter half of 1919
there were 26 race riots in American cities. Simmons realized that
there were plenty of things to be afraid of. Americanism needed protecting, and the Ku Klux Klan was his money-spinning way of doing
just that. When newspapers began to criticize the organization, appli-
cations for membership soared. What really made certain the wildfire
growth of the Ku Klux Klan, however, was not self-promotion, but
the initiation into the controversial secret society of one man: the
president of the United States, Warren G. Harding.

By late 1924 there were an estimated 4 million members of the Ku
Klux Klan, and people still continued to join. The society rode a tidal
wave of patriotism, Christian fundamentalism and white power that
was exceeded only by the patriotic white power growth of National
Socialism in Germany. The narrow racial and moral perspective and a
disdain, even hatred, for democratic government make for an interesting comparison. Totalitarian leadership was a cherished dream, as this
passage from the 1924 edition of the *Klansman's Manual* describes:

> The military form of government must and will be preserved for the
> sake of true, patriotic Americanism, because it is the only form of
> government that gives any guarantee of success. Both experience and
> history demonstrate the fallacy and futility of a so-called democratic
> form of government for any such movement as the [Ku Klux Klan].

Klan meetings (or Klonklaves in the 'KL' mania of Simmons's ritual
titles) were attended by rich and poor, educated and ignorant. New
titles, such as 'Kleagle', were invented to give the Klan a richer sound-
ing pedigree. The Ku Klux Klan, just like the Nazi Party, seems to have
touched a raw nerve, and Americans wanted answers and moral certainties just as much as Germans did. What the Klan lacked was that
immense vision that so motivated the Nazi hierarchy, party workers

and membership. It lacked also the ability to control its high-profile officials. The sickening rape, mutilation and death of a young white girl in March 1925 at the hands of a senior Klansman did irreparable harm to the society's public respectability. Drunken sexual deviant David Stephenson was a Grand Dragon, who commanded Klan activities throughout the 'Realm' of Indiana. He effectively tarnished the name of the Klan and shattered the illusions of hundreds of thousands of loyal followers. That and other Klan misdeeds saw the well-to-do members of the society drop out for good. Within five years the Klansmen numbered around one-hundredth of that promising 4 million.

The 1920s were undoubtedly the golden age of the Ku Klux Klan. Unconnected with the Klan of the Pulaski veterans, Simmons's Klan was a product of its age, reacting and over-reacting to situations and problems that were new – all part of the 'modern age'. The Klan faced fierce opposition from courageous newspaper reporters, but by far the Klan's deadliest enemy had been its own Klansmen. Hypocrisy and criminality had always been the society's chief undoing. In addition, its members felt they were being played for fools by a corrupt leadership. Finally, the Klan had no overall strategy – no great vision of the future to couple with a method of achieving it. Where Hitler was able to rouse the German people into action through the vehicle of the Nazi Party, Imperial Wizard Hiram Evans, leader of the Klan throughout the 1920s, pushed his followers to gain office but without any grand, unifying purpose.

The Depression of the 1930s gave what remained of the Ku Klux Klan something to fight for (or, more accurately, against). Labour unrest increased dramatically throughout the decade, as jobs and the economy became the overriding concern of every American, from wealthy stockholder to penniless dock-worker. The Wall Street Crash of 1929 tumbled not only the USA but the whole of the West into an apparently never-ending downward economic spiral. Labour unions were aided and abetted in their attempt to improve the lot of workers by communist activists, and these agitators were depicted by the Klan as America's greatest enemy.

Violent attacks on union workers, protesters and communist leaders were initiated, as was an entire range of other illegal and distressing activities: kidnappings, floggings, tortures and murder. Local police officers were often in on the violence. On 30 November 1935 in Tampa, Florida, the Ku Klux Klan, assisted by members of the local police force, kidnapped three labour organizers, Shoemaker, Poulnot and Rogers. The three were beaten mercilessly. Shoemaker was singled out for a particularly shocking attack and after being beaten to a pulp was subjected to hideous tortures. He was stripped naked, his genitals were burnt and blistered with a red-hot poker, and his leg was forced into boiling tar, to be charred and mutilated. He died in agony days later, with the Klan members responsible remaining free from prosecution.

Klan 'policy' at this time was mainly anti-union and anti-communist, although the society still retained its Aryan white supremacist beliefs. As Hitler rose to power in the 1930s, comparisons between the Nazi beliefs and those of the Klan were frequently made.

'Papers all state Hitler is trying to copy Mussolini,' said Will Rogers in 1933. 'Looks to me like its the KuKlux that he is copying. He doesn't want to be emperor, he wants to be a Kleagle.' Real sympathy for the American white supremacists actually surfaced in the German tract called *Hammer Magazine*, in which a compliment was paid directly to the Klan:

> We greet the gallant men of the Ku Klux Klan with our warmest
> sympathies and cherish the hope to find such cordial expressions of
> feeling with them in the accomplishment of our mutual aims.

There was a definite admiration within the ranks of the Klan for what Hitler was doing in Germany. In some isolated and extraordinary incidents the Ku Klux Klan and the Nazi Party made each other's acquaintance. They were to be brief encounters.

One prominent Klansman, the Reverend Otto Strohschein, was a German-born naturalized American. He returned to Berlin with his son in 1923, taking with him the basic tenets of the racist American secret society. His German Order of the Fiery Cross was essentially a Klan Den, ruled not by an Exalted Cyclops but by an Exalted Wotan. Initiates knelt before a cross that was flanked by a German and an American flag. Its goals were to win freedom for the German people and to rid the nation of undesirables (by opposing the Jewish population). At its height, the obscure German Klan boasted 300 members, but it suffered the fate of all cults and secret societies under Hitler. It was banned by the Nazi Party and ceased to exist.

German-Americans soon began establishing their own sympathetic Nazi groups throughout the United States, but Hitler thought little of them. In 1936 these small cultural heritage groups, including Friends of Hitler, Teutonia and the Swastika Group, merged to form the *Amerika-Deutscher Volksbund* or, simply, the Bund. Members of this organization celebrated the German heritage on which Hitler placed such emphasis, and camps were established in which German-Americans could gather and their children be properly 'educated' and in which Nazi propaganda could be circulated or discussed. Camp Nordland in New Jersey was one of the main Bund centres, and the setting for a remarkable meeting of minds. A joint Bund-Klan rally took place there on 18 August 1940, where 800 Bundsmen met and pledged a friendship with 200 Klansmen.

During the 1930s the Federal Bureau of Investigation (FBI) had done absolutely nothing to bring Klan crimes to justice, but it could hardly resist this provocation, and the Federal government became more alarmed at the so-called 'patriotism' of a society that openly admired Adolf Hitler and his dark designs. Hit with a tax bill for $685,000 in April 1944, the Klan teetered on the edge of existence. Calculated on Klan earnings from the 1920s, the bill instantly wiped out the society, and Imperial Wizard Colescott officially disbanded the Ku Klux Klan. The second great period of Klan history was over. It had lasted for far longer than the first period, from 1866 to 1871, and had welcomed millions of followers – and even a president – into its Klonkaves. The 29-year reign of terror, from 1915 to 1944, encompassed an untold number of hate crimes – beatings, tortures and murders – against innocent men, women and children. Many were not sad to see it go and hoped that in the post-war America of justice and peace, the Ku Klux Klan would never again rear its ugly, white-robed head.

Unfortunately, there lay ahead one final chapter in the blood-soaked history of the Ku Klux Klan. Klaverns in and around Atlanta, Georgia, had informally continued their Klan practices, and barely two months after VJ day (when peace was finally declared at the end of the war with Japan) a Klan ceremony was held on Georgia's Stone Mountain. It involved igniting a vast fiery cross that had been laid out on the side of the mountain, a cross of burning fuel oil. The Klan revival that followed could not match the wave of public support that the Klan had enjoyed in the early 1920s, but it found adherents. The new organization was officially founded in Atlanta by Dr Samuel Green soon after, and called itself the Association of Georgia Klans. Its diverse membership, from middle-class businessmen to police officers and war veterans, was drawn together by a common sense of inadequacy and frustration. Having fought a war against tyranny, oppression and ultra-right fascism, the government of President Truman moved quickly to improve America's human rights situation. This was made even more imperative now that the US had now become the seat of the United Nations. For blacks in southern USA, this could only be a good thing.

In 1947 the Klan's charter, under which it had operated since the First World War, was suddenly revoked. The Klan was also placed on the government's subversive list by the Attorney General. In response, the would-be Klansmen began to reorganize. By the early 1950s there was a multitude of different Ku Klux Klans, and no longer would a single group dominate the race-hate field. Florida, for example, could boast the Knights of the Ku Klux Klan in Florida, the Association of Florida Klans and the Southern Knights of the Ku Klux Klan.

Although the name of the Klan had changed, its tactics had not. On 17 May 1954 the Supreme Court declared that racial segregation within the nation's schools was unconstitutional. This spurred the Klan into action. Throughout the 1950s a campaign of terror was directed against the black population of the south. After the famous bus boycott that protested at the segregation policies of the city of Montgomery, Alabama, the Klan burned down black churches and homes. One group of crazed Klan fanatics, led by a man called Asa Carter, operated in Alabama and was known for committing particularly horrific crimes. Occasionally, such as the incident in which black Birmingham man Edward Aaron was castrated and tortured, the crimes were mere bravado – tests conducted in order to earn promotion in Carter's Original Ku Klux Klan of the Confederacy.

Civil rights activists were well on their way to winning several major concessions, and things improved immeasurably under President John F. Kennedy and his successor, Lyndon B. Johnson. The Klans began to co-ordinate their strategy to undermine these victories. Influential in this anti-black campaign was Bobby Shelton, Imperial Wizard of the United Klans of America (UKA), which was established in 1961. While the black activists used persuasion, peaceful protest and legislation to fight their war, the Klan continued with its tried and tested methods. The UKA was particularly fond of bombs, and the house of Martin Luther King's brother was demolished by a UKA device.

Samuel Bowers, described by some as an 'unasylumed lunatic', was a dangerous man who was to rise to a position of great power in Mississippi. There, as Imperial Wizard, he presided over the White Knights of the Ku Klux Klan from 1964. For five years he coordinated a fearsome campaign of violence on the state's black population. By the early 1970s there had been 75 bombings of black churches, over 300 beatings and numerous murders. Bowers, along with Shelton, was soon to face cross-examination by the House Un-American Activities Committee (HUAC). Congress was at last becoming concerned by the terrorist activities of the Klans. With Federal attention now focused on the Klan and its membership, the society began a retreat. By 1968 J. Edgar Hoover, director of the FBI, estimated that total Klan membership had shrunk from 40,000 in 1965 to 14,000. Within six years this estimate would be revised downwards to perhaps 1,500 – an all-time low for a society that had once boasted over 4 million members.

As the Vietnam War reached its bloody crescendo in Southeast Asia, it was becoming clear that the Ku Klux Klan was out for the count. The acceptance of black rights throughout the southern states, which the Klan had resisted with violence and terror, had eventually triumphed. Just as the original Klansmen spurred Washington to implement greater concessions to the black freedmen one hundred years before, so the UKA and its sociopathic cousins actually quickened the pace of civil rights. The Klan's cause had been lost through flagging support and by the attentions of HUAC. This third phase in the history of the Ku Klux Klan had come to an end. It would never again attain the nationwide status it had enjoyed, off and on over the previous century of violence, but it exists today nonetheless.

In the post-Vietnam era of American history, the Ku Klux Klan has become enmeshed in the sudden and unwelcome growth of the American neo-Nazi and Christian fundamentalist movements. Although the Klan dominated race-hate for three decades following the Second World War, in recent years it has been eclipsed by less formal and fraternally orientated organizations. Today the Klans are just one of many fanatical groups preaching similar Christian fundamentalist, white supremacist rhetoric.

White Supremacy in the USA

The post-Vietnam fascist movement centred on organized violence in a way the Ku Klux Klan never had. Men with unorthodox right-wing racist views who returned from the paddy fields and jungles of that war showed little compunction in using what they had learned in a new fight against American blacks. These fanatics were just a tiny minority. Firearms, military training and bomb manufacture were the new trends in race war, typified by the group set up by veteran Louis Beam. The Grand Dragon of Texas within the most prominent Klan faction, the Knights of the Ku Klux Klan, Beam burned with a fanatical, homicidal hatred for blacks. 'I've got the Bible in one hand and a .38 in the other hand,' he once screamed, and his obsession with paramilitary training bore fruit with a string of training camps, fully kitted out with US Army surplus equipment. Klansmen from across the country enrolled into these camps, learning the finer points of marksmanship, close-quarter fighting and survivalism. Many of his followers were themselves Vietnam veterans, and their combat experience, coupled with a huge armoury that included M16 assault rifles, made them dangerous indeed.

Louis Beam was part of a new trend of activists that were making determined preparations for a violent paramilitary campaign. His backwoods camps symbolized the movement's abject defeat at the hands of the 1960s' civil rights legislation. The far-right preoccupation now revolved around the preparation for some apocalyptic 'fightback'. With his back to the wall, the modern American fascist is fanatical and desperate.

Louis Beam's Alabama counterpart, Grand Dragon Don Black, was actually caught and charged by the FBI for attempting to overthrow a foreign country. Black had conspired with a US mercenary and the deposed Dominican prime minister, Patrick John, to overthrow the government of that nation and re-install John as the new leader. In return for the help of the Klan, the Grand Dragon was promised ample land on the island for use as a refuge from justice and for the establishment of a paramilitary training centre. This doomed plot echoed the failed dreams of the Knights of the Golden Circle, who had planned to create black slave states throughout the Caribbean in the 1850s.

Another Klansman who embraced the paramilitary strategy was Bill Wilkinson, yet another Imperial Wizard leading yet another Klan faction. His entourage regularly toted a small arsenal of deadly weaponry, and as he himself boasted, 'they're to waste *people*'. Wilkinson's training camp was named Camp My Lai after the brutal massacre of hundreds of innocent villagers by US soldiers during the Vietnam War. His followers were thoroughly trained – trained to kill. Perhaps Wilkinson's most bizarre move was his recruitment of 'Ku Klux Kids'. Establishing a Klan Youth Corps enabled the Imperial Wizard fully to indoctrinate young minds with his bigoted race hate propaganda and Christian fundamentalist teaching.

This mix of fanatical Christian belief and racism has, unfortunately, had a long history, and it is today embodied by the (quite legitimate) sect called the Church of Jesus Christ Christian-Aryan Nations. This militaristic cult was established in the years following the end of the Second World War by Klansman and minister Wesley Swift. It remains one of the most dangerous and dedicated cults operating within the United States today. Membership of the Aryan Nations is broad – it recruits Klansmen, neo-Nazis, Christian fundamentalists, ex-convicts and survivalists, labourers, office workers and even academics. The cult is strongest in the south, but also operates in California and in some states in the industrial northeast.

No commentary can fully do justice to the remarkable theology of the Aryan Nations. J.B. Stoner, an influential member and spokesperson for the sect, is a convicted bomber and has nurtured a rabid hatred of Jews and blacks for half a century. Few Klans have welcomed his membership, and he has repeatedly called for the total extermination of the Jewish race. In Stoner's own words:

> I've been fighting against the Jews and niggers and for our Lord Jesus Christ and the white race ever since I was a child ... We had lost the fight for the preservation of the white race until God himself intervened in earthly affairs with AIDS to rescue and preserve the white race that He had created. So AIDS is a great racial miracle. I praise God all the time for AIDS.

In the beliefs of the Church of Jesus Christ Christian, Adam is the progenitor of the white race *only*. Not only that, but the members believe that the 12 tribes of Israel were actually the Anglo-Saxons, the Scandinavians, Germans and Celts. Each of these races is supposedly descended from Abraham, father of the Jewish people. The Aryan

Nations dispute Abraham's role in the Bible, claiming for themselves the entire history of the Israelites:

> We believe that there is a battle being fought this day between the children of darkness (today known as the Jews) and the children of light (Yaweh, The Everliving God), the Aryan Race, the true Israel of the Bible'

Today, the sect is led by Reverend Richard G. Butler, and it operates from its headquarters at Hayden Lake in Idaho. Meanwhile, J.B. Stoner acts as an 'ambassador' for the cult, speaking on its behalf to sympathetic audiences. The church does not renounce, but rather embraces, violence, and it sponsors the Order, a terrorist organization that carries out anonymous attacks on the enemies of the Aryan Nations. The Order perpetrates beatings, assassinations and robberies, and the latter help to finance both itself and (allegedly) the Aryan Nations. In early 1997 an Aryan Nations minister, Pastor Mark Thomas, was arrested for conspiracy to commit bank robbery and for handling stolen money. A group calling itself the Aryan Republican Army was mentioned in connection with his arrest.

Where do the Aryan Nations end and the apocalyptic cults begin? Butler's cult preaches extreme and utterly fanatical racial hatred based on little more than badly interpreted Bible texts, but, like the fledgling Nazi Party, it predicts a great struggle followed by the founding of a blessed kingdom:

> The usurper (the Jewish conspiracy supposed to be controlling all governments) will be thrown out by the terrible might of Yahweh's people ... there is to be a Day of Judgement and a day when Christ's Kingdom (government) will be established on earth, as it is in heaven.

This prediction of violence and warfare prior to a divine paradise is typical of the more fatalistic and suicide-prone groups, which are discussed in Chapter 7. There are, indeed, definite connections between the militiamen responsible for the deaths of almost 200 people in the Oklahoma bombing in 1995 and the Aryan Nations. Timothy McVeigh, the man who planted the bomb, had previously been a member of the Ku Klux Klan. The Aryan Nations, the Klan and the militiamen all have an overriding fear of the US government.

Linking the Church of Jesus Christ Christian-Aryan Nations inextricably with fundamentalist anti-government survivalist movements is the church's unsubstantiated belief in a 'Zionist Occupational Government'. Washington is (allegedly) controlled completely by Jewish forces, and the government must be overthrown before the Aryan revolution can succeed. The Aryan Nations blur the distinction between fundamentalist Christians, neo-Nazis, anti-Semitic hate groups and apocalyptic anti-government revolutionaries. All we can say for certain about this far-right Christian movement is that its membership is consumed by an irrational fear of non-white peoples. From this fear has emerged a dangerous and unbridled hatred.

Other US fascist groups do not have such confusing physiognomies. The familiar-sounding National Socialist White People's Party (NSWP) makes no secret of the debt it owes to Hitler's own National Socialist Party. Founded in 1958 by George Rockwell, a naval officer and ardent neo-Nazi, the NSWP was originally (and rather tactlessly) named the American Nazi Party. Politically, the party reflects a common view among other white supremacist groups: that the white race is under attack from non-whites via liberalism, racial equality and immigration. 'We believe that the Aryan race is our nation, rather than any particular piece of geography or any specific government,' declares a party tract. The NSWP seeks to unite the Aryan peoples and to defend the Aryan bloodline from contamination. 'To do this it is necessary to ... return control of [North America] to the Aryan peoples who originally conquered, populated, and created its culture and political institutions.' Of course, there is no mention in the bigoted tract of returning the continent to the Native Americans who first colonized it 10,000 years ago.

One of the weapons in the NSWP's war against the much-hated Jewish people is its refutation that the Holocaust actually took place. 'Take away the Holocaust,' says Harold Covington, the party's leader, 'and one is stunned with admiration for the brilliance of Adolf Hitler, the vision and accomplishments of the Third Reich, and the incredible military heroism of the German people.' For American (as well as European) fascists, the Holocaust is an indelible stain on Hitler's career as a politician and war leader. Historians agree: Adolf Hitler *did* turn around the Depression-hit Germany of the 1930s, he virtually ended unemployment, and he provided the nation with a viable and energetic economy. Unfortunately for neo-Nazi 'revisionists', Hitler also initiated the bloodiest and most widely fought war in human history, and he *did* perpetrate one of the most terrible crimes against humanity. Hitler undeniably sent over 6 million people, mainly Jews, into the Zyklon-B gas chambers for mass-extermination. Truly sickening experiments were also carried out on inmates of the concentration camps, not just Jews but also national Poles and Russians.

Neo-Nazi groups like the National Socialist White People's Party, which try to pretend that the Holocaust was all a fiction, are desperately trying to give credence to a movement that is utterly devoid of all credibility and respectability. The Holocaust is a shackle that has, for these fringe societies, hindered any attempts they make to rehabilitate their cherished totalitarian leader. We must pray that it stays that way.

European Neo-Nazis

In the mid-1990s Hitler's last-stand bunker in Berlin was rediscovered and explored by archaeologists. Within the cold, wet, concrete labyrinth were found rich and colourful wall paintings that bring to life visions of a lost dream. Aryan men and proud German storm-troopers were depicted holding banners and flags – Aryo-heroics symbolizing a failed crusade. But rather than restore the building's grim interior as a museum, a moment in time from one of history's very worst times, the German government has been forced to re-seal the bunker and keep its exact location hidden. It fears that the bunker will become an infernal shrine to a disenchanted youth cult in modern Germany. The Nazi ideology of the 1930s has been reworked and rediscovered; it has been given new strength in an attempt to utilize its ancient and arcane properties. Today we have a new movement: the neo-Nazis.

The neo-Nazi network spreads across western Europe and deep into Russia, and across the Atlantic it connects into the world's Aryan hotbed, the USA. As we have seen, the American far right encompasses a host of neo-Nazi groups, Aryan brotherhoods, anti-black groups, anti-Semitic groups, anti-Catholic groups – the list is depressingly long. In Britain the neo-Nazis are well represented. Politically, the old National Front and the more modern British National Party hustle their racist policies and fundamental white-power messages. Meanwhile, a tiny but violent Nazi terror group, which calls itself Combat 18, threatens a campaign of racist terrorism never before seen in the UK. Taking its numerical designation from the alphabetical placing of Adolf Hitler's initials, Combat 18 is a product of the 1990s. It is a vocal and violent group of right-wing extremists who employ traditional terrorist tactics to pursue their aims. Members claim that 'white revolution is the only solution', and the goal is to foment race hatred within Britain's inner cities. Combat 18 makes no secret of its supposed links with the Ulster loyalist terror groups, and senior police officers have officially referred to Combat 18 as a 'terrorist organization' (much to its delight). For many people, Combat 18 came to prominence in the media as the main culprit behind the mass soccer violence in 1995 during England's friendly match against Ireland. The group had always found the football terraces a useful outlet for its violent potential. After it had whipped some of the English supporters into a frenzy, Combat 18 weakly declared that the rioting that followed was a pre-planned protest against the Anglo-Irish peace process.

Combat 18 does not just indulge in instigating riots but also in more personal and horrifying acts of brutal aggression. Critics of the group, anti-fascist protesters and writers, as well as more 'liberal' right-wing racists, have been systematically beaten, threatened and terrified. One critic has even been nailed to the floor through his hands and feet. These people are thugs with an ideology of hatred and racial purity that has no basis, no social backing and no logic. Their avowed intention is to 'secure the existence of our people and a future for white children'. This involves harassing, assaulting and killing members of ethnic minorities and creating a crippling climate of fear and terror. In the mid-1990s some gains were made and finances were secured by way of the lucrative neo-Nazi music industry. This churns out ultra-racist material for the back-street dives, off-limits pubs and shady clubs of the largest cities. Bands like Screwdriver preach open race hate and street violence to a loyal audience of young skinhead males. Leading Combat 18 through its bloody peak was drug pusher Paul Sargent, known to his followers as 'Ginger Pig', a dangerous and violent man who evaded police attention until early 1997.

The police crackdown forced the membership to splinter, and a letter-bombing campaign linked to Combat 18 in January 1997 disguised even deeper fissures. At first it seemed that intercepted letter-bombs sent from neo-Nazis in Denmark were targeted at enemies of the radical group. In particular, well-known mixed-race couples, such as sports competitors Sharon Davies and husband Derek Redmond, were to be the first victims in a new race war. But soon material came to light indicating that the other targets were actually members of the fascist far right. Combat 18 was in a fight for survival against its rivals at home and abroad. Sargent was summarily expelled from the organization, and other, equally sinister groups readied themselves to emerge from the shadows. The future for Combat 18 is uncertain, but there is no end of extremist neo-Nazi factions in Britain that are willing and able to beat, torture and kill. Big names include Blood and Honour and the newly formed British Hammerskins. The successful usurper will have sole domination of the neo-Nazi music business, a multi-million pound industry that has already sustained Combat 18 through five years of urban mayhem.

It would be a mistake to think that all neo-Nazi activists in Britain and Europe fit the skinhead, bully-boy image that dominates the movement. The neo-Nazi political movement also circulates Hitler's racist doctrines in a more refined manner, even though the Nazi dictator died over half a century ago. John Tyndall, former leader of the National Front organization, once commentated that his (and the group's) firm Nazi beliefs had to be hidden beneath a veneer of cultivated British patriotism and nationalism. 'The NF could not be openly Nazi because it would be stuck in the mire of the Second World War and the death camps,' wrote Tyndall in a letter to American colleagues. Consequently, the National Front replaced its swastika emblem with a Union Jack. Although a national flag often carries little if any party political association in other countries (such as the USA, for example), in Britain the Union Jack seems to embody right-wing ideology. Ultra-nationalists, right-wing traditionalists and racists have often rallied around the national flag. The National Front and other intolerant groups have done much to create this sad association. The latest incarnation of the fascist right, the British National Party, shot into the headlines in 1993 when the residents of London's poorest borough elected a BNP member, Derek Beackon, to a council seat. This was achieved by the promulgation of unsubstantiated rhetoric claiming that minorities were being given priority over whites in the allocation of public housing. Twisting facts and playing on people's fears and concerns are the standard tactics of a party that can achieve nothing by more respectable methods. Violent crime dogs all aspects of the neo-Nazi movement. BNP leaders like John Tyndall (having moved on from the National Front), Richard Edmonds and Anthony Lecomber have criminal convictions for violent attacks, and several BNP members are serving jail sentences on similar charges. Combat 18 has served the BNP's needs quite usefully in this capacity, both as a hit squad targeting vocal anti-fascists and protecting neo-Nazi writers and speakers.

Where violence fails, the BNP and its associates disseminate Nazi propaganda among the target audience. More than 100,000 copies of an anti-Semitic leaflet, 'Holocaust News', were handed out to school pupils recently, and the BNP was found to be behind this campaign. Why neo-Nazis should repeatedly publish propaganda material about the Holocaust is an interesting question. The subject has become an obsession for many in the movement who wish to see neo-Nazism widen its popular appeal.

The most frightening aspect of the 1997 Combat 18 débâcle was the fact that international forces were at work. Until recently, many of Europe's neo-Nazi groups have been focused inward, and their activities have rarely strayed over their respective national borders. This even included the bland-sounding International Third Position (a splinter group of the National Front movement). Recently, however, the neo-Nazi movement as a whole has networked, creating loose and informal cross-border ties through the use of the phone, fax and Internet. The letter-bombs intercepted by Scotland Yard were sent by neo-Nazis from Denmark. This nation has been a hot-bed of racist Aryan ideology, and three main factions (*Nationalpartiet Danmark, Partiet De Nationale* and *Danmarks Nationalsocialistiske Bevægelse,* DNSB) dominate the Danish right wing. Of all the Danish neo-Nazi groups, the DNSB is the most vocal, the most dangerous and the most notorious, and, like all of these tiny factions, it keeps in touch with other groups across Europe. Some evidence of close contacts with a banned German neo-Nazi power group, the *Nationalistische Front,* has recently been uncovered.

For many neo-Nazis, scattered as they are throughout the length and breadth of Europe, the German racists are the pure-blood of the entire movement, and the neo-Nazi groups there have become a fountainhead of Aryan ideology. Germany itself has seen a staggering and frightening resurgence in racist attacks since the late 1980s, and in particular since the reunification of East and West Germany. For a period immediately following the collapse of the Berlin Wall, rival gangs fought across the rooftops of Berlin, the anarchist *Autonomen* versus the neo-Nazis. There were, incredibly, 372 anti-Semitic attacks in early 1995, more than occurred in the five years before 1933 (the period of Hitler's rise to power). Compounding this horror, is the fact that anti-Semitism forms only a small part of the neo-Nazi agenda. German Nazis have carried out 13,000 attacks since 1990, with the main targets being foreign workers and asylum seekers. But the homeless, the handicapped and members of the Jewish population are also targeted.

This reign of mindless terror has resulted in at least 75 murders, the destruction of homes and hostels and the desecration of graveyards and synagogues. There have been 'pogroms' at Rostock and Hoyerswerda, targeting not just Jewish people, but the numerically stronger immigrant minorities of the 1990s, in particular the Turks. Murder, mutilation and suffering are the tools in trade of a sadistic and desperate movement that is driven by hatred yet is devoid of logic. It seems that logic rarely has a place, even in the established political arena. Some Germans have endorsed the policies of the main racist parties, such as the *Republikaner Partei* (RP).

In 1992 ex-Waffen SS officer Franz Sconhuber, standing as a representative of the RP, won half a million votes in rich Baden-Württemberg. A year later the equally bigoted organization *Deutsche Volksunion* was able to secure a quarter of a million votes in Hessen. Other, more violence-orientated neo-Nazi groups, include the *Gesinnungsgemeinschaft der Neue Front* (GdNF), *Direkte Aktion* and the *Freiheitliche Deutsche Arbeiter Partei* (FAP). The GdNF, for one, has proven links with the American Nazi organization, NSDAP-AO.

Some estimates have put the number of German fascist activists at 66,000, spread among approximately 80 different ultra-right groups, some large, some small. Government bans on these cults of violence seem to have had little real effect, and, according to some, are merely a cosmetic attempt carried out by a government that wants to be seen to be doing something. What can be done? If the problem were localized, a one-off aberration depending on local support, the German, and European authorities would more easily be able to target the problem. But on a continent-wide scale, the neo-Nazi phenomenon must be seen as a social ill of the first order, rather than as a gang of sick thugs who get their thrills from attacking defenceless minorities.

Adolf Hitler's failed crusade is often seen as a blueprint to be copied and improved upon by today's fascists. In Austria, the birthplace of

Hitler, a man named Gottfried Kussel was jailed in 1993 for attempting to revive the National Socialist (Nazi) Party. In retaliation, his neo-Nazi organization, the *Volkstreue Ausserparlamenarische Opposition* (VAPO), initiated a merciless letter-bombing campaign that resulted in the mutilation of three innocent people. When the Vienna police raided VAPO property, they discovered a cache of weapons capable of equipping an entire army battalion. Hundreds of fully automatic assault rifles, handguns, anti-personnel grenades, mines and anti-tank rocket launchers were stored ready for use in a wave of racist violence. VAPO members were not urban kids dreaming of some fascist revolution; several members of the group had fought as mercenaries in former Yugoslavia alongside the Croatian army.

Just as in Britain and Germany, every neo-Nazi hit squad has its 'soft' political wing. In Austria the *Freiheitliche Partei Osterreichs* (FRO) campaigns for seats, and in 1993 the party's leader, Jorg Haider, was able to secure 780,000 signatures for an official petition that opposed immigration. His party ranks as the third biggest political party in Austria.

Almost every western European state harbours its violent neo-Nazis: the *Vlaams Blok* (VB), the *Parti des Nouvelles* and *L'Assaut* in Belgium; the *Centrumdemocraten* (CD), *Voorpost* and *Aktiefront Nationale Socialisten* (ANS) in the Netherlands; and the *Front National* (FN), led by Jean-Marie Le Penn in France. Unlike the British National Party, Le Penn's movement has made significant political gains, and (like the BNP) regularly employs neo-Nazi thugs from more openly violent terror gangs as street enforcers. There are Italian neo-Nazis (the Armed Revolutionary Nuclei), Swedish neo-Nazis (*Vitt Ariskt Mostand*), Norwegian neo-Nazis (*Hvit Arisk Motstand*), Polish, Czech and Hungarian neo-Nazis – even (ironically) Russian and Ukrainian neo-Nazis.

In Russia the greatest prize for any ultra-right party is the state's valuable nuclear capability and a legacy of strident militarism that dominated half a century of global politics. Vladimir Zhirinovsky, political demagogue and outspoken fascist activist, won 23.4 per cent of the votes during the 1993 elections to the Russian parliament. He still retains links with the German neo-Nazi *Deutsche Volksunion* and openly displays his admiration for that most famous of moustachioed German dictators. With world media attention focusing on him during the 1993 election campaign, Zhirinovsky preached isolationism, Cold War rhetoric and racial hatred. Of all the current far-right fanatics, Vladimir Zhirinovsky and his innocuously titled Liberal-Democrat Party may yet prove to be the deadliest and most catastrophic heir to Adolf Hitler. Throughout the war Hitler had a team of under-funded atomic scientists working to produce an atomic bomb. The team failed in its task, but the Russian Zhirinovsky, or someone like him, may yet attempt to use nuclear weapons in an act of racial genocide.

CHAPTER THREE

Architects of Terror

At the very end of the 1980s our television screens were filled with conflict and horror. The so-called 'Velvet Revolution', which saw the overthrow of communism in eastern Europe and the institution of democracy, had taken the world by surprise. For the intransigent dictator of Romania, Nikolae Ceausescu, the revolution came as a complete shock. Immensely destructive fighting followed the people's uprising, and battles raged with assault rifles, grenades and armoured vehicles in the streets for several weeks.

On the other side of the globe, another conflict hit the headlines: Panama. President George Bush had sent in an array of US military forces to capture the nation's drug-dealing ex-CIA ruler, General Noriega. It was an explosive, no-holds-barred police action, which resulted in massive amounts of property damage, numerous civilian casualties and the deployment of various experimental weapons (such as the F-117 Stealth bomber) for the first time. With these two conflicts competing for air-time around Christmas 1989, a colleague of mine wryly commented on the timing of the Panamanian invasion: 'You don't think the Romanian uprising is an accident do you? What better way to keep your invasion out of the news.'

No expert in international affairs, this observer was voicing a sentiment that has become current in today's multi-layered society: 'None of us can truly know the reality of what is going on around us.' And in the area of spontaneous revolutions, a fear often exists that they have been purposely engineered by unseen forces for their own ends. This fear is not new. Bolshevik revolutionaries, fighting to overthrow Russia's tsarist government in 1917, were seen by elements in the West as part of an evil international conspiracy, the first shock troops in an endless chain of revolutions that would encircle the world like beacons. Dark and mysterious forces were reputed to be at work within the Russian Revolution. Its detractors continued to ascribe a hidden level of purpose behind its social reorganization and its radical economic policies. One group in particular was accused of orchestrating the Russian Revolution. That group was the Freemasons.

This (often misplaced) fear that unseen forces are manipulating important world events can be traced even further back to the fiery political events of the eighteenth century. It was a century of revolution and of change, with two of the most momentous popular uprisings of human history taking place within two decades of one another. They were the American War of Independence (1776) and the French Revolution (1789). The murky political scene of that period was shot through with unsubstantiated rumours, with hidden agendas and with secret and not so secret societies. The alleged involvement of these secret societies in the two greatest revolutions in history has raised questions about the motives and the motivators of revolutions ever since. It is not just more recent, well-intentioned uprisings that have been tarnished by the legacy of eighteenth-century paranoia but also the chief suspect in all of these revolutions – Freemasonry. Whereas Freemasons today depict themselves as right-thinking members of the Establishment and benevolent businessmen involved in low-key charity work, the modern organization has had trouble shaking off this unwanted and unflattering sinister image from the past.

The truth is that Freemasons *have* been associated with revolutionary forces during several crucial periods in European history. Definite masonic links have been established with the Jacobite Rebellions, the Irish Rebellions and the unification of Italy. While Freemasonry is in *no* way a violent organization, is it so difficult to believe that Freemasons participated in the American, French and Russian Revolutions ?

The First Freemasons

There are many versions of the actual origins of the secret fraternal society known as Freemasonry. Modern Freemasons like to trace the rituals and customs of the organization back to the days of the Egyptian pharaohs, to King Solomon and the builders of his famous Temple. Any associations of masonic history with biblical figures, however, rank as pure mythology. Hard evidence of a masonic order goes back only as far as the 1600s and seems to have been based on already existing guilds of practising stonemasons. What could possibly be the connection between medieval stonemasons and later revolutionary secret societies?

It seems that the stonemason enjoyed some prestige in medieval society. Those who carved in free-stone (which was used for arches and intricate decoration) had a particularly elevated status among other craftsmen. Other masons earned their living carving rough stone blocks and were not 'free' to travel where they liked. Thus these skilled stonemasons became known as 'free' masons. To prevent themselves from being exploited, the freemasons banded together into cooperative guilds, called lodges. The master mason on each building site ran the lodge, and members employed a series of grips and passwords with which they could identify one another. Although these lodges sprang up wherever work existed – the building of a new cathedral, for example – in London there became established a permanent London Masons Company. Masons across Europe banded together into similar fraternal organizations; there were the Compagnonnages in France and the Steinmetzen in Germany, and in Scotland, too, masons were developing their own system of passwords.

It was in Scotland that the most influential member of the new organization came to prominence. King James VI of Scotland became also king of England as James I in 1603, and his accession to the English throne united the two countries and established the Stuart dynasty as the legitimate royal family. Some writers have attributed the sudden emergence of 'speculative' Freemasonry to this monarch. 'Speculative' Freemasonry, which began to spread throughout Britain in the seventeenth century, differed from 'operative' Freemasonry in that its members were not actually masons. The lodge system, the secret signs and the ritual of the Freemasons were all employed, but the fundamental reason for the lodge meetings was now quite different. Members used the secret lodge meetings as clubs within which the conversational atmosphere turned to the underground topics of the day, especially to the esoteric subjects filtering in from the continent – philosophy, science, alchemy and medicine. In addition, the growing fascination of wealthy young men for art and architecture and the secrets of the ancients provided reason enough for them to seek membership into Freemasonry. The architect Elias Ashmole (1617–92) and, later, the noted antiquary William Stukeley (1687–1765) joined the movement to discover the hidden traditions of the ancient builders. Such was the enthusiasm of educated non-masons to join the London Masons Company that a parallel group, called Acception, was established in 1619 purely to cater for them.

Following the dark and chaotic years of the English Civil War and the Restoration of the Stuart monarchy in 1660, Freemasonry blossomed. It blended progressive ideas from the continent (a movement calling itself Rosicrucianism) with a general freedom of thought among the educated. Freemasonry seemed to act as a binding agent throughout the tumultuous seventeenth century, providing for a well-educated and liberal-minded group of men in British society a well-protected (because of its inherent secrecy) association. In a world of divisions and inequalities, the masonic lodge became a leveller, allowing people to talk together who would otherwise never have met. Within this enlightened and tolerant atmosphere the Royal Society was born, one year after the Restoration of the Stuart monarchy. Although modern Freemasons claim always to have remained non-partisan, the lodges owed their existence to the House of Stuart. This climate of toleration contrasted sharply with that of the oppressive

Catholic governments across the Channel. Many of the Rosicrucian thinkers who had contributed so much to the growth of Freemasonry were actually refugees from German principalities and France.

Between 1660 and 1688 Freemasonry reached its historical apogee. As a select club for cultured, thinking men, for common craftsmen and for members of the nobility, the movement proved incredibly influential. Following the Great Fire of London in 1666 an immense period of rebuilding was begun. Both 'operative' and 'speculative' Freemasons were able to take the credit for the achievements of this impressive building project. Christopher Wren, designer of St Paul's Cathedral (among many other grandiose buildings), was not only a brilliant architect but also a founder member of the Royal Society and a Freemason. Two decades later he achieved the honoured position of Grand Master.

Ending the 'honeymoon period' of the new and vibrant society was a revolution that would split the nation and split English society. The Glorious Revolution of 1688 would also inextricably link the Free-masons with sedition and revolution – whether such links were justi-fied or not. King James II converted to Catholicism in 1685, causing tension and suspicion within Parliament, and many feared a Catholic backlash against those Protestants who were active and vocal. In a deft *coup d'état*, Parliament offered the British throne to James's sister Mary, who was married to the Protestant William, the Dutch Prince of Orange (the House of Orange was the ruling dynasty in the Nether-lands). William accepted and landed on English soil on 5 November 1688. James II did not give up his crown without a fight and, after fleeing from the country for a time, returned to fight the Battle of the Boyne on 1 July 1690. The battle lost, the last Stuart to reign as king of Britain fled the country and lived in exile forever after. But the secret society he had helped to create remained in place, although some Freemasons did cross the Channel to live in exile with James Stuart.

A foreign king now occupied the English throne, and although there were several dissenters, the change of monarch was accepted rela-tively calmly. The throne would soon be occupied by a German claimant, George I, but the pro-Stuart cause did not give up hope of regaining the crown. Even though the deposed James II died in exile in 1701, his son, James – known as the Old Pretender – carried on the struggle. In turn, his son, Charles Edward – known as Bonnie Prince Charlie or the Young Pretender – sought to mount an invasion and claim what he regarded as his rightful inheritance.

The exiled Stuarts were not lone figures dreaming of a return that could never come to pass. They were backed by an intricate and enthusiastic network of supporters in both France and England. Named 'Jacobites' after *Jacobus*, which is the Latin form of the name James, these supporters helped to coordinate several armed attempts at ousting the Hanoverian kings. The first took place in 1708. With a French fleet and manpower, a Jacobite invasion force readied itself to sail against England, but poor organization led to the entire project being cancelled. Many Jacobites were Catholic, and many more were Scottish, the original home of the Stuart dynasty. Scottish hatred of the Hanoverian kings boiled over into open warfare, which the Jacobite movement encouraged and assisted. Two great campaigns were fought by the Stuart monarchs-in-exile: in 1715 and in 1745–6. Both were failures for the Stuart cause, and following the defeat of the Scottish clans at Culloden in 1746, no further attempts were made to take the crown.

Freemasonry attempted to remain outwardly neutral during the Jacobite rebellions, but the network of secret lodges had proved highly advantageous to the Jacobite cause. Freemasons and Jacobites had become popularly associated with one another, and this led to the execution of several aristocratic Freemasons. For the new rulers, the Freemasons were a dangerous and unwanted group, hiding their traitorous beliefs behind a veil of secrecy and subterfuge. Not all Freemasons were Jacobites, but many were, and following the 1715 uprising it was decided to form a purely English branch of Freemasonry. Founded in 1717, the Grand Lodge was a counter to the Scottish brand of Freemasonry, which was dominated by Jacobites and Catholics. From its very inception, the Grand Lodge was shot through with a thick vein of patriotism. Toasts to King George and rousing songs designed to display the patriotism and loyalty of the membership were a prominent feature of the opening ceremony. The many degrees of rank that had become a feature of the established lodges were abandoned and replaced with the three basic degrees: Apprentice, Fellow Craft and Master. This attempt to hijack the social and political influence enjoyed by Scottish Freemasonry soon made headway. However, only five years after the founding of the Grand Lodge, the worst fears of the Protestant establishment were realized. A Jacobite conspiracy to overthrow the capital with help from exiles in France was uncovered. One of the ringleaders proved to be Dr John Arbuthnot (1667–1735), an influential Freemason and member of the newly formed Grand Lodge – and also a Scot.

With the publication of the 'Constitutions of the Freemasons' by the Grand Lodge in 1723, the organization made every effort to emphasize its patriotism and religious neutrality. The document called for religious tolerance and for harmony and friendship across social divides. More importantly, it declared in black and white that Freemasons of the Grand Lodge should not 'be concerned in Plots and Conspiracies'. The radical intellectual liberalism that characterized Scottish Freemasonry was gone. What the Grand Lodge put in its place was a fraternal brotherhood that came to value tolerance, culture and social harmony. Without a religious or political agenda, Freemasonry became an enlightened society in which up-to-date ideas could be freely discussed among open-minded individuals. Charity and the duty of all members to come to the aid of their fellows also became quite prominent aspects to the movement.

After 1746 and the defeat of Jacobite forces at the Battle of Culloden, the pro-Stuart cause ended. Scottish Freemasonry was not now considered to be the hotbed of revolutionaries that it once had been, and some English lodges began offering the 'higher' degrees to their members. The very real threat of revolution that had been nurtured within Jacobite Freemasonry had a profound impact on the course of later English masonic history. Members of the Grand Lodge would always make it very clear that their society was apolitical and that it would never become mixed up in political squabbles, conspiracies or revolutions. What happened within masonic lodges overseas was another matter entirely, as the American colonies were to discover.

Revolution in America

A certain degree of controversy surrounds the argument that Freemasonry had an important influence on the American Revolution. Certain facts are, however, undeniable. The most important leaders of the revolutionary cause to free the American colonies from British control were all Freemasons. They included George Washington, Paul Revere, Admiral John Paul Jones, Alexander Hamilton and Benjamin Franklin. Ideas and concepts held dear by the Freemasons, such as liberty, freedom of speech and of the press and fully representative government, were all incorporated into the American Constitution. Finally, one of the symbols of Freemasonry, the pyramid emblazoned with the image of an 'all-seeing eye', was placed on every dollar bill in the country. Beneath this symbol the words *Novus Ordo Seclorum* (A New Secular Order) announced to the world the intentions of this masonic state: to rule without religious bias or prejudice – to be, as the Freemasons had declared in their Constitution, wholly apolitical.

But to declare that those men who were responsible for finally drafting the constitution of this new state were members of, and influenced by, Freemasonry tells us nothing of their previous involvement. Did Freemasons pursue an agenda during the War of Independence? Did Freemasons actually foment the revolt in the first place?

Of course, Freemasons arrived in the American Colonies just as many other, non-masonic English and Scottish travellers did. One of the earliest recorded Freemasons to settle in America was John Skene, who became the deputy governor of New Jersey. Several other American colonists are known to have joined lodges during their visits to England. It was only to be expected that these isolated and outnumbered Freemasons would come together to create their own American lodges. Benjamin Franklin (1706–90), scientist and author, was fascinated with the growing phenomenon of Freemasonry, and in 1731 he became a member of a local lodge. At that time several lodges were already in existence. Rising rapidly in such a small order, Franklin soon became the Grand Master of the Pennsylvanian Freemasons.

Britain's Grand Lodge took note of the situation in the American Colonies and during the 1730s began sponsoring masonic lodges there, as off-shoots of the Grand Lodge itself. By the end of the decade it had established affiliated lodges in Georgia, New Hampshire, New York, Pennsylvania, South Carolina and Massachusetts. The growth of the secret society continued during the following decades. When friction developed between the colonies and the mother country, Freemasonry may have acted as a conduit for intelligence as well as a forum for debate. The British government continued to press for increased tax levies on its colonies, and discontent erupted into public outrage. Two American Freemasons were behind a condemnation of British policies by the Virginia Assembly in 1769. In the following years British forces used violence to quell dissent, eventually leading, in 1773, to the spoiling of an entire cargo of tea that sat within the hold of a ship in Boston harbour. The Boston Tea Party, as the incident came to be known, was a non-violent act whereby 342 chests of tea (which were to be sold at a greatly reduced price, undercutting all local tea merchants) were heaved overboard by a large group of colonial activists disguised as Mohawk Indians. This bloodless incident marked the beginning of the American War of Independence, and in April 1775 hostilities-proper were initiated at Concord, just outside Boston. The actual Declaration of Independence, signed on 4 July 1776, placed the united opposition of the 13 American colonies under the revolutionary leadership of George Washington.

Few non-violent events can have had as much effect on the history of the United States of America as the Boston Tea Party, and a convincing argument can be made to show that the protest was actually orchestrated by Boston Freemasons. Boston's Freemasons' Hall was used not just by Freemasons attending regular meetings but also by a number of other secret societies. Shadowy groups, such as the Committee of Correspondence, the Long Room Club and the Sons of Liberty, were all attended by Freemasons. It was the Sons of Liberty (of which Paul Revere was a member) that really turned covert dissent into overt action. Demonstrations and public disorder were the society's weapon against British domination, and a third of the group's leadership were Bostonian Freemasons. It might be said that Freemasons were highly influential in lighting the touch-paper of the American Revolution, but there is less certainty that Freemasonry itself was involved. There is a difference. Minutes of masonic meetings in Boston during the period of the Tea Party fail to indicate any kind of conspiracy or revolutionary master-plan. The lodges of St Andrew's and St John's are unlikely to have planned and orchestrated the act of rebellion. Nevertheless, individual Freemasons, driven by the beliefs and philosophy of their brotherhood, *did* decide to take action.

The Sons of Liberty provided the main vehicle that allowed motivated brethren to organize and direct the Boston Tea Party. The War of Independence was fought and won in a similar manner. There was no secret conclave of Freemasons directing the war from some remote location, but there were instead members of disparate lodges at the forefront of the independence movement. A number of the colonial generals were Freemasons, but a number were not. A number of the signatories to the Declaration of Independence in 1776 were Freemasons, but others, again, were not. And then, of course, there were Freemasons fighting from the ranks of the British army 'redcoats'. The tide of war ebbed and flowed until 1783. No major decisive engagement took place, and the reasons for this are partly military, partly logistical and partly social. At least one writer has suggested that the common masonic ties that linked American and British commanders were in some way responsible for the poor showing of the British forces. At the Peace of Paris in 1783, Britain formally acknowledged the independence of the colonies.

The American colonies were now free to establish their own government, and just as Freemasonry had been there at the start of the war, it was there at the end. Conspiracy historians see in the creation of the American government the machinations of a masonic élite. But like the Boston Tea Party, the founding of the Constitution was influenced more by the masonic beliefs of its perpetrators than by the secret society itself. When the Constitutional Convention met in 1787, several notable ideals held in high regard by members of the brethren were put into practice. Democracy and social justice were to underpin the laws governing this new nation. It was to be the office, and not the man who occupied that office, that would be the key to power. And this power would be transient. Once in office, a despot would be forced to leave at the end of his fixed term, by being impeached or deposed. This new republican government became a model of the Freemasonry ideal. When George Washington took up the presidency of the new-born American government on 4 February 1789, Freemasons occupied many of the important positions.

Both the national currency and the national capital would succumb to the ministrations of masonic influence. The 13-stepped, 4-sided pyramid topped by the mystical 'all-seeing eye', which still adorns dollar bills, is an unashamed symbol of Freemasonry. Any modern street map of Washington will illustrate the scale of the influence that enthusiastic Freemasons had on the city's design. Both the Capitol and the White House became crucial foci in the awesome building project. Architecture would come to symbolize the construction of not just a new city, but a new society, regulated, ordered and harmonious. Christopher Wren, Freemason and architect, had attempted a similar feat over a century before in the ruins of London.

As the first president of the fledgling government and the highest placed Freemason in the land, George Washington was invited to lay the cornerstone of the Capitol building. Supervising the ceremony was the Grand Lodge of the state of Maryland, and Washington was asked to serve as the Master. Lodge members wore their exotic masonic costumes, as did Washington and the members of his own Virginian lodge. The items used by him in the ceremony were the basic symbols of Freemasonry: the trowel, set square, level and gavel. These precious tools are today in safekeeping at a masonic lodge in the Federal District of Columbia.

The achievements of the American revolutionaries would soon provide a model and an inspiration for those fighting oppression in France. However, it was to be a Reign of Terror that would fill the vacuum there, not an egalitarian state designed to mimic the principles of the masonic lodge. Freemasonry did not suddenly initiate revolutions across the globe in imitation of the American success. For one thing, there was no single organization called Freemasonry, only numerous competing traditions and thousands of unconnected and independent lodges. The organization, the resources and even the desire to begin such an outrageous plan had never existed. But Freemasonry had shown that its members, even when operating without direction from the hierarchy, could put its philosophies into practice. The secret society could influence nations, help overthrow governments and even found new nation-states.

The Reign of Terror

European Freemasonry, in comparison, had a far from easy existence. In many areas the movement was tolerated, and even patronized, by national leaders (such as Frederick the Great, ruler of Prussia, 1740–86). But as a pioneer of liberal and egalitarian ideas, the society came under fire from others. The Roman Catholic Church, in particular, was afraid of Freemasonry's attitude to religion and the Establishment. Pope Clement XII (reigned 1730–40) denounced the order in 1738 and officially forbade members of the Catholic Church from joining it. Spain and Portugal, both fiercely Catholic countries, were eager to follow up the pope's appeals, and the Inquisition there was turned against Freemasonry. Many of the society's members were summarily arrested and tortured. The shadow of the Inquisition was long. Even as a machine of the Middle Ages, it still operated in the middle of the eighteenth century – a century often called the Age of Enlightenment or the Age of Reason.

In France the edicts of the pope on the matter were not taken too seriously, but the seeds of doubt and suspicion had been planted. Clement had stated that an organization that fostered secrecy must have something to hide. Not only did he suspect its members of heresy, but he claimed Freemasons were 'depraved and perverted'. Jacobite Freemasons, in exile with their Stuart king, found allies among the new-born French network of lodges. In fact, some historians have suggested that the exiled Jacobite Freemasons were themselves responsible for establishing the order in that country. In order to cement an alliance, a prominent Scotsman called Michael Ramsay helped to introduce a new set of 'Scottish' masonic rites and degrees into French Freemasonry. For members of the Jesuits, the Catholic Church's loyal missionary organization, this cooperation resulted in a strange paradox. Instructed by the Church to have no truck with Freemasonry, they were compelled by loyalty to the Catholic Stuarts to support its Jacobite Freemasons.

With the collapse of the Stuart cause and the Jacobite Rebellions in 1746 following the defeat at Culloden, Scottish Freemasonry in France also died out. The scene was to be dominated by the French masonic organization entitled the Grand Orient. In the latter half of the 1700s its lodges recruited members from all walks of life and all strata of society. Businessmen and craftsmen still joined, but the ranks of the Grand Orient were swollen by the initiation of aristocrats. By 1789, the year of the French Revolution, the order could boast something between 20,000 and 30,000 members, spread among more than 600 lodges. There *were* other lodges outside the Grand Orient – even in France Freemasonry competed with itself. While the Grand Orient tailored its recruitment to titled aristocrats from across France, its rival the Grand Loge (initially established by the London Grand Lodge as a counter to Jacobite Freemasonry in France) generally initiated members of the French middle class.

For the following decade, the kingdom of France was rocked by a violent and far-reaching social revolution. Tension and anger among the populace in the period leading up to the Revolution had been rising to dangerous levels. A rich, untaxed aristocracy lorded it over a poverty-stricken and over-taxed peasantry. Businessmen and professionals also suffered under the burden of French taxation. Inequality, oppression and social division were pushing the poor to the brink of toleration. Leading the social debate in higher circles were thinkers such as Voltaire, Montesquieu and Rousseau, and the Freemasons the Marquis de Lafayette and Danton. Lafayette, especially, was enthusiastic about the ideals that he had seen put into practice in America.

Exactly how much effect Freemasonry had on the events of 1789 may never fully be understood. The subject is – and was then – highly controversial. What is certain is that the lodge network acted as a repository of intelligence and organization in the early days of the Revolution. Militant conspirators found it a useful mechanism for discussing ideas and for coordinating action.

When the government in Paris wanted to press taxation even further in May 1789 it summoned the States-General, at which the three sections of French society, aristocrats, clergy and commoners, were represented. Rather than ratify the tax proposals, the 'third estate', the commoners, demanded the establishment of a National Assembly composed of all three estates. On 14 July the citizens of Paris formed a Civic Guard and stormed the city's prison-fortress, the Bastille. The Revolution had begun in earnest. As the Assembly began drawing up a new constitution that would provide jobs and better standards of living for members of the impoverished third estate, the jobless and hungry flooded into Paris. Meanwhile, members of the French nobility fled the country. King Louis XVI and his queen Marie Antoinette, however, found themselves trapped in Paris and at the mercy of the mob.

By the end of 1791 the king was forced to accept the new constitution, the vast properties of the Church were seized, and a landmark document, the Declaration of the Rights of Man, was adopted. The new republic was proclaimed by the National Convention, a body that replaced the now defunct National Assembly. Neighbouring kingdoms – Austria, Prussia, Holland and Sardinia – feared the politically active and highly unstable French Republic, and it did not help that Marie Antoinette was the daughter of the Emperor of Austria. War was declared, and during the years of fighting that followed, fear and paranoia ran riot through France. In January 1793 Louis XVI was executed. Responsible for the death of the king and for the blood-soaked years of revenge that followed was a small but powerful political sect called the Jacobins. Maximilien Robespierre led the group, which was named after the old convent in Paris where it met. The Jacobins were initially involved in moderate constitutional reform during the Revolution, but this moderation was replaced by a fervent wish to execute all enemies of the newly created state.

Legitimate power was rapidly lost in the following months to a clique of committees and councils, foremost of which were the Committee of Public Safety and the Revolutionary Tribunal. Together they began the Reign of Terror, which shocked the civilized world with its ferocity and ruthlessness. The Jacobins were responsible for the establishment of the Committee of Public Safety and for the motivation and organization of the Reign of Terror. It was the aim of this campaign to capture and behead (with the mechanized execution machine, the guillotine) any remaining French aristocrats, and all those who might represent a threat to the new order. Neither gender, nor age, nor infirmity could offer a means of avoiding the guillotine. Beginning in September 1793, the Reign of Terror lasted until the fall of its leader, Robespierre, on 27 July 1794. Within just the last six weeks of the killing frenzy, almost 1400 people were executed in Paris alone. This bloody climax to the frightening policy of mass-murder had its own name, the Red Terror.

The Jacobins had little to do with Freemasonry and everything to do with fear, death and paranoia. The name of the sect is still used today to identify someone as an extreme political radical. Few cult leaders have had the deadly vision and macabre motivation to initiate the cold extermination of so many innocent people. Those that do so by edict are ruthless dictators, those that do so by manipulating the fervour of their followers are cult leaders of the highest order. Robespierre and his Jacobin sect were able to organize a terrifying vengeance on those thought to be responsible for decades of misrule and poverty. Robespierre was no Hitler, and the Jacobins never in any way resembled the Nazi Party, but the methods were strikingly similar.

Paranoia and suspicion understandably festered in the unhealthy climate of the Revolution, and they gripped French Freemasons as strongly as anyone else. Once in power and despite the active participation of Freemasons in the early stages of the political upheaval, the leaders of the Revolution had outlawed the fraternal society, both the Grand Lodge and the Grand Orient. Certainly Denis Diderot (the influential French philosopher) and probably also Voltaire were both members of Freemasonry. Some writers have suggested that the Revolution was, in fact, masterminded by a small gathering of 27 politically motivated Freemasons, but this view is not favoured by modern historians and contradicts the well-established fact that Freemasonry was outlawed by the new leadership.

It is not impossible that the order played a significant role at the start of the Revolution, fostering and trumpeting the masonic ideals of liberty, democracy and equality. Much like the German *Völkischen* cults a century later, these intellectual and philosophical ideas would be adopted by those of a more practical nature. In Germany in the 1920s Adolf Hitler took the racial theories of Adolf Lanz and the Teutonic ideals of groups like the Germanic Order and the Thule Society and used them to overthrow the government. He immediately banned the secret societies and cults that he had so casually plagiarized. The enlightened and revolutionary spirit of the Freemasons, coupled with their propensity for secrecy and cooperation, deeply frightened the Revolutionaries. If they could channel the people's frustrations and desire for change once, it was thought, then they could do it again. The fact that the organization was banned points to some involvement in the French Revolution, however small.

Certainly there were those at the time who believed (or wanted to believe) that the Revolution had been one vast masonic conspiracy. In 1797, almost a decade after the upheavals, an outspoken abbot, Augustin de Barruel, published a book that voiced this very opinion. The tone was dark, and it would mar the image of Freemasonry for the following two centuries. Barruel and others were accusing the order of being an international revolutionary group dedicated to overthrowing all forms of established government and all forms of organized religion. A wave of hysteria followed as the public became preoccupied with the notion of Freemasons and other secret conspirators plotting to overthrow the modern world. The early years of the nineteenth century were to be marred by fears of this kind.

Barruel was perhaps reacting to the emergence of a strange anticlerical cult that had become established in the wake of the Revolution. This cult of 'Reason', which became the officially sanctioned religion of the revolutionaries, was rich with pagan ideas and mood. The cult of Reason prospered because the Christian Church was put under terrific pressure to bow to the wishes of the state. Members of the clergy were now elected by property owners and not selected by the Church hierarchy. Worst of all, it was a requirement that all priests should take an oath of loyalty to the Revolution, a move that the pope vigorously condemned. As the church became more 'secularized' and the churchmen were seen more and more as Establishment enemies of the Revolution, the cult gained further ground.

This split between the state and the Church enabled the abstract ideas of liberty, reason and philosophy to prosper and take shape. The cult of Reason could be a new revolutionary religion, not based on clerical authority and obedience to strict Catholic ritual but on the very virtues espoused by the leading masonic philosophers of the day. Many churches were being converted into temples to the new cult. There, ceremonies were held to celebrate the goddess of Reason. Her statues began to replace those of the Christian saints and especially those of the Virgin Mary. A French writer, Adrien Dansette, describes a scene from within Notre-Dame, then a temple to Reason:

> A rock was placed in the choir of [the church] and on it a circular
> temple was erected, dedicated to 'philosophy'... a procession of girls
> marched up and down the sides of the rock, saluting as they passed the
> Flame of Truth which burned half-way up. An actress from the opera,
> dressed in white and wearing an azure cloak and red bonnet, came out
> of the temple and seated herself on a grass-covered throne. She was
> Reason and the girls chanted a hymn to her.

Barruel was convinced that the anti-clerical aspect of the Revolution was clearly indicative of masonic interference. Clearly the entire

Revolution had been a conspiracy plotted and hatched at every level by members of Freemasonry. What was the cult of Reason except the actual incarnation of masonic beliefs? Didn't the Freemasons oppose the Church as well as dictatorial government? The cult of Reason did not have a long life, however. When Napoleon rose to power in France he quickly re-instated the Roman Catholic Church. It was, after all, a necessary tool of strong government in the country.

But Barruel's accusations were not forgotten. The public mind became almost obsessed with the idea of secret masonic lodges and other covert conclaves. Rumour and gossip provided the engine for the manufacture of real fears and worries. For some, the appeal became compulsive. Such was the alluring glamour of the secret societies, that Charles Nodier and Filippo Buonarotti began inventing their own. They created, wrote about and disseminated information and rumours about wholly fictional secret societies. Unfortunately, the authorities were also obsessively fascinated with this growing phenomenon and began to pursue these fictional cults. Innocent people were rounded up, investigated and arrested in connection with membership of these societies. In response, those under suspicion began banding together for self-protection, creating passwords and signs, establishing secret meeting places and adopting false, ritualistic names. In this way a number of French secret societies were given life in the 1800s. Fiction had become fact in an unusual and highly disturbing example of nineteenth-century witch-hunting. Nodier had created a self-fulfilling prophecy.

Nodier was also heavily involved in the French occult revival of that century. Various mysterious and secretive occult groups merged and dissolved, as members moved from one to another. Dabblers in the occult included such notables as Charles Baudelaire, Théophile Gautier and Victor Hugo. They revelled in their participation in the secret societies and also in the forbidden nature of their interests. These societies were parlour-room gatherings, however, not the high-level conspiratorial councils that the government and people feared were out there, plotting the next revolution.

The Charcoal Burners

In Italy a secret society composed mainly of Freemasons was plotting a revolution that would eventually unify the divided Italian states. Italy in the early nineteenth century lay far from the forefront of economic and political dynamism. While Britain, Spain and France had achieved political unity, the Italian peninsula was divided politically into a number of separate city-states and principalities. In addition, the states of the Church cut the peninsula in half, further impeding any kind of unity. Italians considered themselves as one people, just as the classical Greeks had done, but they remained divided and ineffectual. Napoleon invaded the Italian states in the final years of the eighteenth century. In place of the northern states, the French ruler created a French puppet kingdom, the Kingdom of Italy. This collapsed in 1815 with the fortunes of Napoleon himself, but the fact that such a political entity could exist had been proven beyond doubt.

When French domination of northern Italy slackened, Austria moved in to take France's place. Not only were the Italian states divided, but the ominous shadow of Austria guaranteed that no revolutionary movement could easily unite them and bring an end to foreign intervention. But the nationalist spirit had been kindled within the hearts of numerous proud Italians. Napoleon had shown how easily the ruling families of the Italian states could be displaced and how Italians could work together when necessary. The French dictator also symbolized the bitter truth that foreign powers had always played a significant part in the future of the Italian people. A patriotic secret society called Young Italy was established, under the leadership of a young revolutionary called Giuseppe Mazzini. In 1831 the Young Italy membership swore to fight for the unity and freedom of the fatherland under the cry *Risorgimento* (resurgence). The Young Italy movement was certainly neither appreciated nor tolerated by the authorities, and Mazzini was driven into exile to London. From there he continued to work towards his society's ultimate goal.

Without warning, in 1848 revolutions broke out across Europe in a triumphant declaration of the people's wish for self-determination. Mazzini rushed back to his homeland, and Young Italy led the uprisings in the Italian peninsula. Although most of these were quickly suppressed, the society was able to establish republics in both Rome and Venice that were to last for several months. Mazzini once again fled from Italy after the republics foundered, and the nationalist reins there passed to another secret sect called the Carbonari (Charcoal Burners). Mazzini had been initiated into the Carbonari in 1827, and its greatest activist was a popular hero named Guiseppe Garibaldi. The Carbonari was a fraternal organization that took its title from the mutual-aid groups of charcoal burners that had existed in Italy since medieval times. According to tradition, the earliest lodges were established in Capua sometime between 1802 and 1810 by French army officers hostile to Napoleon. The first recruits were officers of the Italian military, rich landowners and civil servants, and the organization flourished particularly in Piedmont, where its members were free from persecution. With membership almost wholly middle class and a strong impetus from Italian Freemasonry, the Carbonari never was, nor did it pretend to be, a society of the masses. Both its purposes and its methods were well delineated.

As a dedicated revolutionary organization, the Carbonari created lodges abroad (in France, Spain and Germany) and coordinated these lodges in a grand revolutionary strategy to overthrow governments across Europe. The secret society was responsible, in 1820 and 1821, for the independence of Greece and for the formation of new constitutions in Spain as well as some of the Italian states. The final victory of the international Carbonari campaign was the Decembrist uprising against Tsar Nicholas I in Russia in 1825. This coup fell through, however, and its previous gains were quickly and completely reversed by the powerful European governments of the day. The most effective tactic of the Carbonari was the co-opting of disaffected young army officers. They had little reputation to ruin and often commanded the loyalty of their troops.

With so many Freemasons involved in the Carbonari, it was not unexpected that the secret society had a good deal of arcane, masonic-style ritual. Candidates for initiation were blindfolded and were tested against various symbolic objects – an axe, a Cross and a flame. With his hand holding the axe, the initiate vowed:

> upon this steel, the avenging instrument of the perjured, scrupulously
> to keep the secret of Carbonarism; and neither to write, engrave,
> or paint anything concerning it, without having obtained written
> permission.

It is true that most Carbonari were Freemasons and that most Italian Freemasons were Carbonari. There was a great deal of overlap.

The greatest triumph of Carbonarism was without question the society's role in the unity of the Italian states in 1861. Giuseppe Garibaldi led the movement and once unity had been achieved, he became the Grand Master of the entire organization. To succeed in their goal, the Carbonari had to contend with the Papal States that lay across the centre of Italy. While most of the Italian city-states were led by undemocratic royal families, it was the pope who controlled the Papal States and who had a vested interest in seeing that both his carefully contrived web of alliances and his spiritual leadership should remain intact. Freemasons and Carbonari both wanted to see a secular Italian state built on the ruins of the squabbling city and Papal States – and so Freemasonry and the pope were put into direct opposition. Freemasons at the time made no secret of this hostility. Grand Master Lemmi wanted the loyal brethren 'to scatter the stones of the Vatican, so as to build with them the Temple of the Emancipated Nation'. Similarly, the pope issued several encyclicals against Freemasonry for primarily political motives. These bans were enjoined on all Roman Catholics everywhere, although the pope's fight for survival lay specifically with the Italian Freemasons and the Carbonari. Roman Catholic opposition to Freemasonry has dogged the fraternal society ever since. What began as unsubstantiated rumour in the aftermath of the French

Revolution became full-scale conflict during the unity of the Italian states.

The liberal ideas and political victories secured by Freemasons in Italy provided fuel for those detractors who sought to identify some malign masonic conspiracy. Freemasons did want revolution and were capable of organizing violent opposition, its critics were able to write. But again, there is little evidence to support the theory that the exploits of the Carbonari disguised some deeper, darker secret. The nineteenth-century obsession with secret societies and their unseen influence manifested itself in an undying belief in the existence of a masonic plot to overthrow the ordered world and create chaos and anarchy. Subtle, unseen and silent, the hidden cabal of Grand Masters was feared to be plotting political events that would send shock-waves throughout modern society: left-wing activism in France, the 1917 Russian Revolution, the assassination of Archduke Franz Ferdinand, German inter-war inflation and the Spanish Civil War. Undecided, some modern critics have claimed that Freemasons and Jews work together in this ceaseless capitalist conspiracy; others argue that it is Communism and Freemasonry that are co-conspirators in the headlong plunge for world domination; some desperately try to reconcile both arguments.

If Freemasonry really was planning worldwide domination through an intricate network of spies, agents and collaborators, how would it actually go about such a venture? The machinations of one Adam Weishaupt give us some idea of the methods (and the immense troubles) of such a movement. His masonic society, the Illuminati, is believed by some of the fringe conspiracy writers to exist today. Its grandiose plans were equal to the most fevered nightmares of the Abbé Barruel, and even after it was suppressed, the Illuminati has festered in the imaginations of those who had convinced themselves that the masonic conspiracy was out there.

The Illuminati

On 1 May 1776 a young professor at the Bavarian university of Ingolstadt began the formulation of a new secret society based on masonic lines. This man was Adam Weishaupt (1748–1830). He had been educated by his godfather, Baron von Ickstatt, following the death of his own father (also a professor). Of the greatest influences on Weishaupt were his years of study at a Jesuit college. The Jesuit order was an élite and highly educated organization within the Catholic Church, and its members were universally respected. Weishaupt, though, looked back on that period of Jesuit instruction with contempt. His orthodox education was supplemented by study of the 'enlightened' French authors of the day. Following his graduation and appointment to a teaching post at the university in 1772, Weishaupt gained a reputation for academic brilliance and intellectual scepticism. Although he taught law, he was still greatly interested in the Jesuits and their role. His first writings, however, were heavily influenced by Protestant writers such as the Dutchman, Hugo Grotius (Huig de Groot), and it was clear that Weishaupt was not going to follow the Jesuit tradition that he had absorbed. This was to cause a degree of friction and political infighting among the university's academic hierarchy.

Baron von Ickstatt was an influential man in Ingolstadt. Not only was he a member of the Electoral privy council, but he was also co-director of the university that was attended by his spirited godson. Weishaupt, sharpening his skills at intrigue and power politics, ably recruited the other co-director as a patron and in 1773 secured for himself the chair of canon law at the university. For over ninety years this esteemed post had been held by a Jesuit, but Pope Clement XIV (reigned 1769–74) had that year 'annulled and extinguished the Jesuit order', leaving the chair of canon law open for Weishaupt. This radical move deeply upset the academic establishment. From spite, it refused to award him a salary, which provided Weishaupt with the opportunity to begin intriguing on a much greater scale in order to achieve what he wanted. He dabbled in the affairs of other university faculties, he spread rumours about his colleagues and his superiors, and he kept in close contact with anti-clerical writers and ex-Jesuits. The university provided a perfect training ground for his later career, a harmless hotbed of conflicting political aims, which he could manipulate and reorganize.

Disenchanted with the powerful forces of religion that maintained a strong grip over the German states, Weishaupt also became disenchanted with Freemasonry, to which many intellectuals were turning as a legitimate alternative to the Christian Church. In 1774 a friend introduced him to a Protestant Freemason, who encouraged him to apply for membership. Weishaupt's hopes for the fraternal society were not borne out, and he quickly became disillusioned. The fees were high, and the much trumpeted masonic secrets were little more than elaborations on the rituals that were, by now, well known to the world. Rejecting academia and both organized religion and its intellectual rival, Weishaupt decided to form his own movement. A secret society along the lines of Freemasonry, but with unique methods and goals.

Initially called the Perfectibilists, later the Illuminati, the secret society was originally intended to sever the perfidious influence of the ex-Jesuits within the university. However, its potential for greater things was quickly realized, and Weishaupt began recruiting well-educated radicals into the society. Its stated aims were:

to make the perfecting of the reasoning powers interesting to mankind, to spread the knowledge of sentiments both humane and social, to check wicked inclinations, to stand up for suffering and oppressed virtue ... to facilitate the acquirement of knowledge and science.

This egalitarian mood paralleled the aspirations of the American colonists struggling for independence on the other side of the world. Weishaupt saw the Illuminati as a harbinger of freedom and liberty for mankind, and the extraordinary scale of his vision is hinted at in his own writings. 'Princes and nations,' he predicted, 'will disappear without violence from the earth, the human race will become one family and the world the abode of reasonable men. Morality alone will bring about this change imperceptibly.' This aim, the promotion of a non-violent revolution to liberate mankind, was radical indeed!

Membership of the Illuminati was restricted to cultured sophisticates who would study under Weishaupt. Many of the university professors were won over and all but two joined the Illuminati within the order's first two years of existence. The education provided by Weishaupt would promote the powers of the mind and an appreciation of egalitarian thinking. According to the Illuminati:

Man is not bad except as he is made so by arbitrary morality. He is bad because religion, the state and bad examples pervert him. When at last reason becomes the religion of men, then will the problem be solved.

The Illuminati brethren were not simply scholars, but conspirators in a political power game that they hoped would bring about the desired revolution. Each initiate was gradually led through a series of secret doctrines and accepted into higher degrees. Its teachings were not the ritualistic mumbo-jumbo of Freemasonry but the writings of classical moralists and others, and its claim to be a secret society easily outclassed traditional masonic lodges. The Illuminati went much further. Each initiate, who was supervised by a senior initiate and owed absolute obedience to this superior, vowed to sever his ties to friends, family and Church. By diligent learning, the initiate rose through the order's grades. He would be intensely scrutinized and would not be made aware of the Illuminati's real purpose, of Adam Weishaupt's true identity or of the strategy by which the order would achieve its aims.

From the initial five members in 1776, the Illuminati rapidly developed, and by 1779 it had 54 members and 'chapters' in four other Bavarian cities. Weishaupt's tactics were revolutionary. Members would, by various means, attain positions of importance and power while retaining loyalty to the Illuminati. This peaceful corruption of the established order spread the Illuminati's influence upwards into the highest strata of society. These well-placed members were then in a position to assist other members in achieving equally powerful positions. They were also encouraged to recruit suitable (that is, wealthy and powerful) candidates from among the upper echelons of society. Recruitment was a highly secret operation, often taking place without the recruit's knowledge! A suitable candidate was selected, trained and put up for election by the Illuminati inner circle. Only when the candidate had succeeded in gaining membership, was he told of the existence of the order.

Weishaupt had mastered the art of the conspiracy, both in the methods he used to co-opt other organizations and in the sophisticated approach that he adopted to manipulate them. To coerce a group radically to alter its official stance or policy on one particular subject, Weishaupt realized that the very worst approach to take was indignantly to oppose that policy at every turn. Where lay the deceit in that? The Ku Klux Klan discovered this 200 years later in its violent and sadistic fight to prevent the implementation of the civil rights legislation of President Johnson. The pressure of attack increases the victim's resolve to defend himself. Weishaupt realized that by establishing a similar organization to the one he wished to manipulate or by co-opting one influential member of the target group the task became much easier. The new mouthpiece would be ordered to proclaim itself a radical version of the official organization and begin an ever-more outspoken and outrageous series of claims and pronouncements. In an effort to distance itself from this Illuminati-controlled pawn, the target organization would tone down its own approach, even changing its own policies to demonstrate how different it was. In effect it moved in the opposite direction to that in which it was headed, and straight into the arms of Adam Weishaupt. The strategy was simple and effective.

Freemasonry had always denied that it was a society of intellectual revolutionaries opposed to God, Church and state. The Illuminati, on the other hand, embodied that very vision. It truly was the nightmare of the Bavarian establishment. Its meetings were filled with anti-clerical, anti-religious spirit, and its members actively opposed the totalitarian measures imposed by both Church and state. Banned literature found its way into the Illuminati's library, and topics of conversation never discussed in Bavaria (focusing on philosophy, politics and the role of religion) became subjects of debate. In these early years the Illuminati flourished. Its members revelled in the secrecy and subterfuge, the multi-layered organization and the radical ideology that it espoused. When they were operating on Illuminati business, members were given pseudonyms, often the names of historical personalities. Adam Weishaupt was called Spartacus, after the gladiator-slave who challenged the might of Rome by raising his own army of runaway slaves. Other pseudonyms included Tamburlane, Socrates and Cato.

By 1779 the idea of the Illuminati had grown a little stale and several of the senior membership (those 12 élite 'disciples' called the

Areopagites) were becoming bored with the movement. Weishaupt worked hard behind the scenes to keep the order together, but discipline and enthusiasm waned once it became apparent that the cherished goals of egalitarian revolution were remote and almost impossible objectives. At meetings, there was much talk, open debate and plotting, but what were the real achievements of the Illuminati?

Weishaupt needed a fresh influx of recruits and some kind of ritualistic ceremony with which to distract the short-term frustrations of his members. For this he returned to Freemasonry. In an inspirational move, Weishaupt did not merely copy its ceremony and organization, but actually infiltrated local lodges, tapping off Freemasons for his own secret society and inextricably intermingling German Freemasonry with the Illuminati. The master-intriguer, Weishaupt joined a lodge of Munich Freemasons in 1777 with the aim of copying much of the arcane ritual that it employed. Another Illuminati, Xavier Zwack (known within the order as Cato), began recruiting Freemasons in Munich and convinced Adam Weishaupt that some of the Areopagites should become Freemasons, linking the two systems inextricably. Thus, the Illuminati became almost an off-shoot order of German Freemasonry, but one that accepted only the most trusted and well-thought-of members. Plugged parasitically into the fraternal brotherhood in this way, the secret order gained secret access to legitimate masonic lodges and their brethren and enabled it to disseminate its radical propaganda throughout the lodges. Those initiates thought unworthy of promotion into the élite higher grades of the Illuminati could be pushed back into the harmless masonic lodges. The Bavarian Illuminati was probably the very first secret society to use (or abuse) the machinery of Freemasonry for nefarious purposes. While most people considered Freemasonry to be a secret group within society operating with their own hidden agendas, few realized that another group operated inside Freemasonry itself, pursuing its own hidden agenda.

Using this mechanism, the Illuminati flourished rapidly, and from 1779 new lodges were opened with little fanfare across the rest of Germany, and in Austria, Bohemia, Hungary and Italy. Within the space of only a few years, the revolutionary cabal had 300 members, including some of the most prominent or powerful men in Europe, such as Goethe, Schiller, Kolowrat, Cobenzl, Mozart and Hardenberg. With the growing wealth and influence of the Illuminati in such a short period, several Areopagites discussed infiltrating and dominating the whole of German Freemasonry. Such was the demoralized and fragmented character of the fraternal orders across Central Europe that a plan was hatched to realize this dream. A confederation of lodges would be assembled under the control of a (non-existent) Ancient Scots Superior. This front organization would communicate the commands of the Illuminati directly to the disparate fraternal lodges. Although seriously contemplated, this plan was never in fact, brought to fruition.

From July 1781 the Illuminati became an oligarchy as Weishaupt handed over control of the organization to his Areopagites. Adolf von Knigge (1752–96), who was known as Philo, helped him to reshape the order and began to recruit fresh Areopagites. Mysticism, occultism and elaborate quasi-religious ceremonies were introduced that paralleled some of the more extreme practices of the masonic lodges. The early 1780s could be considered the climax of the Illuminati – dissension and persecution soon followed. At its height there were four grades of membership, beginning with the Initiate Grades, the Masonic Grades and the Scots Grades and finally the enigmatic Mystery Grades. Each of these was further subdivided – for example, the Mystery Grades included the ranks of Priest, Reigning Priest, Grand Magus and, at the pinnacle of the Illuminati's hierarchy, the Man-King.

The year 1784 marked the beginning of the end for the Illuminati. Both Knigge and Weishaupt were forceful and fanatical characters, and quarrels soon broke out. Particularly annoying for Weishaupt was Knigge's passion for elaborate ritual and ceremony that did little to secure the goals and aspirations of the Illuminati. As far as Weishaupt was concerned, the Illuminati was destined to reach across the world in an ever-tightening web of conspiracy and intrigue, but Knigge did not share his megalomaniacal plans, and by July 1784 it was agreed that he should leave the organization. This was to be the first of several crushing blows. They followed in rapid succession. Rumours of Illuminati conspiracy and evil-doing circulated wildly throughout Bavaria, and both the public and the government began to become more than a little interested in its activities, especially since many of these rumours hinted that the order had penetrated the ruling administration and was pursuing its own agenda. Fears of an imminent revolution forced an outcry. This outcry involved the Catholic Church, the academic establishment and the police. Ex-Jesuits were also enmeshed in the investigation and pursuit of members.

Although Weishaupt's Illuminati was not mentioned specifically by name, the Elector of Bavaria published an official edict that forbade members of the public from joining any secret society. The ex-Jesuit community began collecting captured Illuminati literature, and much of it was used to charge the membership with various serious crimes. These included moral corruption, political intrigue, treason and irreligion. Although Weishaupt approached the Elector in a desperate attempt to prove the Illuminati's innocence, the persecutions continued. On 2 March 1784 another edict was published that specifically condemned the Illuminati and its activities. All of the order's members were now in danger, arrests were made, interrogations carried out, witnesses came forward with exaggerated stories, and lodges were raided. Officials discovered quantities of poison, invisible inks, a mass of incriminating literature and also documentary evidence of initiations.

Weishaupt, Knigge and others who had escaped the Elector's attacks began to publish pamphlets in their defence during the following years. Weishaupt wrote an *Apologie der Illuminaten* (1786), and Knigge followed suit two years later with an article of his own. By the end of the decade around 50 pro-Illuminati documents had been published in London, Paris and Copenhagen, and in Bavaria. The turn of the century ushered in a more tolerant mood in Bavaria, resulting in an amnesty for political exiles. A number of Illuminati returned to take up seats in the government. Weishaupt himself never returned to Bavaria, however, and he died in 1830. His plan to overthrow world governments and their Churches through a vast international conspiracy of highly placed agents had failed. The Illuminati simply faded away. Although a group calling itself the Order of the Illuminati was established in Dresden in 1896, it seems to have had no real connection to the original and never achieved the notoriety of its namesake.

French Freemasonry was always very wary of the Illuminati, and there were few if any collaborations between them. Nonetheless, the Illuminati was accused by some of instigating the French Revolution. The Abbé Barruel explicitly mentioned Weishaupt's secret society in his vehement writings on the conspiratorial movement. Because of the order's intimate connection with legitimate Freemasonry, the latter found itself tarred with the conspiracy brush. No one could now believe that Freemasons were not wholly free from secret machinations, plots and political intrigues behind closed doors. The Illuminati provided all European governments with a perfect example of the 'hidden enemy', and public suspicion festered in the early years of the nineteenth century. The aftermath of the French Revolution was awash with rumour, suspicion, cynicism and real fear. Haunting memories of the Illuminati, stopped just in time by the Bavarian authorities, would have kept alive the belief that just beneath civilized society lay covert groups plotting the downfall of established governments and established religions.

The legacy of Adam Weishaupt and his Illuminati is the enduring belief that almost any political event could actually be the calculated act of some unknown, utterly secret cabal of nameless and powerful men. As the author Arthur Edward Waite cynically wrote: 'Beneath the broad tide of human history there flow the stealthy undercurrents of the secret societies, which frequently determine in the depths the changes that take place on the surface.'

The Army of General Ludd

Fear and suspicion always intensified during periods of warfare. Since 1803 Britain had been locked in a hugely expensive war with

Napoleon that seemed to be draining the entire economy. At the end of 1811 the Duke of Newcastle, Lord Lieutenant of Nottinghamshire, sent urgent reports to London about violent attacks on the machinery that was used to manufacture stockings. He attributed these attacks to French activists, working secretly in the depressed towns and villages of Nottinghamshire to foment riot and criminal damage. Rumours abounded. Not only were there men with French accents operating in the area, it was said, but Napoleon had offered local men £4000 to smash these machines. Since the attackers operated at night, with masked faces, it was a rumour that few found difficult to believe.

The truth, however, was far less romantic – and far more desperate. At the beginning of 1812 the British economy had rarely looked worse. Taxation was high to pay for the war against the French, overseas trade had virtually ceased, and the prices of goods had soared. Bankruptcy and unemployment were becoming commonplace, and more and more families were experiencing the bitter realities of poverty. Some of this bitterness sprang from the memory of better times, when food was affordable and there were decent jobs for those who were skilled enough to take them.

Some of the blame for these desperate times, when a family had to sell everything they owned just to eat, can be laid at the door of Parliament. Land had been snatched from the common people during the field enclosures, and this took away the poor's ability to feed themselves. Workers' rights were being steadily eroded, minimum standards on the quality of work and the wages paid were abandoned, as was legislation that regulated the introduction of industrial machinery that might disrupt the security of workers. Things were going from bad to worse, and the disenfranchised workers in the worst hit areas saw no possibility that their lives would improve.

In control of this madness was the Tory Prime Minister, Spencer Perceval (1762–1812), who, along with the rest of the party he led, believed wholeheartedly in *laisser-faire* economics. This meant non-intervention in such important aspects of the country's economy as labour relations, the plight of the poor or the encouragement of trade. The desperately poor had to fend for themselves. And in 1811 and 1812 that is just what they did.

Throughout 1811 Sherwood Forest became the secret encampment for a number of men calling themselves Luddites. They established themselves as a well-organized clandestine society, employing oaths and passwords and enjoying the support of the local community. It is not known exactly who formulated the idea of a violent secret society, perhaps James Towle or the trade unionist Gravener Henson. We know for certain it was not a man called Ned Ludd. The character of Ludd was semi-mythical, a Leicester stocking-maker who, frustrated with his frame, had broken it to pieces with a hammer in 1782. The leader of the new society called himself 'General Ned Ludd' and has remained anonymous ever since.

Stocking frames in villages across Nottinghamshire were smashed by the Luddites. It was not the use of machinery they were reacting against, but against the most unpopular master hosiers, who demanded the shoddiest work at the lowest wages. By the end of 1811 there were several thousand troops on alert, ready to chase down the Luddites, whose numbers and acts of violence were growing and who enjoyed widespread local support. Frame-smashing occurred almost nightly, with the result that in February 1812 the death penalty was introduced for the crime of frame-breaking. From the forests of Sherwood, General Ludd sent a letter to Prime Minister Perceval to protest at this measure. He was not alone: several Nottinghamshire officials also questioned the wisdom of such a move. What would prevent the Luddites from taking a life while they vented their anger on the machines? As one Luddite song put it:

> You might as well be hung for death
> As breaking a machine,
> So now, my lad, your sword unsheath,
> And make it sharp and keen

In January 1812 Luddism reached Yorkshire. Here though, the men involved worked in the woollen industry, not in stocking making. New machinery, such as Richard Arkwright's spinning frame and James Hargreaves's carding machine, had turned a cottage industry into a labour-saving factory industry. Those men finding their skills redundant (especially the élite woollen workers – the croppers) protested, petitioned and campaigned to save their jobs. To no avail. The croppers formed the nucleus of the newly formed Yorkshire Luddites. On 19 January Luddites from Leeds set fire to Oatlands Mill, a factory in which machinery had been installed. Although the factory was not too badly damaged, the government offered a huge cash reward for anyone with information. No one came forward. The leader of the Yorkshire Luddites, one George Mellor, commanded the loyalty of the local populace as well as of '2782 sworn heroes'. These Luddites were drilled on night-time manoeuvres on the moors above Huddersfield, practising with whatever weapons they could lay their hands on – pistols, clubs, knives, hammers and axes. Mellor wanted a distinctly military organization, which could make swift and effective raids on the hated machines.

With the frames making easy targets for a small group of armed men, the Luddites were successful in destroying most of those in the area in which they operated. Becoming bolder, they turned their attention to the larger mills. On 9 April 1812 Mellor led a force of 300 Luddites to Joseph Foster's mill at Horbury. Achieving complete surprise, the gang forced two of Foster's sons onto the floor and his other two sons to unlock the mill for them. This done, they smashed every machine within the building and set fire to the remains. As the mill began to burn, the Fosters listened as Mellor gave a roll call to the assembled Luddites, and then marched them off into the darkness. That 300 armed men could commit such an act of destruction naturally frightened the public. Were these the actions of disgruntled labourers or something more sinister? The French Revolution haunted the imagination of newspaper editors, government ministers and members of the public alike. It had been just over 20 years since the oppressed peasantry of France had risen up in revolt to seize the government and conduct their own Reign of Terror.

This fear – that Luddism represented the first tentative steps towards an English revolution – seemed to be validated during the investigation that followed the attack on Foster's mill. Papers had been found, dropped in the lane near the mill, that outlined a plan for wholesale revolution. They were identical to a set of revolutionary plans found on an Irish activist called Colonel Edmund Despard, who had been executed for treasonous activities ten years before. What interest the Luddites had in a revolution is unknown. Certainly several of their members, such as John Baines and John Booth, had revolutionary sympathies, and it is likely that one of these was responsible for dropping the papers. But a potential link between Luddites and French revolutionaries thoroughly alarmed a nation that was at war with France at the time.

Most Luddites had little interest in overthrowing the government; they simply wanted redress for the indignities and poverty imposed on them by tyrannical mill-owners. One of the most hated of the mill-owners, William Cartwright, had a certain prominence. The owner of Rawfolds Mill near Liversedge, Cartwright acknowledged the Luddite threat and duly took precautions. On the night of 11 April 150 Luddites, led by George Mellor, attacked the mill. They little expected such a ferocious welcome. Soldiers opened fire on the masked marauders, wounding several, and a bell rang out summoning further defenders. All the while the panicking Luddites tried vainly to smash down the mill doors to gain access, but Mellor and his followers broke and ran. All but two of the wounded were dragged away into the woods. These two unfortunates, Samuel Hartley and John Booth, died from their wounds – taking to the grave the identity of their fellows.

Revenge burned in Mellor, and when Cartwright rode to Huddersfield to give evidence about the Luddite attack, a group of Luddites opened fire on him, but Cartwright was unharmed.

If they couldn't get at Cartwright, the Luddites decided, they would strike at another hated mill-owner, William Horsfall. Horsfall ran Ottiwells Mill at Marsden, and, expecting the worst, he had asked for extra troops and a cannon to be garrisoned there. It was decided to

assassinate the man, and on 28 April Mellor, accompanied by his lieutenant, William Thorpe, and two croppers, Thomas Smith and
Benjamin Walker, organized an ambush on the road out of Huddersfield. This time the Luddites were successful, and Horsfall died soon
after the shooting.

Things were getting out of hand. To combat Luddism, a new strategy was formulated that would be eminently more effective than any
squadron of cavalry troopers. In Manchester, where Luddite uprisings
had led to the destruction of steam-looms and factories, the authorities had begun to infiltrate the society with paid informers. Known
simply by specific initials (such as S), these agents were encouraged
to incite trouble and violent activity. In Yorkshire plain-clothes soldiers roamed the roads at night looking for Luddite activity. Trotting
noisily around on horseback the cavalry patrols had no chance whatsoever of catching the conspirators en masse. One essential infiltration
point for the soldiers (and for croppers from other parts of Britain
hired especially for the task) was the St Crispin Inn at Halifax. A back-
room there had been used for months as the meeting room and place
of initiation for the Luddites. Handshakes and passwords were briefly
exchanged before the assembled men sat down to business by the dim
glow of candlelight. John Baines and George Mellor met at the St
Crispin, and 'twissed in' (initiated) new Luddites with a simple ceremony in which candidates swore allegiance to the cause over the
Bible. Their oath would be binding:

> I … swear that I will use my best endeavour to punish by death any traitor
> or traitors should any rise up among us he or them and tho' he should fly
> to the verge of nature I will pursue him with unceasing vengeance.

Once 'twissed in', a couple of workers from Manchester in the pay of
the authorities were able to report on the secret meetings. John Baines
was arrested, and by October Mellor had been arrested too. George
Mellor had dominated the Halifax Luddites with his imposing manner
and physical presence, but this tough leader now faced execution for
his part in the Rawfolds attack and for his murder of William Horsfall.
Other Luddites were hanged, and many more were transported to
Australia. Many, however, were released through lack of evidence, for
the Luddites operated at night, in disguise, and were bound by oaths
of secrecy. It was often very difficult for the courts to build up convincing evidence of Luddite activities in these circumstances.

Luddites continued to smash machines and openly declare their
defiance of a regime that tolerated, even fostered, the crushing poverty
in which they were forced to live. A free pardon in 1813 allowed
many Luddites to throw off their criminal allegiance and return to
their lives of hardship, but Luddism was not as easily suppressed.
General Ludd continued to fight the machines and their owners in

Nottinghamshire. From April 1814 until mid-1816 frame-breaking continued to be reported. James Towle, the most likely candidate for the identity of General Ned Ludd, organized a particularly successful raid on a lace factory at Loughborough in June 1816. Some 17 Luddites were involved, and all were betrayed by one of their number, John Blackburne. Towle was one of those caught, and he was hanged at Nottingham along with five of his comrades. Perhaps he had been General Ludd after all – with Towle's death the Nottinghamshire Luddites turned their backs on the movement.

Seen by the government of the day as un-patriotic criminals and terrorists, the Luddites were, in fact, a highly focused group of desperate men with no alternative course open to them. Pushed into action by crippling hunger and unimaginable poverty, these otherwise honest workmen had struck out at the immediate causes of their hardship. Local people saw the Luddites as heroes, and many songs and rhymes were composed in their honour. This, perhaps more than the financial costs of machine-breaking, caused the government considerable worry.

Like all such subversive organizations, certain individuals used the cloak of secrecy as a cover for more criminal activities. On the whole, however, the Luddites remained true to their cause. Their strength came from their oaths of secrecy, while their weakness came from the limited manner in which they could display their outrage. Luddism could so easily have been the spark that ignited an English revolution. It was an attempt to improve the desperate plight of common men, but without enough broad appeal to spread throughout the nation's poor in a single fiery wave. Machine-breaking as a revolutionary movement was crippled by the rigorous demands of secrecy, the lack of any voice among the organization and the Luddite tendency to look back on better days and not forwards. This last point is perfectly illustrated by a handful of lines in one of the popular Luddite ballads:

> Let the wise and the great lend their aid and advice
> Nor e'er their assistance withdraw,
> Till full-fashioned work at the old-fashioned price
> Is established by custom and law.

Anxious about their immediate concerns, and those of their fellow workers, the Luddites lacked any inspirational vision and any lofty thoughts about freeing the British working classes from the harsh inequalities of the class system. Other revolutions, in France and North America, were directed by educated men of such vision. Liberal movements that were so popular among Freemasons provided the goals that popular uprisings could hope to attain. The Luddites were utterly self-reliant and fought their battles without the aid of middle-class sympathizers. Such liberal-minded activists of this sort had been crucial in various popular uprisings, as we have already seen.

International Anarchy

'The bourgeois have sown the wind, they shall reap the tempest.'

If 1968 is to be seen as the pivotal year of social revolution in the twentieth century, 1848 should be considered its nineteenth-century equal. Revolution spread like wildfire from capital to capital, whipping up riots and civil disorder. Both Paris and Berlin saw fierce uprisings. Successes were generally short lived, since the tiny political clubs that were hastily formed during the revolutions were split by division and rivalry. Before 1848, the political societies had represented the aspirations of the middle classes, desperate to win power from the entrenched aristocratic regimes.

Two of the major activists of this kind were François-Noël Babeuf (1760–97) and Filippo Buonarotti (1761–1837), both of whom were involved in the 1796 Conspiracy of Equals. Babeuf, the founder of the Society of Equals, claimed that the French Revolution had been a failed attempt that had not delivered what it had promised. Buonarotti was a member not just of the Freemasons but of the Carbonari and Mazzini's Young Italy group. They were in love with the idea of revolution, and both were professional revolutionaries, dedicated to overthrowing the Establishment in order to fulfil their idealistic dreams.

After 1848 the membership and aims of these groups underwent a radical shift. In the latter half of the nineteenth century it was not the educated middle classes who sought a voice, but the working classes and their middle-class spokesmen. Louis-Auguste Blanqui (1805–81) was one such spokesman who, after many years of planning, gained the support of the Parisian working classes through his League of the Just. A similar secret society of his, the League of Outlaws, united the German workers who were living in Paris at that time.

Less fundamentally nationalistic than before, the revolutionary secret societies were now more international in scope. The founders of communism, Karl Marx (1818–83) and Friedrich Engels (1820–95), for example, preached the waging of a class war that would cross national boundaries. In the late nineteenth century the violent and fragmented revolutionary movement calling itself anarchism earned itself lasting notoriety. These revolutionary terrorists operated without regard for national frontiers, and saw as their goal the destruction of established governments. Like the Illuminati, the anarchists envisioned a time when all repressive regimes would collapse, making way for a new order. Unlike the Illuminati, which saw the penetration and corruption of the Establishment as the chief weapon in this fight, the anarchists favoured direct, violent action. Mikhail Bakunin (1814–76), an influential anarchist, shared the common revolutionary belief that the French upheaval of 1789 was only the first in a long series of social revolutions that would culminate in the emergence of a new phase in human affairs. Bakunin and his comrades saw themselves as an élite band of dedicated fighters, and although there seemed to be little actual organization, little coordination and no established agenda, on paper their successes looked very impressive.

The tsar of Russia, Alexander II, was shockingly murdered by an anarchist in 1881. Other political murders followed: the president of France, Sadi Carnot, in 1894, the Italian king, Umberto I, in 1900 and even the president of the United States, William McKinley, a year later. Anarchists claimed responsibility for all of these alarming assassinations, yet the collapse of established governments did not occur as predicted. Chaos and anarchy failed to erupt in the period following the murders, and the popular uprisings that were expected also failed to materialize. Life and politics continued as they always had, but now with a new personality at the head of government, but with little else to show for the 'violent reaction against the established order', as condemned anarchist Émile Henry described the movement. It was not just political leaders who found themselves targeted by this shadowy group of murderers, but also police stations, churches, law courts and Establishment figures. From 1880 until the First World War, bombs were exploded, fires started and innocent men shot to death for the cause of anarchism.

As a political force, anarchism was weak, having no central authority and no representative organization. Lacking a practical way to achieve the anarchists' dream of a utopian society in which the rights of men and women were respected above all things, the movement attracted only dreamers. More than that, it attracted a certain type of dreamer. Many, though by no means all, anarchists were driven by two factors: extreme poverty and an assertive independence. Bitter loners, these fanatics nurtured a deeply held desire to strike back at an uncaring and machine-like society that trampled over the lives of the poor and hard-pressed.

Unlike some of the liberal thinkers, the intellectuals and the Marxists, the anarchists wanted total and uncompromising change. And they wanted it now. Their way was through direct action – which meant violence against both property and people. In Russia, one anarchist group called for 'mighty and ruthless, total and bloody, people's vengeance'. It was an article of anarchist faith that the Establishment had achieved its position through the murder of innocents and that to dislodge it, the same tactics would have to be employed. As one English paper, *The Anarchist*, openly declared: 'Our modern civilization is a Moloch temple reared upon the bodies of slaughtered slaves. Let the terrorists do what they will, they cannot equal the crimes of our masters.' This almost indiscriminate use of deadly violence did little to endear the anarchist cause to the public.

The suddenness and ferocity of an anarchist attack always shocked. Santiago Salvador, a 33-year-old Spanish anarchist, detonated two bombs inside Barcelona's Liceo Theatre in November 1893. The well-dressed and refined audience were at that moment enjoying a performance of *William Tell*. Without warning, the bombs exploded and killed 20 people. Salvador had killed these people in revenge for the execution of his friend, Pallas, who had himself killed six innocent people for the cause.

Anarchists, by the very nature of their high-profile murders, soon began to earn a fearsome and myth-clouded reputation. The classic stereotype began to emerge of a criminal psychopath, a mad, twisted bomb-thrower with a foreign name and a bad accent. When an anarchist bomb was thrown into a crowd at Chicago's Haymarket Square in 1886, the authorities were incensed with anger. During the ensuing investigation it was discovered that there were perhaps 3000 anarchists operating in Chicago alone and that many were of European origin. President McKinley was assassinated in 1901 at close range with a revolver. It came as no surprise to the public that the killer was an immigrant: a Polish anarchist named Leon Czolgosz. Theodore Roosevelt voiced the feelings of many Americans when he judged anarchism to be 'a crime against the whole human race', and he demanded that 'all mankind should band against the anarchists'. Portrayed as the 'enemy of humanity', individual anarchists responsible for planting bombs were ruthlessly pursued by the outraged governments of Europe and the United States.

The 1890s saw a climax of anarchist violence, with a surge of support from intellectual anarchists who looked forwards to the demise of the bourgeois society. Names like Ravachol and Auguste Vaillant became the rallying cries of anarchists who wanted to revenge the execution of their heroes and to continue the bloody slaughter. After 1900, however, the terrorist movement found fewer adherents. Russian anarchists, organized into two secret societies, the Black Banner and Without Authority, tried to overthrow the tsar in 1905, but the plot ultimately failed. Elsewhere, the anarchist found himself isolated and vilified. The last of the famous activists was the Frenchman Bonnot, who indulged in a frenzied life of crime between 1911 and 1913. Bonnot ended his life wrapped in a mattress as he shielded himself from a hail of bullets in the most ferocious gunfight of his career.

Today historians see the work of lone activists in those bombings and assassinations, the work of men fuelled by a passion for social justice and for revenge against an unjust society. The governments of the day, however, were incapable of seeing them in this light. 'There are thousands to continue the work,' proclaimed one condemned anarchist, and the international support that he and others boasted of was considered a dark reality. Police forces everywhere feared that an international conspiracy worked tirelessly behind the scenes to unseat every national leader and to bring about the collapse of every national government. The simultaneous rise of anarchist violence in Britain, France, Italy, Spain, Russia and the USA was not considered to be some bizarre coincidence – it was perceived as the strategy of a powerful secret organization.

The Black International, a shadowy congress of anarchists who met only once in London during 1881, provided a suitable name with which to label this conspiracy. But the Black International never met again, and never coordinated the campaign of death it had promised. Anarchist papers, like the French *Black Flag*, also promised much and delivered little. They discussed anarchist philosophy, talked about bombs and bomb-making and urged their readers to take direct action. However, the anarchist meetings, newspapers and handbills were all exercises in propaganda, showing no evidence of an organized strategy or of a master-plan.

The Black Hand

Just as anarchist terrorism entered a rapid decline, newspapers across Europe were filled with accounts of another shockingly brutal assassination. Were the anarchists trying to make a come back? Within days, however, it became apparent that the murder of Archduke Franz Ferdinand of Austria was of major importance. From our perspective, almost ninety years on, his assassination could be seen as the single most important political murder of the twentieth century. Anarchists representing the Black International were not involved – the facts were even more sinister. Evidence seemed to point to the machinations of a powerful secret society operating within the Balkan peninsula and calling itself the Black Hand. From that single murder, more death, chaos and anarchy erupted than even the most optimistic anarchist could have dreamed of. The First World War became mankind's first collective nightmare.

The Serbian Black Hand society originally developed from a group calling itself *Omladina* (from a Serbian word meaning 'youth'). In Bohemia the *Omladina* was divided into groups called Hands, which gives some idea of how the rest of the society was organized and also helps to explain why the Black Hand splinter group was so-named. Each Hand consisted of five society members, the chief of whom was named the Thumb. The most senior Hand (the so-called Upper Hand) was made up purely of Thumbs who elected their own leader.

Founded in the mid-nineteenth century, the *Omladina* sought the establishment of a Slavic state that would unite Romania, Bohemia, Moravia, Silesia, the Balkan states and some parts of Poland. The

Slavic peoples of Central Europe have never been united in this way, and the secret society worked steadily towards this goal with a campaign of assassination and organized terror. High on the group's list of targets was Serbia, a powerful state that dominated the region between Greece and Austria-Hungary. Two rival Serbian families dominated political life in the latter decades of the century, their bitter rivalry eventually precipitating the start of the First World War. The Karadjordjevich were supported by Russia, while the Obrenoviy looked to the mighty Austro-Hungarian Empire for support. Serbia's first king, coming to power in 1878, was an Obrenoviy, and the influence of Austria-Hungary on Serbia that resulted was deeply unpopular.

The Russian tsar found it expedient to fund the *Omladina* and have this secret organization carry out activities against the Serbian government. Agents of the society were responsible for shooting Prince Michael in 1868 and also for kidnapping the Serbian prince, Alexander. In a stunning coup, they smuggled Alexander to Russia where he underwent radical indoctrination, and when he was finally returned to Serbia, the prince immediately abdicated. Working on behalf of the Russians in their support of the rival Karadjordjevich family, the *Omladina* continued to wreak havoc. After a failed attempt at overthrowing the ruling dynasty in a spectacular *coup d'état*, the society proceeded to assassinate the young King Alexander Obrenovic and Queen Draga in 1903.

One of the agents involved in the killings, Colonel Dragutin Dmitrievich, was badly wounded by gunfire, yet he miraculously survived. This Serbian army officer later went on to plan and lead the Black Hand society. Under the assumed name of Apis, Dmitrievich recruited his future Black Hand assassins and was at pains to ensure that they were not only very young but also suffered from tuberculosis. They were, therefore, going to die, whether they carried out the planned murders or not. The first planned Black Hand assassination, of no less a person than the Emperor of Austria, was a failed attempt made in 1911 by a tubercular young man named Jovanovich. Three years later, the secret society's most famous murder, of Archduke Franz Ferdinand and his wife, was also carried out by agents who suffered from varying conditions of tuberculosis. They were schoolboys who swore the oath of the Black Hand:

> By the sun that warms me, by the earth that feeds me, by God, by the blood of my ancestors, by my honour and my life, I swear fidelity to the cause of Serbian nationalism, and to sacrifice my life for it.

The Archduke was an heir to the Austrian throne and destined for great things, and as he toured Sarajevo, the capital of Bosnia, which was then part of the Austro-Hungarian Empire, the Black Hand moved in to kill him. With the death of King Alexander Obrenovic in 1903, the cries for a 'Greater Serbia' among the population had begun to disturb the Austrians, who were now much more isolated from events there. On 28 June 1914 the Archduke and his wife Sophie were shot to death as they toured the streets in their open-topped car. The security arrangements were abominable, and the Black Hand agents actually botched one attempt. A second attempt succeeded, and Gavrilo Princip was apprehended and convicted of the double murder. His two accomplices had been two boys called Tchabrinovich and Grabezh. All had cyanide capsules, which had failed to work.

Austria-Hungary used the assassination as a pretext for a military invasion of troublesome Serbia, a move that upset the delicate balance of European treaties and obligations.

Russia, supporter of both the Serbian Karadjordjevich dynasty and the Black Hand secret society, began to muster troops in retaliation. Germany supported Austria and mobilized its own armies, causing every other European state to react. The result was a war that exploded across Europe. The horrors that followed the declaration of the First World War (ironically called, by those who fought in it, the 'Great' War) are well documented and will stand for all time as a testament to the dark depths to which the human race can sink. By 1918 and after four years of unremitting warfare, 20 million people had been killed and millions more maimed. Europe was devastated and lost its dominance in the world, the ruling dynasties of the Russian, Austrian, German and Ottoman empires were toppled, and the mighty colonial empires of Britain and France were dealt a fatal blow.

Historians consider that it was the precarious military and political situation that was responsible for the misery, death and destruction that followed, but there is no doubt that the Black Hand played its part. Could Apis and the Black Hand have seen the possible repercussions of the assassination? Did it ever consider that Austria would intervene directly in Serbian affairs? We may never know the full details of how and why the sinister Black Hand acted as it did. What we can be sure of is that its single greatest triumph touched off the First World War, which, unresolved, was re-fought by Adolf Hitler in the 1940s. How many other secret societies can boast such a litany of mass-murder?

As an indication of how little notice the human race takes of the lessons that history teaches us, the Black Hand has resurfaced among the Serbs of the 1990s. Like its ancestor, this gang of killers is interested in securing the freedoms of Serbians in Bosnia, at the bloody cost of innocent Muslim lives. Although its namesake touched off one of the bloodiest wars in human history, the Black Hand is seen as a patriotic organization by the Serbs who know of its existence.

CHAPTER FOUR

The Invisible Armies

North of Tokyo, amid the sparsely populated mountains, a band of men and women assembled to prepare themselves for a momentous battle with the forces of law and order. It was late 1971. The group called itself Rengo Sekigun, and its fanatical leader, the 27-year-old Tsureo Mori, had become obsessed with the idea of overthrowing the Japanese government and smashing the imperialist domination of the United States.

The 30 members of Rengo Sekigun were to form three armed suicide squads that would assassinate important Japanese citizens as well as key government ministers. The group had already carried out a limited campaign of murder; now it would go one step further. Like the anarchists before them, the group believed that the corrupt system would inevitably come crashing down. But not all of Mori's followers at the isolated training camp were convinced by this strategy. When these doubts were raised in 1972, Hiroka Nagata, an influential female member of the organization and a dangerous fanatic, ordered that a 'people's court' be held in which to try these doubters. Uncontrolled savagery followed. Those found guilty of abandoning the goals of Rengo Sekigun were systematically tortured, tied to stakes set in the ground and whipped with wires. All were then left to die of exposure in the mountains after being stripped naked. One of the women killed in this way was eight months pregnant – Nagata had always considered sex to be 'unrevolutionary'.

News of the atrocities featured in newspapers around the world. What kind of people were these? Why would the leaders of Rengo Sekigun torture and murder half of their own followers?

The organization is known to intelligence agencies by the more familiar name of the United Red Army or the Japanese Red Army (JRA), and it is one of the most dangerously unpredictable terrorist groups to have emerged in the post-war world. Yet its behaviour has almost resembled that of a fanatical cult, more concerned with strict observance of belief than with the prosecution of an armed struggle. In the 1990s Japan was hit again by a wave of violence that shocked the world. This time it was not directed by a terrorist group, but by a religious cult. Aum Supreme Truth, like the JRA, blurred the definitions and refused to be easily categorized.

Terrorism itself, although easily stereotyped by the media as the act of blowing up civilians, hijacking planes or gunning down innocent bystanders, is a complex and ill-defined subject. George Bush provided a working definition of what constitutes terrorism: 'Terrorists,' he said, 'deliberately target non-combatants for their own cynical purposes. They kill and maim defenceless men, women and children ... and others who defend the values of civilized society.'

Many terrorist groups are the covert armies of governments in exile or the paramilitary force of a disgruntled minority, fighting for a voice or for survival. In this category we can place the Irish Republican Army (IRA), whose members claim to represent the discriminated Catholic minority in Northern Ireland and by acts of terrorism want to unite the UK province with the rest of Catholic Ireland. We can place in this category, also, the Peruvian Shining Path (*Sendero Luminoso*), which wages a guerrilla war in the Andes, the African National Congress (ANC), as it existed during South Africa's years of apartheid, and the Workers' Party of Kurdistan (PKK), which fights for Kurdish independence in southeastern Turkey. Similar separatist organizations include the Corsican National Liberation Front (*Front de la libération nationale de la Corse*, FLNC), the Sri Lankan Tamil Tigers and the Basque separatist group ETA (*Euzkadi ta Askatasuna*). The motivations of these terror groups are often quite clear cut, and their goals in many cases are realistic expectations of a desired political situation. This is not to say that their violent activities can in any way be condoned.

Distinct from the terrorist driven by nationalist or separatist fervour is the idealist. Unlike his cousins fighting on behalf of a region or a people, the idealist is isolated from the people around him. He fights for a radical cause, a religious belief, a hatred of some abstract force or for a redundant political ideology that does not seem to represent any one section of society. Such groups often cross national boundaries to carry their fight to all corners of the world. Technically referred to as terrorists, such a group easily falls within our definition of a 'brotherhood of fear'. Without an established power base, such a group is able to mould its own ideology as it sees fit and can freely make alliances with the strangest of bedfellows. Naturally, there are terrorist organizations that seem to encompass both of these categories. Pre-eminent among these is the Palestine Liberation Organization (PLO), which has links with an array of diverse terrorist groups around the world.

The fact that these idealistic terrorists wage a war on their own terms without recourse to a predetermined agenda does not mean that their fight is any the less bloody. In the past dedicated ideological terror groups have caused some considerable unease within the international community. In this chapter we will examine the rise of some of these terror groups and look at how they emerged from obscurity, conducted the most appalling crimes against innocent people and were finally suppressed or were disbanded in a fit of disillusionment.

Samurai Swords and Flame-throwers

What became known as the Japanese Red Army actually began as two separate leftist groups that merged in 1970. Both groups, the Red Army (led by Tsureo Mori) and the Tokyo-Yokohama Joint Struggle Committee against the Japan-United States Security Treaty (led by Hiroka Nagata), protested against US-Japanese cooperation. Their first public act as a unified organization was a hijack. Armed with sharpened samurai swords, the elegant weaponry of a bygone era, the JRA terrorists forced a plane belonging to Japanese Air Lines (JAL) to fly to communist North Korea.

The movement rapidly upgraded its killing technology and over the next two years carried out terror attacks and murders throughout the country. Several of its members had sought the backing of experts in the terrorist field and had travelled to Lebanon, where Palestinian guerrillas were active. There, the Japanese fanatics were taught the skills of the international terrorist, from hijack and hostage-taking techniques to familiarization with firearms and explosives.

Only a few months after the shocking mass-murder of their own followers in 1972, three of these Arab-trained activists put their newfound skills to use in the service of the Palestinian cause. Travelling incognito from Paris into Tel Aviv's Lod airport, the three Red Army terrorists left the Air France plane on the tarmac and took the bus to the terminal. After proceeding past the usual customs checks, the three collected their luggage and calmly proceeded to pull out submachine-guns and hand grenades. Turning their guns and grenades on the massed crowds within the terminal building, the three Japanese wounded 76 people and killed 26. In the confusing and bloody mêlée, one of the terrorists was accidentally shot to death by one of his fellows, and another was killed by the blast of one of his own grenades. The single survivor was arrested by Israeli forces and imprisoned.

The Lod airport incident illustrated the savagery and fanaticism of the Japanese Red Army and the willingness of the Japanese terrorists to kill on behalf of the Palestinians. This was a disturbing new phenomenon. Further acts of terror were carried out, in particular a JAL hijack in 1973 and an attack on a Western-owned oil refinery in Singapore in January 1974. Both Japanese and Palestinian terrorists took part in the refinery attack, and after hostages had been taken, the group demanded the release of several imprisoned JRA members from Japanese jails. When this demand was refused, Palestinian terrorists, acting on behalf of their JRA comrades, infiltrated the Japanese embassy in Kuwait a week later. Hostages were taken, and the demand was repeated. This time the Japanese government acceded to the demands.

More acts of terror were perpetrated by the group in the 1970s. One attack carried out in July 1974, was particularly noteworthy, since it involved the Euro-Palestinian terrorist known as Carlos the Jackal. Neither Arab nor Japanese, Carlos carried out a grenade attack on a Parisian store in support of JRA's seizure of a French embassy. Such international cooperation seemed to prove the point of some analysts that a Soviet-backed international conspiracy was at work here. According to the theory, all terrorists were funded by the KGB and fought on its behalf. The theory went some way to explain the varied acts of cooperation between terrorist groups but could not explain why some terrorist groups expended so much energy fighting one another.

The late 1970s saw repeated JRA attacks and hijacks, but the movement then suddenly dropped out of sight. A decade later the group re-emerged to shock the public with a spate of bombings in Italy. During the investigation of a bombing in Naples in 1988, the Italian police became convinced that JRA was now working hand in glove with Libya. The Arab regime in Libya made no secret of its hatred for the Western powers and was said to fund terrorist activities abroad. It mattered little which actual organization did the killing.

No evidence came to light, however, of links between Libya and Japan's other extreme groups. Pre-eminent among these far-left factions is the terror organization calling itself New Left, a hotchpotch of competing radicals that actively campaigns for unconditional revolution by violent means. Attacks on Japanese airports by New Left in the late 1980s have been accompanied by more daring feats. A garage-manufactured flame-thrower was used to burn down a political head-quarters building in 1984, and in 1986 homemade rockets were fired at Tokyo's historic Imperial Palace. Rather than procure expensive military-grade weaponry from the arsenals of more established terrorist networks, Japan's New Left has resorted to equipping itself with homemade – but no less devastating – fire-power. Both New Left and the JRA are still considered to be active and are thought to be as highly motivated as ever.

The Palestinian links forged by the Red Army movement were not unique. For Western powers, fighting a limited counter-terrorist campaign individually against small, well-organized bands of fanatical killers, this fact has proved immensely worrying. One dedicated group of West German terrorists struck at the very heart of Europe in the 1970s. It forged links with Arab terrorists that equalled and even surpassed those of the JRA, and it actually took its name – the Red Army Faction – from its Japanese namesake. As one 'red army' began to copy the name and techniques of another, an array of left-wing 'red armies' sprang up across Europe. But the most influential – and most feared – of these revolutionary terrorist organizations was the West German-based Red Army Faction.

Baader-Meinhof

An extraordinary wave of protest swept through the industrialized nations during the late 1960s. Much of the protest called for an end to military intervention in Vietnam, but it also included vociferous calls for nuclear disarmament and for the dismantling of the NATO alliance. Caught up within the burgeoning youth rebellion of the day, the protests became international in scope, embracing people in North America, Japan, Britain and the rest of Europe. Not all left-wing activists found this form of protest acceptable. In particular, a disenchanted core of educated middle-class men and women found that traditional democratic politics had abandoned them. With their ardent left-wing zeal unrecognized and unrepresented, these youths considered themselves a shunned minority, a revolutionary élite with a vital message. Some of these people turned to violence in order to make themselves heard.

The unbalanced radicals of the Japanese Red Army were made up of just such an educated élite (both leaders of the group were 27 years old when it was founded). In West Germany, too, the most notorious terror group in the nation's post-war history was established by disillusioned intellectuals. Andreas Baader (aged 24) and Gudrun Esslin (aged 27) were the founder members of the movement, which was born in Frankfurt in 1968. Baader argued that support for the communist peasants fighting against the Americans in Vietnam was only part of the left's obligations. American imperialism and the entire capitalist system were at fault and had to be destroyed. These idealistic revolutionary sentiments were given practical shape on 12 April when the terrorists set fire to a department store in protest against the materialist consumer society. Although arrested, the arsonists jumped bail and joined the left-wing underground to plan a campaign of violence. They were joined in 1970 by two respectable professionals, the journalist Ulrike Meinhof and lawyer Horst Mahler. From this time , the group, which called itself the Red Army Faction (RAF), became known as the Baader-Meinhof gang, and it hit the headlines with a string of bank raids intended to fund their forthcoming terrorist attacks.

By 1972 the RAF had amassed enough firearms, explosives and technical training to carry out its violent campaign. Beginning in May of that year a series of shocking bomb attacks rocked the nation. A total of 15 bombs was exploded, the most devastating of which were targeted against a US army headquarters in Frankfurt and a newspaper office in Hamburg. Government officials whose views were considered by the RAF to be damaging to the 'people's interests' were also targeted, and several were assassinated. Finding sympathizers in neighbouring countries, the RAF set up contacts with like-minded organizations. The Red Army Faction had taken its name, first, from the radical Japanese Red Army and, second, from the concept of an international left-wing movement that would rise up across the industrialized world. The Baader-Meinhof gang was to be just a part, a splinter or 'faction' of this violent uprising. In fact, the intellectual, bourgeois leadership of the terror group was dismayed to find that its attempts to liberate the nation were not welcomed by the working classes. The idealists had no popular support, just radical ideas and an unreceptive audience.

To many Germans, now proud of the way in which their country had embraced the ethics of the post-war world, the Baader-Meinhof gang was seen as a dangerous throwback to the 1930s. Just as the Nazis subverted the democratic system with a campaign of organized terror, these new radicals abandoned the democratic process in favour of violent revolution. Accordingly, these young men and women were disparagingly described as 'Hitler's Children'. Without a set agenda or a realistic method of achieving their political goals, the RAF were little more than anarchists, updating their killing techniques with plastic explosives and concealable sub-machine-guns. However, the West German authorities were not going to let the Baader-Meinhof gang continue to murder and maim. Within only a few years most of the RAF, including both Baader and Meinhof, were apprehended, although the underground organization proved more resilient than expected and survived the suppression.

In the mid-1970s RAF activities proved more ruthless, more violent and more dangerous than ever before. A new breed of revolutionary had taken up the fight. Younger, more professional and more detached than their predecessors, the new RAF continued to detonate bombs on US military facilities, in banks and in government buildings. These indiscriminate attacks were supported by a well-planned campaign of assassination and kidnap. Günter von Drenkmann, President of the Supreme Court, was killed by gunfire at his own front door in November 1974. The following year terrorists from the RAF kidnapped the leader of the West Berlin Christian Democratic party, Peter Lorenz. In return for Lorenz, the RAF was able to secure the release of five of their comrades from prison. Other high-profile attacks included the seizure of the West German embassy in Stockholm in April 1975, a bloody raid on the OPEC meeting in Vienna in December of the same year and the kidnap and murder of businessman Hans-Martin Schleyer in September 1977. The Schleyer kidnap had been an attempt to gain the release of some of the original terrorist gang, and the failure of this plan ended with the suicide of Andreas Baader, Gudrun Esslin and Jan-Carl Raspe in their jail cells (Ulrike Meinhof had hanged herself in May 1976). With the death of the original RAF founders, it seemed that West Germany's bloodiest chapter had come to a halt.

The RAF of the late 1970s had shown itself to be a formidable opponent, not least because of the way in which it was able to reach out to other terror groups. In particular, the RAF cooperated spectacularly with the Arab terrorist group calling itself the Popular Front for the Liberation of Palestine (PFLP) in two headline-grabbing plane hijacks. The first took place in June 1976, when armed terrorists from both the RAF and the PFLP hijacked an Air France flight from Paris to Tel Aviv and diverted it to Entebbe in Uganda. Their demands included the release of both Palestinian and RAF prisoners, and the hijackers were confident of success. Not only were they isolated from both Israel and West Germany in the depths of Africa, but they had the support of Ugandan troops at Entebbe airport. Israel's stance on terrorism was, however, unequivocal, and a daring raid was staged in which Israeli paratroopers stormed the terminal building, killing all 13 terrorists and rescuing all but three of the 53 hostages.

This cooperative effort did not bode well for the future of counter-terrorist operations. Allied with the well-funded and highly efficient terrorist networks of the Middle East, the fanatical radicals of the Red Army Faction were capable of unprecedented horrors. If any observers thought that such an alliance had been a one-off, they were proved wrong less than a year later. A second hijacking, this time of a Lufthansa jet by PFLP terrorists, ended in stalemate at Mogadishu airport in Somalia. They demanded that the West German government release several of the imprisoned RAF terrorists. This demand was rebuffed, and an Entebbe-style rescue mission was hastily prepared. Soldiers of the élite West German counter-terrorist unit GSG9, which had been specifically set-up to counter RAF activities, worked with the British Special Air Service (SAS) to storm the plane and successfully free all the hostages.

As the decade came to an end the RAF had been squeezed almost into oblivion by the determined West German government. Just as the terror groups began cooperating across international frontiers, sharing information and resources, opening up their training facilities to other groups and acting in concert, so too did the world's *counter*-terrorist groups.

Yet the Red Army Faction survived into the 1980s, carrying out numerous attacks with guns, bombs and even rockets on NATO targets and personnel. In 1985 13 of the group's 22 core activists were women – an indication of the faction's wide, if numerically small, appeal. Names such as Susanne Albrecht, Brigitte Mohnhaupt and

Adelheid Schultz show how dominant the role of women had become. But then, two of the RAF's most famous terrorists, Meinhof and Esslin, had been women. This gender slant was not coincidental. Red Zora, a left-wing terrorist group in the early 1980s, recruited only women and attacked targets associated with prominent social issues.

There was considerable overlap in membership between Red Zora and the RAF and between the Revolutionary Cells (*Revolutionare Zellen*, RZ) terror group and the RAF, although the RZ was primarily concerned with industrial disputes. Between them, Red Zora and RZ were responsible for over 600 bombings in one year alone (1982). RAF activities from 1985 onwards saw some considerable degree of collaboration with other 'red armies' in Europe, in particular *Action Directe* (based in France) and the Italian Red Brigades. Victims of this international left-wing terrorism continued to be NATO facilities and personnel but also included industrialists and businessmen. The deaths were relentless, brutal and pointless. When La Belle Disco was bombed in 1986 with Arab assistance, President Reagan used the incident as a pretext to mount a bombing raid on the Libyan capital of Tripoli. The West Berlin club was often frequented by US servicemen, one of whom was killed in the bombing. Again, this Arab connection illustrated the complex and confusing network of organized international terror that seemed to penetrate almost every modern state. With a suspect, Christine Endrigkeit, and her Arab terrorist boyfriend, Mansour Hazi, apprehended, the German authorities are confident that the latest incarnation of the Red Army Faction has been eliminated. That there may yet be another phase in the ultra-left terror campaign cannot be ruled out, despite a singular lack of real purpose, of aims or of successes.

Driven by a determined sense of social injustice, the RAF terrorists have struck at figures of authority as well as at other aspects of the Establishment. Fighting from a platform of middle-class indignation on behalf of the oppressed working classes, they have failed to deliver anything but misery and death in an uncoordinated and naive blitz on modern society. Although the RAF saw itself as an urban Marxist-Leninist revolutionary guerrilla army, it was never anything more than a well-armed and efficient band of anarchists. The faction's organization eventually proved its undoing, the police were able to dismantle the terror group piece by piece, tracing an incriminating trail of contacts and links. The remainder of Germany's 'red armies' have been less easy to eradicate. Wise to the vulnerability of a well-ordered operation, today's heirs to the Baader-Meinhof legacy have opted to use discrete terrorist cells. Each cell is an autonomous unit – hence their name, the *Autonomen* – which directs its own terrorist campaign with little regard for the activities of other *Autonomen* or for the rest of the ultra-left movement in general.

Europe's Other Red Armies

Germany has proved to be the home of Europe's most international terrorist organization, and several of the continent's other nations have suffered accordingly. It was the active involvement of several West German terrorists living in France that helped the French terror group *Action Directe* (AD) become established in 1979. Régis Schleicher, Jean-Marc Rouillan and his girlfriend, Nathalie Ménigon, were AD's leaders during the group's first few years. Despite several violent attacks in 1980 and 1981, the French authorities took little notice of this upstart organization. Following a series of bank robberies, with which AD was able to grow in both size and offensive ability, the terrorists soon hit the headlines. Six people died in a restaurant bombing in the summer of 1982, and police were able to trace the involvement of both AD as well as a gang of ruthless freelance Arab terrorists led by Abu Nidal. Further outrages committed by various Middle Eastern terror groups shook France simultaneously, and the police began a vigorous crackdown – *Action Directe* now came high on their hit-list.

The Red Army Faction continued to take an interest in this newly created terror group. A secret Lisbon conference in 1984 was held by, and for, European terrorist groups dedicated to thwarting the imperialist policies of NATO and the United States. The conspiratorial pact that they approved was even given a name, the Political-Military Front. Although terrorists from Belgium, France, Italy and Portugal were represented at the covert summit, the real driving power behind the international sweep of violence was the RAF. By far the most vocal, the most radical and the most violent of Europe's burgeoning fanatics, the RAF and AD spear-headed the anarchistic revolution. Representing the working classes of Europe as well as the hungry masses of the Third World, these idealistic killers claimed to oppose modern industrialization and consumerism as well as the Western exploitation of the world's developing nations. In essence, they opposed modern society, assassinating businessmen involved with electronics, computing and nuclear energy and detonating bombs at various corporate headquarters. Like the RAF, AD also waged a terror campaign against NATO, and when it found the opportunity, struck out at the Establishment. *Action Directe* blew up part of the Interpol headquarters in 1986 and tried to kill a defence official in 1985 and a former minister for Justice in 1987.

Although the history of AD was violent and bloody, it was also a mercifully short one. Despite extensive international connections, the membership continued to fall into police traps, with the result that by 1988, AD had little, if any, momentum left. Key players, such as André

Olivier, who was arrested in 1986 with a car packed with firearms, were being routinely taken out of commission. Crucial to the destruction of this fanatical gang was the discovery of an AD safe-house established at a farmhouse outside Orléans. There, in February 1987, four out of the five remaining leaders were apprehended, including both Ménigon and Rouillan. The fifth member of AD's inner circle, Maxime Frerot, was captured by police later that year, a fugitive from justice, living rough and on the run, with scant support from the now-defeated organization.

Italian revolutionaries far outnumbered the well-prepared and influential RAF. Like the members of the German Baader-Meinhof gang, the Italian Red Brigades (the *Brigate Rosse*) were composed almost exclusively of disenchanted intellectuals and middle-class drop-outs. Like their West German cousins, they fought on behalf of (an imagined) long-suffering working class. However, the Red Brigades proved extremely fanatical and far more dangerous. The movement initially gained its momentum during the student troubles of 1968, and it was supported by a radical millionaire businessman named Giangiacomo Feltrinelli. A committed revolutionary, Feltrinelli organized his own revolutionary terrorist group called the Proletarian Action Group (GAP). He died while planting explosives in 1972, and a right-wing fascist backlash ensued. Left-wing ideologies and right-wing fascism have been constantly at odds in Italy since the end of the Second World War. The fascists began a bombing campaign that murdered innocent civilians and that lasted well into the 1980s.

Left-wing revolutionary groups seemed to proliferate in Italy during the 1970s. At one point during the decade of violence there were 150 individual terror groups – a prominent example of which was the Front Line. Bombings, murders and assorted acts of criminal sabotage escalated to unbelievable proportions, and as the decade came to a close 2000 acts of left-wing Red Brigades terror were being committed each year. Often it was policemen and magistrates who were the targets. Italy became almost paralysed with fear and frustration by these *brigadistas*. Renato Curcio was a leading figure in the left-wing movement, a hardened terrorist and one of the founding members of the Red Brigades. His wife, who joined him in the struggle to bring down the Establishment, died in a gunfight with the authorities. Curcio's eventual arrest helped spark off the most publicized Red Brigades atrocity – the kidnapping of Aldo Moro.

Aldo Moro was a Christian Democrat politician who had been crucial in preparing a compromise between his own party and the rival Italian Communist Party. Both parties planned to act together to oppose the bloody wave of Red Brigades terrorism. For this, Moro was kidnapped, his five bodyguards were shot dead, and he was held by the Red Brigades for two months. Their intended goal – the isolation of the Communist Party and a return to its radical left-wing political stance – failed. Their revolutionary strategy centred on the idea of forcing the communists into ever more radical and confrontational positions. Meanwhile, the fascist terror gangs were attempting to achieve the same. The climate of fear that their bombs created was intended to incite the Italian military to stage a *coup d'état*. Both movements failed. Moro's kidnap jolted the government into action, and an anti-terrorist campaign was soon established. Safe-houses were discovered, arms caches were uncovered, and numerous terrorists were apprehended. On 10 May 1978, two months after being snatched, Aldo Moro was found in Rome, shot in the head and stuffed into the boot of a car. The crackdown had definite results, turning public opinion against the Red Brigades and closing down much of their operation.

Organized terror, however, only requires the dedication and determination of a few fanatics. While a good deal of the Red Brigades' apparatus had been dismantled, the core terrorists continued to pose a threat to 'imperialist capitalism'. This hard core was responsible for the kidnapping of US Brigadier General James Dozier in December 1981. For the revolutionaries, Dozier represented the militaristic and imperialist powers of NATO and the United States. He was, without doubt, the most senior American officer in Italy at that time. Like the RAF, the Red Brigades were vehemently anti-American and were participating in a Europe-wide swipe at NATO and its members. This shift from local political activism to AD- and RAF-style international terror deeply troubled the Italian authorities. Dozier was luckier than Moro – he was rescued on 28 January 1982. Ten armed counter-terrorist police stormed a flat on a tip-off from Red Brigades prisoners and discovered Dozier tied up inside a tent that had been pitched within the flat.

Continued pressure and the infiltration of brigades by ice-cool plain-clothes policemen, virtually destroyed the Red Brigades. What survived the early 1980s eventually reformed as the Fighting Communist Cells in 1985. These new brigades continued to kill and maim, beginning with a noted political economist called Ezio Tarantelli. Tarantelli had advised the government to scrap the sliding wage system then employed by Italian industries, and his assassination was a calculated move by the PCC brigades to secure the support of the working classes. Predictably, it failed. The sheer hopelessness of their position did not deter the brigades from further acts of violence, and high-profile assassinations were attempted in 1986 (Antonio de Empoli and Lando Conti) and in 1988 (Roberto Ruffilli). Later that year, using informers and tip-offs from previously captured *brigadistas*, the remaining Red Brigades manpower was arrested and imprisoned. Little now remains of the movement outside the Italian prison system. That it (or the RAF) may reappear, phoenix-like, is a threat that the Italian and German authorities live with constantly. Sympathizers, survivors or fresh idealists may well pick up where the original terrorists left off. In some cases the *brigadistas*, newly released from jail, may want to return to the armed revolution. Time will tell.

Belgium, too, had its own Fighting Communists. Called the *Cellules Communistes Combattantes* (CCC), this ultra-left terror group began a bombing campaign in 1984. Sympathetic with the Red Brigades and the Red Army Faction, the CCC targeted local NATO facilities and various industrial targets said to represent the hated influence of capitalism. The greatest impact that the CCC and its founder, Pierre Carette, had on the European terrorist scene was as a haven for members of *Action Directe* and the Red Army Faction. Together, the three terror groups created the ephemeral and ineffectual Anti-Imperialist Armed Front. Perhaps this umbrella label gave the disparate groups a feeling of solidarity. Although each faction fought its own battles within its own country, they did indeed share similar aims and target broadly similar targets. The CCC provided assistance for both AD and the RAF, especially when security crack-downs made life in their native countries difficult.

Unlike its dangerous and fanatical allies, the CCC murdered no one during its brief existence. However, two firemen were killed extinguishing the after-effects of one of its fire-bombs. Carette and three accomplices were arrested by Belgian police at the end of 1985, bringing to an end the group's short-lived campaign.

Other European terror groups have been less squeamish about murdering innocent men and women. Portugal's little-known FP-25 (*Forces Populares 25 de Abril*, named after the revolution of 25 April 1974) claimed the lives of a number of innocent Portuguese civilians. It espoused a second revolution that would smash the power of the right-wing capitalist Establishment and sever the imperialist links with NATO and the United States. It was a familiar manifesto, with predictably familiar results. By 1985 most of FP-25, including the organization's leader, Lieutenant-Colonel Otelo Carvalho, were imprisoned.

Activists in neighbouring Spain have been equally blood-thirsty. The now-defunct Spanish terrorist group, First of October Anti-Fascist Group (*Grupo de Resistencia Antifascista Primero de Octubre*, GRAPO), killed 20 people between 1975 and 1985 and kidnapped a number of others. Figures of authority, right-wingers and several banks and international offices were GRAPO's preferred targets. Since 1985, following a concerted anti-terrorist investigation, GRAPO has been rendered lifeless. Again worrying to the Spanish authorities were the faction's links with RAF, AD and the Red Brigades.

Greece's revolutionary terror group called November Seventeen appears not to have had the close ties that so many of the other Euro-terrorists enjoyed. November Seventeen has flourished in a nation that has a poor anti-terrorist record and a long-established tradition as a Palestinian haven. All the traditional revolutionary targets feature on the group's agenda, from NATO officers to government leaders and 'capitalist sharks'. Of all the Euro-terrorist factions, it has not yet been brought to heel and remains the most sinister and dangerous élite in southeast Europe.

Euro-terrorism has taken the world by storm. Isolated gangs of intellectuals have taken up guns and bombs against the representative democracies and multinational corporations. Their mandates are based on ideological fantasy, unachievable dreams of a society that, in practical terms, could never exist. Fighting their guerrilla wars from the (seemingly) secure hideout of the urban jungle, the terrorists can strike randomly with shocking force and are able to coordinate their attacks with other cells only a phone call away. Their ultimate weakness is crippling – they lack popular support. Royal Ulster Constabulary (RUC) policemen who chase up leads on an IRA bombing in Northern Ireland will inevitably find the trail blocked. Witnesses refuse to come forward, and the type of public support that is of such great help in police investigations – reporting suspicious behaviour or suspicious neighbours, for instance – does not exist. Operating from within a loyal and supportive community, the IRA is almost 'untouchable'. No such support existed for the élite terrorists of the 'red armies'. Fighting for aims almost incomprehensible to the general public, with a campaign of deadly violence that sickens most people, the idealists can never achieve their lofty goals. Mao Zedong's oft-repeated analogy of the guerrilla as a fish swimming within a sea of peasants, stands true for such rural revolutions. But the modern urban guerrilla had little protection from the 'capitalist sharks' he sought to destroy and often suffered a long prison sentence or death as a result.

Traditional revolutionary activity postulates a general uprising of the working classes with an armed struggle to throw off the shackles of tyrannical government. Public support in the villages and cities contributes to the struggle and provides recruits, food and shelter for the guerrillas. Thus went the successful revolutions in China, Vietnam and Cuba. If Che Guevara and Mao Zedong can be described as the father and grandfather of revolutionary guerrilla warfare, the Latin American revolutionary leader Carlos Marighela could be described as the father of *urban* guerrilla warfare. Marighela's ideas and his writings were studied, digested and put into practice by the 'red armies'. Many looked to Marighela in the same way that the North Vietnamese peasants looked to their revolutionary leader, Ho Chi Minh.

Like Che Guevara, one of Fidel Castro's most trusted activists, Carlos Marighela had abandoned the Maoist view that the revolutionary should slowly build up support until revolution breaks out – at which point the guerrillas take charge of the uprising. Tipping the theory on its head, he advocated immediate violent action in order to trigger the desired revolution. Only a small élite of revolutionary activists need engage in this fight. For Guevara, the guerrilla vanguard would emerge from the rural communities of the troubled Latin American nations. For Marighela, the cities would become the central arena for the revolution and any rural uprising could succeed only in partnership with a simultaneous urban revolt. With many Central and South American states becoming increasingly and dramatically urbanized, it is easy to see how this change in ideology came about.

This new thinking radically changed the very tactics of revolution. Typical rural movements usually measured success by the control of hamlets, villages, towns and (ultimately) provinces. As the guerrillas advanced on their beleaguered capital, the central government usually found its population divided and its provincial hold slowly slipping away until a stranglehold of guerrilla-held territory encircled the loyalist strong-point. In 1950s Malaya, rebel-held territories were termed 'black', while those provinces still loyal to the government were termed 'white'. A similar strategy of slow asphyxiation was later adopted in Vietnam and was itself based on an eminently successful strategy used by Mao in China.

The urban terrorist wasn't interested in 'taking' villages and towns. Marighela and his Brazilian revolutionaries, the National Liberation Army (*Acçâo Libertadora Nacionale*, ALN) carried out bombings, acts of sabotage, kidnappings and assassinations in order to frustrate and intimidate the Brazilian government throughout the 1960s. The aim of such apparently mindless violence and terror was to force the authorities to institute a rigorous security crackdown. This situation was intended to precipitate a social crisis that would trigger a revolution, and it was predicted that the people would rise up against the oppressive state. The ALN was savagely crushed by the Brazilian government, whose authority was never challenged by any kind of revolutionary uprising. Marighela himself was killed in a gun-battle with São Paulo policemen in November 1969. He had failed to illustrate the effectiveness of his strategy. Later, urban guerrillas in both Uruguay and Argentina attempted Marighela-style urban campaigns and, like the ALN, failed to prove the viability of the concept.

Carlos Marighela's definitive treatise on the subject of urban revolutionary warfare (what we have been describing as terrorism) was *The Mini-manual of the Urban Guerrilla*. This document, perhaps more than any other, had a great impact on the 'red armies' of the West. Eager to make a difference and without popular support or a properly thought-out strategy, they were forced to resort to this very limited concept of political revolution through the use of indiscriminate violence. But Marighela's urban guerrilla strategy was fatally flawed. As we can see, few of these ideological factions remain in operation today.

Rather than armed struggle following on from a revolution, the ideologists attempted to spark such a revolution through direct violence. Challenging the authority of the state with guns and bombs was (and still is) considered to be a legitimate form of protest by alienated groups of individuals. If peasants in Cuba can pick up rifles and overthrow their own government, setting up one of their own, what moral force prevents the urban terrorist from doing the same? So the ideologists' argument may run. But it is the weight of popular support, from whichever quarter – racial, religious or social – it is derived, that determines the legitimacy of a revolution. For example, few Westerners condemned the armed revolution of Shiites in southern Iraq following the Gulf War of 1991. The desperate plight of the people there and the tyrannical government of Saddam Hussein were seen as justification enough for this minority to fight back. Unfortunately, the uprising came to nothing and Hussein used extreme force against those cities that had dared to rebel.

Today, the technology of death has reached highly affordable and highly portable levels. Modern sub-machine-guns (such as the Ingram MAC-10) can put all 32 bullets in their magazine into a target in less than two seconds, and this weapon folds to under 27cm (10½in) in length, easily hidden beneath a jacket. More readily available firearms, such as the familiar semi-automatic pistol, provide unprecedented amounts of fire-power to a team of determined and well-trained terrorists. Just one or two shots from a pistol at close range are quite enough to kill a target. In addition, bomb-making techniques are now widely disseminated through various military-style publications and on the Internet. A terrorist bomb factory need not now be run by an ex-army explosives expert. Self-taught skills coupled with stolen quarry explosives or common chemicals can be quite enough to manufacture the deadliest of bombs.

It is the ease with which a lone individual can produce such a devastating weapon that has gravely troubled police forces. With such awesome fire-power available to a single disturbed fanatic, the police cannot necessarily deduce that a particular terrorist network is responsible. One such bombing campaign took the police force of Kent in England quite by surprise. Throughout 1995 three homemade bombs exploded at points along the M2 motorway. Two of these destroyed roadside telephone boxes. No warnings were given, no demands or threats were made, and no clues were left as to the identity of those responsible. Eventually apprehended, the culprit proved to be a man, acting on his own, without any definable reason other than to shock.

Taking the radical politics, non-conformity and elitist stance of the ideological terrorists to their extremes, one could foresee a time when one-man terror factions fight their own bloody struggles. Armed with a bomb-making manual, a fanatical and unpopular belief, and the relative anonymity of privacy, one man might kill and maim to force his extremist views on the population at large.

But it has already happened.

Terrorism USA

Between 1978 and 1995 United States Federal agents had been baffled by a series of sporadic bombings. Many of these bombs were sent through the mail to previously selected targets. The first, on 26 May 1978, injured a police officer who had been handed a suspect package sent to a university professor. At the same university in Illinois, almost exactly one year later, a second package left on campus exploded, injuring one student. Because of the academic nature of his targets, the unknown terrorist was given the name 'Unabomber'.

Further injuries were inflicted on plane passengers and airline staff over the next couple of years. From then on, individual students, staff and professors suffered the bizarre attentions of the Unabomber over a period of ten years – at Vanderbilt University, the University of California at Berkeley and at San Francisco, the University of Michigan and also at Yale University. In the mid-1980s the burgeoning computer industry attracted the wrath of the mysterious Unabomber. It was inevitable that some unfortunate member of the public would one day become a victim of the Unabomber, and on 11 December 1985 the owner of a Sacramento computer store was killed by an explosive device. This man became the Unabomber's first victim in the 17-year bombing campaign.

Whoever he was and whatever he wanted, the Unabomber continued to terrorize people who were involved in various key aspects of modern society. He carried on his violent activities into the 1990s. An advertising executive was killed by a letter-bomb in 1994, and the president of the California Forestry Association died when a bomb sent to his office in 1995 exploded in his hands. Clearly the culprit had time and plenty of it. It wasn't until June 1995 that any word was received from the bomber concerning demands or details of his terrorist beliefs. At last, 17 years after sending his first device, he had approached two prominent newspapers with a 35,000-word manifesto. If they were to print this voluminous tract, wrote the Unabomber, he would bring an end to his campaign of murder and mayhem. On 19 June they complied with his demands. The manifesto told the FBI investigators much about the psychology of the criminal; essentially, it formed a very complete and very sophisticated condemnation of the technological world in which we live. Whoever he was, he was well-educated, patient and untroubled, and also incredibly fanatical about his carefully thought-out beliefs.

Within months the authorities had apprehended a suspect, and he appeared to match this strange profile closely. Theodore Kaczynski had been a model academic, a successful professor of mathematics at the University of California at Berkeley, but inexplicably, he had abandoned the university in 1969 for life as a low-paid manual labourer. Later buying land in rural Montana, he retired from the world, building himself a log cabin and living the life of an eccentric hermit. Without a car, a telephone or even the necessity of electricity, the vegetarian Kaczynski seems to have revelled in his abandonment of the technological luxuries of the modern world. And as the Unabomber he could fight his one-man war from the safety of this rural hideout.

Officially, the US government did not class the Unabomber as a terrorist until the *New York Times* and *The Washington Post* received his socio-political manifesto. According to the FBI, bombings, shootings and acts of sabotage and arson carried out to change public opinion or government policy are not terrorism until a group has claimed credit for the incident. This clause helps the FBI claim that the terrorist figures are far lower than they really are, for not all acts of terror are claimed by specific terror groups.

Theodore Kaczynski was a lone bomber, driven to strike out against a despised technological society and its representatives. An anarchist of the ultra high-tech world, the Unabomber was a terrorist who acted alone. He had little need of an organization that could protect and support him, keep him in line and ensure he was highly motivated. Professor Franco Ferracuti, terror psychologist and expert criminologist, would also fail to class the Unabomber as a terrorist. He once said that there was 'no such thing as an isolated terrorist – that's a mental case'. Whatever labels are used by the experts, however, the Unabomber fits our profile, even though he acted alone. He did not commit random violence on the whim of a psychological illness; instead, he carried out an organized and systematic campaign that represented his socio-political views and the views of a small clique of sympathizers in America. Just as our 'brotherhoods of fear' defy all the norms of civilized society with their calculated and consistent criminal activities, so Kaczynski fought an armed struggle for a philosophy that he truly believed would be the salvation of mankind.

Kaczynski was a radical spin-off, a one-man revolutionary army straight out of the student revolts of the late 1960s. His belief that the modern capitalist system was failing the human race mirrored the embittered ideologies of the 'red armies', who fought their own war against consumerism, industrialization and American imperialism. We should feel fortunate that Kaczynski acted on his own rather than become entangled in the high-powered all-or-nothing stakes of a radical ultra-left terror faction.

There have been several violent groups dedicated to altering the perceptions of both the American public and its government in recent decades. One loosely organized movement has gone from strength to strength, cruelly feeding off media attention and conflicting party politics. The so-called 'pro-life' movement, which protests against the pregnant woman's right to abortion, has at its heart a core of radical terrorists. Violently fanatical in their belief that the right of the human foetus supersedes the right of the mother, the activists have intimidated, vandalized, injured and, more recently, even murdered. As this anti-abortion movement picked up speed in the mid-1980s, a campaign of bombings and arson began that was to attract the attention of the FBI. In 1984 alone there were 25 such attacks on family planning and abortion clinics. This made 220 acts of violence in total in only four years.

By pursuing a hard-line campaign that resorts to vandalism, threatening behaviour, kidnapping, assault and murder, the anti-abortion terrorists hope to frighten the doctors who perform the abortions into abandoning their work. As a side-effect, patients are intimidated by such action, and the activists hope that this, too, will help their cause. However, by attempting to manipulate a social and political issue in this way, the anti-abortion bombers have become fully fledged terrorists in all but name. By wounding and killing medical staff, the 'pro-life' group immediately loses its credibility: it is impossible to be 'pro-life' by blowing someone to bits.

Throughout the 1980s the anti-abortion attacks did not figure on the government's list of terrorist activity. By failing to claim responsibility for the violence, the anti-abortion terrorists avoided being legally defined as such by the investigating agency, the FBI. Presidents Reagan and Bush had politically aligned themselves with the 'pro-life' movement, while simultaneously committing their administrations to a well-publicized crusade against all forms of terrorism. This dichotomy was resolved in a deal that kept the anti-abortion attacks free from uncomfortable terrorist associations. In addition, the blurring of definitions helped these presidents to minimize America's terrorist statistics.

Terrorism on the scale of that suffered by Britain, Italy, Germany and France had been noticeably absent in the United States until comparatively recently. The rise of militia terrorism since 1993 has changed all that, and the disturbing (sometimes quite bizarre) story of this armed and dangerous movement is fully told in Chapter 7. This is not to say that the American government has never been plagued with terrorism, but the sustained and bloody campaigns that rocked Europe in the 1970s and 1980s are virtually unknown there. Terror groups that *did* develop did so in exactly the same circumstances as their European cousins.

Student protests and rallies in 1968 focused on the war being fought in South Vietnam and were led by the Students for a Democratic Society (SDS). This left-wing protest movement gave birth to a confusing array of radical action groups. Far-left politics and a youthful revolutionary zeal combined to create Red Guerrilla Resistance, Red Guerrilla Defence, the Black Liberation Army, the United Freedom Front, the Prairie Fire Organizing Committee, the May 19 Communist Organization and the Republic of New Africa. Eclipsing them all however, was the Weather Underground, the only revolutionary group seriously to take up arms against 'the system'. Leaders Bernadine Dohrn and Mark Rudd set out their aims in a leaflet entitled 'You Don't Need a Weatherman to Know Which Way the Wind Blows'. Deeds followed words, and the Weather Underground (or 'Weathermen') participated in the violent student attacks on police and government buildings in Chicago that came to be known as the 'Days of Rage'.

In July 1970, although the ringleaders of the organization were still at large, the American government charged them with the execution of numerous bombings. Still their activities continued – until the Weathermen emerged into the public light at the end of the decade. Some doubt exists about the actual extent of their campaign. The group claimed responsibility for 17 bombings in their 1974 book *Prairie Fire*, but the FBI could not accurately verify all of these claims. By far the most spectacular of the Weathermen's bombing attacks took place on 29 January 1975, when the group claimed responsibility for an explosive device that caused $300,000 worth of damage to the US State Department. The Underground, and the vociferous student groups already mentioned, undoubtedly discredited the liberal (but peaceful) student politics of the day.

Joining the broad left-wing radicals were a handful of black-power groups, the most famous of which was the Black Panther Party (BPP). Formed in 1966 as a means of local ghetto self-defence, the Panthers would initially shadow police patrols through the black areas of Oakland, California, in an attempt to curb police harassment and brutality. Leaders Huey Newton and Bobby Seale soon attracted the unwelcome attentions of the authorities, and Newton found himself arrested on trumped-up charges of murder. The nationwide campaign to free him that followed helped to spread the Black Panther organization into new territories.

With the growing discontent against the Vietnam War, the Panther movement found itself allied with a plethora of radical sects and groups, almost all with an anti-government agenda. Little of this energetic coalition survived beyond the end of the Vietnam conflict – more than 1000 Panthers and their sympathizers were eventually arrested, and several members had been shot by the police. While it still existed as a useful force, the Black Panther Party began to focus more on overthrowing the regime that it opposed rather than merely defending the rights of the oppressed.

Black Panther aims were, like those of the student idealists that they associated with, difficult, if not impossible, to achieve. As a revolutionary movement dedicated to seizing control of the state and handing power over to the disenfranchised black masses, the BPP did not stand a chance. Support for such an armed movement was virtually non-existent among middle-class blacks and ineffectual among blacks trapped in ghetto poverty. Although the Panthers ignored the need to recruit the black middle-classes into their struggle, Malcolm X, one of America's greatest activists in the black liberation movement, did not. It was the ballot, as *well* as the bullet, that Malcolm X acknowledged as being central to the liberation movement.

Malcolm X had called for the formation of self-defence groups before his death in 1965, and even for an armed black resistance group, much like the Mau Mau cult of 1950s Kenya. 'In Mississippi we need a Mau Mau,' he had said. 'Right here in Harlem, in New York City, we need a Mau Mau.' His pressure group, the Organization of Afro-American Unity (OAAU), had the avowed aim to 'fight whoever gets in our way, to bring about the complete independence of people of African descent here in the western Hemisphere ... and bring about the freedom of these people by any means necessary.' But it remained essentially a political group, with only abstract pretensions to violent struggle.

According to one of Malcolm X's biographers, the Panthers, like all left-wing ideological movements, became fatally 'caught up in the illusion that the masses are revolutionary in themselves'. Malcolm had advocated violence only as a last resort, yet the extremist Panthers were arming themselves with the intention of using the weaponry to spark a nationwide revolution, just as the 'red armies' would later do in Europe. Malcolm X was tragically assassinated in 1965, his attempts to coordinate both middle-class and poor urban blacks still incomplete.

The guns on which the BPP placed so much reliance proved of little use in liberating the black minorities through the sought-after revolution. Rapid and systematic suppression of the Panthers by the police in the late 1960s prevented any of their vaunted ideas – disconnected as they were from any actual political mechanism – from becoming anything more concrete. The tough handling of these 'terrorists-in-waiting' meant that the Panthers always remained a self-defence force.

The Party's members had virtually no opportunity to carry their message of violent revolution to the people, and the organization disappeared without trace following its comprehensive suppression in the late 1960s and early 1970s.

The Nation of Islam, a more modern incarnation of the Black Panther phenomenon, continues the tradition of community defence without the revolutionary message. As a group of Muslim vigilantes, the movement has helped to clean up crime-ridden estates in some of America's largest cities. The problems of escalation will always exist: the authorities have claimed that the Nation is anti-Semitic. In 1997 the Nation of Islam was invited to help London's Islamic community in the inner-city area of Brixton. A number of shootings had created a worsening climate of fear, and Minister Wayne Muhammed asked the permission of police to organize Nation of Islam patrols. The request was denied.

Both the Panthers and the Weathermen followed a pattern that was being successfully blazed by the coldly efficient Baader-Meinhof gang across the Atlantic. Thankfully, these US terror groups proved far less terrible than their radical agenda suggested. The Weather Underground in particular had all the right ingredients. With its Marxist ideology and fanatical student activists, it was just as committed to the 'overthrow of US Imperialism' as the bloody 'red armies'. What it lacked was a physical connection with another terrorist organization. It lacked the educational experience of mixing with professional, hard-core terrorists. This was something from which the RAF, the Italian Red Brigades and the JRA had all benefited, not just in training opportunities, but also through joint operations and the acquisition of explosives and other military weaponry.

Right-wing Terror

There were – and still are – other malign forces at work among the murky world of the terrorist underground. 'Red armies' and revolutionary anti-capitalists were not alone. In some countries right-wing factions took up the gun and the bomb in order to pursue their own political aims. Italy suffered badly from the frightening attacks of these neo-fascist terrorists, beginning in the 1960s and continuing into the 1990s. Perhaps the worst atrocity committed by these right-wing killers was the bombing of Bologna railway station in August 1980, when more than 80 people were killed and many more were wounded.

The neo-fascists concentrated on exploding bombs in areas crowded with civilians because their aim was to create a climate of fear and tension. It was hoped that this would lead to a hardening of government attitudes and the imposition of martial law. The ultimate aim was some sort of military-backed take-over. When the Red

Brigades began their campaign of terror in the 1970s, they sought much the same goal – but the left-wing dream envisaged a popular uprising at the moment of social collapse, not a military coup.

Who are the neo-fascists? For decades rumours have circulated about the possible links between these right-wing terror gangs and radical elements within the Italian military and secret services. This belief springs more from the military-orientated objectives of the movement than from specific threads of direct evidence. But the rumours persist, and it is unlikely that a terror campaign coordinated with such fanatical zeal, such ruthless efficiency and undepleted resources could maintain a decades-long war against the Italian people without some organizational backing. The great fear of conspiracy theorists is that the neo-fascists represent a secret army, dedicated to 'state terror'.

Such secret armies have actually been formed in a number of unstable countries around the world. Left-wing terrorists waged an urban guerrilla war in Uruguay from 1963 onwards, but their activities were severely curtailed a decade later. The Uruguayan government became repressive and in practical terms allowed the military to take control of the internal affairs of the state. The brutal crackdown on the terrorists, on their sympathizers and on those suspected of being sympathizers was unrelenting. Right-wing death squads sponsored by the military roamed the streets, at first they killed suspects, and then they began murdering anyone – trade unionists, left-wing activists and so on – who had spoken out against the Uruguayan regime. In February 1973 the military actually overthrew the weak democratic government.

Other Latin American nations reeled from the violence of the fascist death squads. In Argentina Juan Perón ruled the country until his death in 1974, when he was succeeded by his wife Isabel. Left-wing terrorists were active in the cities, in particular the People's Revolutionary Army (*Ejército Revolucionario del Pueblo*, ERP) and the Armed Forces of Liberation (*Fuerzas Armadas de Liberación*, FAL). Like many Latin American governments, Argentina's counter-terrorist campaign proved wholly ineffective. The growing danger to the state from the revolutionaries encouraged frustrated members of the police and armed forces to take up the fight themselves. Death squads began a counter-terrorist movement, with terrorist violence of their own. In Argentina these groups boldly called themselves the Argentinian Anti-Communist Alliance (*Alianza Anticommunista Argentina*, AAA). The death squads soon became an unrecognized (yet institutionalized) adjunct to the security forces, and few officers were able to resist their alluring power and effectiveness. That they were effective is undeniable – left-wing terrorism vanished from sight as suspects were kidnapped, tortured and executed, without trial, without ceremony and without anyone ever knowing.

The fate of the accused. A suspected witch is held before an agent of the German Inquisition (*c.* 1600). The barbaric implements of the approaching torture are being prepared nearby. *Mary Evans Picture Library*

Pleading for mercy. Conrad of Marburg, a powerful and sadistic sixteenth-century theologian on a mission from the Pope, sits in judgement. The German Luciferan sect was to be the main target of his savagery. *Mary Evans Picture Library*

As a cover for the die-hard racists and hate-mongers, the BNP touts itself as
a radical new alternative to established political movements. Most European
nations have similar 'front' groups, all dedicated to fear, victimization and
terror. *Robert Todd/Images Sans Frontieres Ltd*

Opposite page
Top left Heinrich Himmler surrounded by a loyal entourage. Himmler
proved to be one of Hitler's most fanatical devotees. As the head of the
feared SS paramilitary organization he set himself up as the leader of a 'cult
within a cult'. *Imperial War Museum*

Top right Adolf Hitler addresses the strategic aspects of his military
campaign. The Nazi Party resembled a modern mind-control cult in several
important ways, with Hitler as the messianic, charismatic and obsessive cult
leader. *Imperial War Museum*

Left Few political movements have gripped a people as fiercely and as
dangerously as Nazism. Here loyal Germans show their respect for the New
Order. *Imperial War Museum*

Above Members of the Klu Klux Klan display the gaudy regalia of their ancient order. Were it not for the organization's campaign of terror, torture and murder, the Klan's ritual could be considered nothing more than amusing pantomime.
Rex Features/Tom Kidd

George Washington at the altar of his lodge (1793). *Mary Evans Picture Library*

Textile workers smash their own machines in order to secure their livelihoods (*c.* 1812). They formed part of the poverty-stricken Luddite movement which took its frustrations out on factory machines at the start of the nineteenth century. *Mary Evans Picture Library*

Archduke Franz Ferdinand and his wife tour Sarajevo in June 1914. The two were shot to death by a schoolboy member of that feared secret society, the Black Hand. Few other assassinations have so dramatically affected world history. *Mary Evans Picture Library*

Co-founder of the infamous Baader-Meinhof terrorist gang in 1968, Andreas Baader was a disenchanted left-wing radical with a penchant for violence. He committed suicide in 1977 leaving the organization, also known as the Red Army Faction, to carry on killing into the 1990s. *Rex Features*

An unmistakable portrait of 'Scarface', otherwise known as Al Capone. Synonymous with organized crime and gangsters, Capone was responsible for creating America's first true criminal syndicate during the 1920s. Nicknamed the 'Outfit', it long outlived its creator. *Rex Features*

Above Devotees of
Voodoo engage in
one of the cult's
ceremonies. The pole
around which they
dance is the entry
into this world for
the spirits which
they call.
Rex Features

Left A rare picture of
Koresh doing what
he did best: turning
the Biblical Book of
Revelation into
gripping oratory. His
in-depth knowledge
of the Bible, and his
passion carried many
of the Waco cultists
along with him to
their death in 1993.
Rex Features

Tokyo decontamination. Only one city on earth has been the victim of a nerve gas attack delivered by subway train. The Japanese cult Aum Supreme Truth attempted to bring about Doomsday in 1995 and injured over 5,500 Tokyo commuters in the attack. *Rex Features*

By ignoring the usual channels and turning to 'state terror', the death squads became intoxicated with power. Almost immediately, they began to kidnap and murder an entire section of the population that had absolutely no connections with terrorism. Anyone with left-wing tendencies, and some without, and on some occasions even children, were taken without warning by unidentified men to military establishments, tortured and then murdered. Thousands were 'disappeared' in this way. In Argentina the mothers of the 'disappeared' protested to the military government, but no formal recognition of the horrible events was made until the junta was overthrown in 1984.

In Italy both left- and right-wing factions misjudged the socio-political situation, the population's abhorrence of terrorism and the government's realization that a trap was being set. Unfortunately, the terror campaigns in Latin America were more successful. It became relatively easy to provoke the military into overthrowing a weak and ineffective democratic regime, bringing about the political crisis that had been the terrorists' aim. However, the military often then began to sponsor its own counter-terror terrorist groups, and these purged the nation without regard for civil liberties or legal niceties. This pattern was repeated across Latin America. Such savage oppression and committed ruthlessness was totally unforeseen by the naive, communist-inspired revolutionaries who had sparked it off. It may be exactly what the Italian neo-fascist gangs are trying to emulate.

The Palestinian Terror Network

Although the old-style nineteenth-century anarchists had been international in vision, their cross-border links did little more than provide morale-boosting support for one another's actions. Today's international terrorists are *truly* international. For the paranoid, such complex links fuel suspicions of a global conspiracy directed at the heart of Western capitalism. But who directs this conspiracy and why?

Most of the 'red armies' have received considerable assistance from Palestinian terrorist organizations. This broad Arab grouping is not the only Arab terrorist sect at large in the Middle East – far from it. Each Arab faction fights for an individual cause, often the same one, but occasionally for mutually opposing causes, leading to bloody internecine conflict. There are even one or two terror groups without a cause of their own, waging a terrorist campaign on behalf of others. However, the Palestinian terrorist network is one of the most active and most efficient of them all – a truly international movement.

Bound between the Jordan River in the east and the Mediterranean in the west, Palestine is a relatively tiny region. Following the Second World War the area was inundated by Jews from Europe who were granted their own nation-state by the Western powers. Outraged

Palestinians and troops from neighbouring Arab countries took up arms in 1948. Their war against the new-born state of Israel ended in failure, and the Palestinians became a minority group in their own land. Hundreds of thousands fled into exile from the region.

When the regular armies of neighbouring Arab states failed to defeat the Israelis in 1948 and 1956, the Palestinians turned to other, more unorthodox methods of liberation. In the 1950s a violent nationalist organization called Al-Fatah was founded by Yasser Arafat, and it soon dominated the umbrella resistance group called the Palestine Liberation Organization (PLO). In 1964, the year the PLO became operational, Al-Fatah fighters carried out a raid into Israel, marking the start of the Palestinian's armed fight to free their people.

During the Six Day War of 1967, PLO terrorists attacked Israeli targets from across the border in neighbouring Syria and Jordan. Led at that time by Ahmed Shukeiri, the PLO's main goal was the formation of an army of freedom fighters with which to liberate the Palestinian homeland, but this goal remained ever-elusive. While the PLO attempted to represent the Palestinians and their struggle, other more radical splinter groups also turned to terrorist violence as a way of achieving the PLO dream.

Defeated and demoralized by the failures of the Six Day War, some Palestinians decided to carry their fight for freedom far beyond Israel's borders. Central to this shift was George Habash, who established the Popular Front for the Liberation of Palestine (PFLP). Unlike the political realist Yasser Arafat, Habash abandoned any hope of liberating Palestine through internal revolution. His answer was a campaign of terror that would illustrate hard-edged Palestinian resolve and strike fear and panic into the Israelis. The PFLP staged the hijack of an Israeli El-Al passenger jet in July 1968, forcing it to divert from Tel Aviv to Algiers. It was a headline-grabbing strategy that would become almost a hallmark of the Palestinian terrorist movement. Habash took the credit for this first operation, and his movement was invited under the PLO umbrella. Arafat gained a degree of credit from later PFLP victories and provided Habash with funds, training camps and equipment.

During the next two years the PFLP hijack campaign was responsible for 14 incidents, and in 1970 it climaxed with the multiple hijack at Dawson's Field in Jordan. The extraordinary event was a bold indicator of just how powerful the PLO-PFLP alliance had become. What was more, it illustrated how the terrorists were able to wage their unique war in the most unexpected of places and in the most unexpected of ways. Dawson's Field was a disused airstrip in Jordan, and in September 1970 PFLP terrorists hijacked three airliners and flew them, and their passengers, to the airfield. PLO troops met the planes, but the usually friendly Jordanian army moved in to surround the site.

After releasing some of the hundreds of hostages, the PLO moved the rest to the city of Amman and blew up the airliners in a spectacular series of explosions.

Both the intense media coverage and the international pressure mounted steadily day by day, forcing the Palestinians to threaten King Hussein of Jordan. Jordan had always provided a safe haven for Palestinian terrorists, but the PLO could see this alliance approaching its end. Fighting broke out between the Jordanian army and the Palestinian factions, a nasty guerrilla war that turned Amman upside down and erupted in every one of the PLO training camps that were scattered around the country. Syria intervened with its own troops when it looked as if King Hussein was about to defeat the Palestinians, a move that seemed to guarantee a PLO victory. In the end, the entire incident – named Black September by the Palestinians – ended in failure. Israel forced the Syrians back across the border and the Jordanian army rescued the hostages and suppressed the PLO network within Jordan. This powerful terror group soon founded a new operational base in Lebanon, another nation that shared a border with Israel. Terror attacks that were planned and launched from Lebanon soon precipitated the civil war that utterly devastated that country.

Black September, a radical terror faction, was formed jointly by the PLO and PFLP following the Dawson's Field débâcle. This group began its guerrilla war by attacking vulnerable civilian Jordanian targets. It was this organization that was responsible for the high-profile hostage situation at the Munich Olympics in 1972. The Israeli team quarters were stormed by seven Black September gunmen, resulting in the deaths of two Israelis. The demands of the gunmen, that the Israeli government free imprisoned Palestinians, were refused and the West German authorities decided to attempt a rescue. A bus was arranged to take the terrorists and their captors to a waiting plane at the airport. In a hurried assault, the West German police stormed the bus before the gunmen could disembark. All nine hostages died from grenades dropped by the Palestinians, while four of the terrorists were killed and three were wounded. This incident, which provoked worldwide outrage at the time and has been remembered at every Olympic meeting ever since, helped (along with the Baader-Meinhof threat) to spur the West German government to set up its highly trained anti-terrorist squad, GSG9.

The Israeli government also established its own élite counter-terrorist organization. Unlike GSG9, the Wrath of God, as the organization was known, dispatched hit squads of ultra-secret plain-clothes assassins across the globe to track down and execute known Palestinian terrorists. In the years following the Munich massacre, the three surviving terrorists were tracked down and killed. In July 1973, members of Wrath of God, travelled incognito to Norway where Ali

Hassan Salameh, co-conspirator of the Munich operation, was believed to be hiding. Following his assassination, the Israeli killers were caught and arrested by the Norwegian police. They had mistaken an innocent Norwegian waiter for the terrorist Salameh. Although it was discredited by this deadly mistake, the Wrath of God did go on to fulfil its intended goals and made raids on PLO camps over the Israeli border in Lebanon. Al-Fatah's chief of staff was assassinated by the group in April 1973, and in 1979 it was a Wrath of God car-bomb planted in a Beirut street that eventually killed Salameh.

When another Palestinian group, the National Arab Youth for the Liberation of Palestine (NAYLP), began a series of devastating attacks on passenger jets, the PLO sought to distance itself from its activities. At least a hundred innocent people were murdered by this organization in 1973 and 1974. Meanwhile, Arafat and Habash had decided to bring an end to Palestinian terrorism outside Israel. Its positive results were non-existent, and world opinion was irrevocably set against the movement. Their decision proved to be a tough one to implement, however. Abu Mahmoud, the leader of the NAYLP, was successfully executed by the PLO, and then Arafat began covertly assisting the American CIA with its counter-terrorist operations. However, the Palestinian liberation movement had mutated and developed beyond the wildest dreams of its initial founders. Splinter groups and radical factions were being led by self-styled terrorist leaders, and the one and only goal of the movement became obscured by a confusing mix of conflicting new aims.

Of interest to us is the disquieting terror organization called the Special Operations Group (SOG). Established in 1972 by Wadi Hadad, Habash's deputy commander, the faction coordinated with a diverse array of terror groups around the world. SOG was purely international in scope, and its broad agenda included striking at Western political and corporate interests. De-stabilizing the West was now perceived to be a legitimate method of hitting back at Israel and its international supporters. One attack in particular was indicative of this new trend in Arab terrorism. An OPEC meeting held in Vienna in 1975 was suddenly disrupted by armed terrorists. One minister and two guards were killed, and the group took 11 oil ministers as hostages and demanded a plane in which to escape. According to one of the surviving terrorists, Wadi Hadad masterminded the OPEC raid, but it was funded by the Libyan leader Colonel Gadaffi, manned by both Palestinian and Red Army Faction terrorists and led by the Venezuelan-born revolutionary killer called Carlos 'the Jackal'. Carlos and Hadad were to cooperate on several major terrorist operations.

In the murky world of international terrorism, Carlos the Jackal played a prominent role. For years this Euro-terrorist acted as a go-between for the Palestinian terror network and for the idealistic revolutionaries waging their urban guerrilla war in Europe. Wadi Hadad had persuaded Carlos, whose real name is Ilich Ramirez Sanchez, to set up a base of operations in London in the early 1970s, and it was from there that the dissident initially began to make contact with the newly established terror groups on the Continent. His career has been well documented, and his name is infamous and synonymous with assassination, deception and international intrigue. Carlos has been associated with some of the most terrifying organizations of violence to have existed in the post-war world. He began to create the first links of this terror conspiracy in 1973, when he subsidized the operations of the Baader-Meinhof gang. The next year he caused death and destruction by throwing a grenade into *Le Drugstore* in Paris, an act of solidarity with members of the Japanese Red Army who were negotiating with the French government at the time.

After the OPEC incident, Carlos planned the audacious Entebbe hijack with his friend, Wilfried Boese, an influential member of the Baader-Meinhof gang. Again directed by Wadi Hadad, Carlos planned the operation, and Boese actually led the terrorists, dying in the Israeli rescue bid. By the start of the 1980s Carlos had vanished from sight, living first in Libya and then in Syria, probably to assist President Assad with his knowledge of the international terrorist network. Carlos was heard of in 1983 after two of his agents, a Swiss and a West German, were apprehended by French security forces. Immediately Carlos (using his real name Ilich Ramirez Sanchez) demanded their release in a Spanish-written letter, authenticated with his own fingerprints. After the detonation of a bomb at Marseilles railway station and two others on express trains, the French government capitulated and released the two international terrorists in 1985.

In October 1994 Carlos was apprehended in Sudan and handed over to the French authorities. He had already been sentenced to life imprisonment *in absentia*, and he now languishes in a French prison. Incredibly, the book *Carlos, The Secret Networks of International Terrorism* by the journalist Bernard Violet inspired Carlos to sue for libel. Claiming that the book had infringed his privacy, the terrorist hired a team of 50 lawyers to fight his case. In 1997 the case was thrown out of court.

Wadi Hadad died of cancer in 1979, and with Carlos in hiding throughout the 1980s, the terrorist scene was left without a leading light. Unfortunately there were quite enough 'leading lights' in the Arab terrorist network to fill this role. Assuming the *nom de guerre* Abu Nidal, the fanatical killer Sabri al-Banna has thoroughly dominated the modern international terrorist scene. World leaders or counter-terrorist chiefs who believe that all terrorists are part of a united whole, a global conspiracy of terror, are mistaken. Abu Nidal is the example that proves this point. So dangerous, so violent and so extreme, he was expelled from the PLO in 1973 and sentenced to death *in absentia*. From that point, Abu Nidal has confounded Arabs and Westerners alike with his commitment to violence and his flexibility of beliefs. During the 1970s the targets of his organization, the Fatah Revolutionary Council (FRC), were mainly Syrian, but attacks aimed at this quarter stopped suddenly in 1977. Several experts in this field tend to believe that Abu Nidal was working for the Iraqi government against the Syrians, but was 'bought off', something that would be considered unthinkable when applied to a typical terrorist movement. But the FRC is un-typical. A ferocious series of attacks on Syria's greatest rival, Jordan, followed. Had Syria recruited Abu Nidal for its own ends? Whatever the case, his terrorist attacks on Jordan continued throughout the 1980s.

It is clear that the PLO and the Fatah Revolutionary Council are mortal enemies. Not only has Al-Fatah sentenced Abu Nidal to death in his absence, but Yasser Arafat has been the target of several assassination attempts, each one coordinated by the FRC. During the latter half of the decade, Abu Nidal's gang began to attack Western targets. In July 1988 passengers on the Greek cruise ship *City of Poros* were sprayed with gunfire, and nine people were killed and almost a hundred wounded. At the port where the vessel was about to dock, two more of Abu Nidal's gang were killed when their bomb exploded prematurely. Where they were about to plant it is still a mystery.

By the end of 1989 there were reports of serious dissensions within the Abu Nidal camp, the murder of six senior members of the FRC and the systematic execution of up to 150 of his followers at the Lebanese headquarters. Even some of Abu Nidal's own officials denounced him as a psychopath, citing as evidence the murder of seven civilians in Sudan in 1988 and of an Arab religious leader in Belgium. Abu Nidal's gang has waged a bloody war in the service of whoever gave it shelter. Without strong beliefs and a fanatical vision of purpose, Nidal's men were little more than international Arab mercenaries. Most of their victims were Arabs, of various persuasions, and many Arab leaders (both terrorist and government) wanted Abu Nidal dead. PLO fighters fought a protracted battle with his men in September 1990 and pushed them out of the refugee camps near Sidon.

Arafat had found support for his leadership of the PLO waning in the 1980s, and he consequently sanctioned a scattered terrorist campaign that included various attacks on Israeli civilian and military targets. It included the famous seizure of the cruise ship *Achille Lauro* off the coast of Egypt. More recently, however, Arafat has wisely reverted to diplomacy and condemns the use of terrorist violence against governments and innocent civilians. His new role as leader of the Palestinians, which was settled in a historic accord with the Israeli government, has meant that the PLO must now abide by international rules. As a legitimate political entity, the Palestinian territories go some way towards an independent Palestinian state – the very goal for which the PLO and its factions had been fighting. With tensions between the new Palestinian state and Israel still on a knife-edge, it remains to be seen what will become of the PLO and its tenacious leader.

Terrorist groups from the Middle East who fight their wars on the international stage have proliferated. Civil war in Lebanon (the PLO base after its expulsion from Jordan) and the fanatical religious revolution that has gripped Iran are the two greatest reasons for this growth. Factions on all sides sponsor terrorists who are willing to bring their struggles to the attention of the Western media. What interests us here, and what is perfectly illustrated by the Palestinian terror network, is the existence of 'pure' international terrorism. Not violent attacks taken abroad to airports, airliners and embassies in the West, but terrorism that does not seem directly to serve the interests of the particular terror group involved. It is a war fought by people who wish to effect a change in their home nation by striking back at the Western industrialized nations as a whole. This strategy presupposes an industrial-capitalist conspiracy of global domination and imperialism (led by the USA), which can be successfully countered only by an equally conspiratorial cross-border terror network. For two decades the PLO has lain at the heart of this network, and actively or through splinter groups and factions, such as the PFLP, Black September and the NAYLP, it has woven an elaborate network of terrorist allies and dependants around the world.

President Ronald Reagan boldly asserted during his tenure in office, that the 'growth in terrorism in recent years ... is part of a pattern, the work of a confederation of terrorist states'. For a time during the Reagan era, the linchpin in this terrorist conspiracy seemed to be Colonel Gadaffi, the Libyan dictator. While it declared Libya as a 'terrorist nation' the US State Department was meanwhile able to show that the country sponsored terrorist acts abroad, posing a great danger to international peace and security. The US government has made much of its 'terrorist nation' blacklist, and has added nations to, or removed them from, the list according to fluctuations in the current political scene. Moreover, the basic evidence linking Libyan sponsorship of global terrorism was never forthcoming. Although there seemed to be little real proof of such an orchestrated campaign, Gadaffi himself boasted of his powerful role within the terrorist community. Vociferous Libyan propaganda certainly gave the impression that the nation played host to all the revolutionary dissidents of the world, and President Reagan, the CIA and the State Department were all ready to believe such self-aggrandizement.

Libya has certainly supported the Palestinian cause – as do most

Arab states with varying degrees of enthusiasm – and has always favoured those factions in the movement dedicated to more extreme methods. In 1985 Gadaffi claimed to have established a 'Pan-Arab Command for Leading the Arab Revolutionary Forces'. The aim of this umbrella force was to instigate an international war against the United States and its Western allies and even against the more liberal-minded Arab states. Publicly offering a wide array of resources for Palestinian terrorists, including weaponry, training facilities and safe havens, Gadaffi openly antagonized the US. The president's pride in the Command's new mission, in the recent deadly results of suicide bombers against US interests and in terrorism in general was never concealed. Quite the contrary. Even so, although he provoked the West to violence against his own people, the nature of his dealings with terrorist groups always remained obscure.

Gadaffi seemed to have little to gain from the various terror campaigns being fought in other countries, but he nevertheless remained adamant about his involvement. There were rumours of material assistance being given to the IRA, rumours that were soon substantiated. In 1987 a consignment of arms and ammunition being shipped to Ireland was seized off the coast of Brittany. The haul, which weighed over 100 tons, included 1000 AK-47s, ten heavy machine-guns and 20 anti-aircraft missiles. In addition, there were rumours of training facilities being made available to activists from the Baader-Meinhof gang, the Italian Red Brigades and even the Japanese Red Army. In the mid-1980s these reports proved worrying, and they convinced many that the world's terror groups were being trained and equipped by Libya to be sent out into the world where they could wreak havoc against that nation's enemies.

Gadaffi's security forces exert a totalitarian grip on the population of Libya, and this has spread overseas to menace or murder innocent Libyans in exile abroad. Libyan terrorists, officially sanctioned by the state, have travelled to other nations in order to seek out and assassinate these dissidents. Such terrorist outrages number in the tens not hundreds, and only one such murder has occurred on American soil. Fisal Abulaze Zagalli, a Libyan dissident, was shot to death at his home in Colorado in 1981. The Libyan terrorists responsible were also thought to have been planning at least two more assassinations on American soil. The fact that Arab gunmen could enter the US and commit a terrorist assassination helped to create a sudden sense of panic within the Reagan administration. It duly announced that Gadaffi had dispatched trained terrorist hit squads to America and that their targets were to be its politicians. Gadaffi had, indeed, sent out assassination teams, but to Egypt and Tunisia, not the USA. These were closer enemies with whom the Libyan leader had long-running grudges. The level of paranoia can be judged by Reagan's immediate action:

trucks full of sand were parked in front of both the White House and the Capitol building to protect them from rocket or bomb attacks. Later these were replaced by concrete barriers.

There is no doubt that Gadaffi has gone to great lengths to appear revolutionary, but his brand of Islamic Marxism has been a failure for the country, and his attempts at flexing his military might have been equally unsuccessful. Time and time again his ineffectual moves to unify the Arab world around him have failed. Mistrusted by his neighbours and hated by the West, Gadaffi had only one way left open to him to satisfy his megalomaniacal thirst for glory. It was terrorism. By associating with the left-wing red armies, Gadaffi could steal some of their thunder; by organizing the murder of Libyans now resident in the West, he could illustrate how long Libya's arm really was. American intervention has not dissuaded Gadaffi. His jet fighters have been shot down in 1981 and again in 1989, and two Libyan attack boats that were sent against a US Navy carrier were sunk in 1986. A month later, in April 1986, President Reagan ordered F-111 bombers based in Britain to bomb targets in Libya. This unexpected move was initiated by a bomb that exploded in a West Berlin bar just days before, killing one US servicemen. However, later investigations revealed that the West Berlin bomb had probably been planted by *Syrian*, not Libyan, terrorists. US paranoia was at its height. Only six months earlier, the government had supposedly uncovered what it had always suspected, 'a radical Islamic infrastructure of terror'. Operated chiefly by Libyan and Iranian terrorists, it was active in the US recruiting local radicals, from black extremists to Puerto Rican and American-Indian separatists. Of course, much of this assertion was a fiction, but a fiction that helped to demonize Gadaffi and enabled the US to strike out at Libya militarily.

However, terrorist attacks of a more definite kind *have* left their mark on the West. In 1991 Libya was accused by a French magistrate of orchestrating the bombing of a passenger jet that exploded over the Sahara in 1989. That same year both Britain and France accused two Libyan agents of planting the bomb that blew up Pan Am flight 103 in 1988. The Boeing 747 exploded over the town of Lockerbie in Scotland at Christmas, killing all 259 passengers and crew and 11 of the townspeople. Gadaffi has refused to extradite the two men, despite the repeated demands of the international community. These two bombing atrocities mark a new phase in Libya's flirtations with terrorism. For over a decade Gadaffi has associated himself with the bloody exploits of international terrorists like the 'red armies', the PLO and the Abu Nidal gang, without directly taking up the fight against the West himself. This tactic has indeed earned him international enmity and has resulted in Libya being labelled a 'terrorist state'. It is unlikely, however, that Libya ever masterminded an elaborate terrorist conspiracy. One journalist visiting the country in the late 1980s, marvelled at the very idea. Stranded for hours at Tripoli airport, hindered by a totally ineffective bureaucracy and intermittent telephone communications, he was amazed that anybody could have thought such a badly run nation could operate anything as complex as a global terror campaign!

If Libya has not, in the end, been at the centre of a worldwide network, the greatest question to trouble Western experts has been: who is? For Reagan and his followers at the beginning of the 1980s the answer was obvious – the Soviet Union. In particular the Soviet secret service, the KGB. Guerrilla armies, fighting for national liberation, had been openly sponsored by the Soviet Union for decades, especially following the end of the Second World War. It seemed a natural assumption that the Soviets would benefit from funding terrorism, just as they had funded the Viet Cong guerrilla fighters in Vietnam. Reagan's Secretary of State, General Alexander Haig, stated quite categorically during his first few days in office that: 'Moscow continues to support terrorism and war by proxy with a conscious policy – programs ... which foster, support, and expand international terrorism.' Terrorists, whether killing in the name of the IRA, the PLO, the RAF or the Tamil Tigers, were all thought to be the dupes of the Kremlin, pawns in a greater game of global domination. Since many terrorists are equipped with Russian-made weaponry, such as the AK-47 assault rifle and the Rocket Propelled Grenade (RPG), the assertion seems to have some validity. But terrorists take weapons from wherever they find them, there are as many US and European weapons in use by terrorists as there are Russian.

Conspiracy theorists saw the PLO as the pivotal organization of the terrorist conspiracy. According to some Russian defectors, PLO fighters had extensive training in Soviet camps, and the organization was well-supplied with Russian arms and ammunition. Few dispute that there was Soviet support for the Palestinian cause, if only because a PLO victory over the Israel regime would have landed Moscow with a new ally in the region. The secondary training and support of other groups, such as the 'red armies' and the IRA, was probably countenanced by the Soviet Union.

Destabilization of the West seems to have been the primary goal, whatever the more immediate aims of the individual terror groups. Thus the PLO, the most powerful and best organized of the world's terrorist groups, acted as a deniable asset, supporting other factions at the behest of the Soviet Union. This secondary assistance was, according to some commentators, payment for the funding and material assistance that the Soviets provided to the Palestinians. The Soviets had a right to expect something in return, and what they wanted was a little of the PLO's experience and skill to be passed on to others further along the chain, to Pakistani terrorists, Indian extremists, 'red army' members and IRA killers.

While the concept of an international terrorist plot trying to overthrow capitalist society at the direction of the KGB might seem far fetched, there may be elements of truth in it. Likewise there may be elements of fantasy too. There has, as yet, been no solid and indisputable proof that the Soviets were masterminding the terrorist campaigns of the world in the 1970s and 1980s. Individual terrorists, often caught unprepared in safe-houses full of weapons, plans, drawings, explosives, membership lists and codes, have never been apprehended with documents that have implicated the Soviet Union. Perhaps the Kremlin was at pains to ensure that its influence among these unstable and violent psychopaths would always remain safely at arm's length. The truth probably skirts the edge of the conspiracy theory. Soviet interest in these terror groups undoubtedly existed, and Soviet links with the PLO would have provided a perfect opportunity to gain some insight, and maybe some influence into these groups. Whether the influence of the superpower went any further than that will probably always remain an open question.

CHAPTER FIVE

Punishment and Profit

Private detective David Hennessey walked out of his small office late on Wednesday, 15 October 1890. With him was Bill O'Conner, a good friend, and a private detective like himself. They dined together at one of New Orleans' restaurants and walked to Girod Street, where they parted company. Hennessey lived only a few doors away and as he approached his home, five men emerged from the shadows. Each one was armed with a shotgun. They opened fire, hitting the detective several times, but he pulled out his revolver and tried to defend himself. His shots went wild, but were enough to scare off his attackers.

Hennessey died from his wounds the next morning, and New Orleans erupted in anger. He had served in the New Orleans police department as a detective in the past and had made enemies among the Sicilian population of the city. Hennessey had made one powerful enemy in particular: a powerful Sicilian businessman called Joseph Macheca. Macheca and Hennessey were to become bitter enemies in a feud over one man – Vincenzo Rebello, America's first-ever Mafia boss.

Back in 1877 an Edinburgh businessman named John Forester Rose had been touring various estates and holdings across Sicily that were owned by his family. Obviously very wealthy, John Rose proved to be an attractive proposition for two influential members of Sicily's Mafia crime gangs. The two men, Leone and Esposito, snatched Rose as he rode south of Palermo and sent a ransom note to his wife in Scotland. When she wrote back to tell the men she did not have the large sum of money that they demanded, they promptly cut off both John Rose's ears and mailed them to her as a warning. Another letter included a slice of the man's nose. Outraged and indignant about the treatment of this man, the British newspapers were able to raise the required amount of money to buy the release of Rose.

It was a year before the Italian authorities caught Leone and Esposito, but their captivity proved a brief one. Leone escaped to North Africa, and Esposito to the United States. With a small gang of comrades, Esposito arrived in New Orleans in 1878, and he saw a great future for the Mafia in this 'land of opportunity'. One of history's most powerful and most ruthless criminal brotherhoods had just arrived in the United States.

Esposito wasted no time in assuming a new name, Vincenzo Rebello, and he quickly established himself as the boss of a Mafia crime syndicate that began relentlessly to squeeze the Sicilian population of the city. Although his tactics and influence inspired fear among his countrymen, someone found the courage to inform on him. The police detective given the task of arresting and charging Esposito was David Hennessey, a man who had always kept a close interest in the Sicilian criminal fraternity. In July 1881 he arrested Esposito, and the Mafia leader was sent to New York to be shipped back to Italy to stand trial. Hennessey would have to give evidence at the New York extradition hearing, but someone attempted to 'buy' him. The Sicilian businessman Joseph Macheca offered Hennessey $50,000 to tell the hearing that he had made a mistake and that the man he had arrested wasn't Esposito after all. By refusing the bribe, Hennessey signed his own death warrant. For the next nine years both men were at each other's throats. Hennessey devoted himself to destroying the newly created Mafia gangs, and Macheca tried to block any move Hennessey made. Grim determination was matched against the corruption and brute force of a sinister and violent network. In the end Hennessey could not overcome his enemies, and he was gunned down in a pool of blood on Girod Street.

Hennessey became the first of many American investigators to be killed trying to stop the rising tide of organized crime. But the Mafia was more than just a criminal syndicate. It was set to become a complex and ritualistic brotherhood, filled with all the fraternal responsibilities of Freemasonry. Unlike the Freemasons, however, the Mafia routinely employs terror, torture and murder to further its aims. These methods are also sometimes used within the brotherhood to sort out internal schisms – Mafia wars.

New Orleans in the 1880s was a more popular destination for immigrants than New York, and as such it was just as cosmopolitan, if not more so. The mix of cultures and peoples that made up the New Orleans population came from across the world – and that included the small island of Sicily. It was in Sicily that the Mafia originated, and at the turn of the millennium the Mafia is as powerful there as it ever was.

Theories differ not only as to the exact meaning of the word 'Mafia', but also to the exact origins of the organization. A popular – and overly romanticized – version tells of a medieval uprising of Sicilian men against the French soldiers who were garrisoned in Palermo, Sicily's capital. Defending the honour of a young woman from a French sergeant, the men killed all the Frenchmen they could find to the cry of 'Death to France is Italy's Cry!' Those that fought in this massacre founded a secret society that survived down the ages. The group took its name from its password, the glorious cry of defiance that echoed through Palermo's streets during those bloody days, 'Morte Alla Francia Italia Anela' – MAFIA. The word is more likely to have been adopted sometime in the mid-1860s following the debut of a popular play called The Braves of Palermo Jail (I Mafiusi di la Vicarria di Palermu). Mafiusi in this sense meant an honourable man, a brave and courageous man. The play proved to be an instant success, and the term entered the national consciousness.

Only a few years before, in 1860, the revolutionary Garibaldi had conquered Sicily as part of the Carbonari strategy to unite the whole of Italy. With his ad hoc fighters were criminals and mercenaries of every sort. To free Sicily he was forced to make use of every advantage he could muster. Once organized, the gangs remained together and began to exploit the rural Sicilians with impunity. Garibaldi's new Italy was committed to the establishment of a just government and was unable to strike hard against the gangs as previous overlords had done. These gangs terrorized the people, they extorted money, they kidnapped, they murdered, and they stole. When their interests over-lapped, the gangs would not hesitate to initiate bloody feuds against one another. As they grew in strength and influence, a hierarchy was developed and the gang chiefs became subordinate to a single leader. Thus small gangs became larger gangs, and the term Mafia was adopted to describe this underworld of crime. Individual members of the crime gangs became known as mafioso.

On the mainland, too, criminal societies had become established in the wake of Garibaldi's victories. Most powerful of all was the Camorra, a secret brotherhood of criminals bound together by solemn oaths, who extorted money from the people of Naples. Their rule of terror waxed and waned with the attitudes of the government, but the move-ment survived until at least as late as 1911. Both the Camorra and the Mafia survived because their existence proved fruitful. The Mafia's grip on the Sicilian countryside was not through fear alone (although that played a huge part of it), but also through a local intolerance of central government. Whether the government of the day was France, Aragon or even Italian, Sicilians have a natural distrust of foreign domination. The Mafia have capitalized on this fear and cultivated a sense of community and self-government, something that the Mafia claimed that only it could adequately provide.

By the 1880s these Mafia gangs were adopting more refined methods of organization, including secret passwords, initiation rituals and an internal structure, designed to insulate sub-groups (regimes) from one another for security reasons. The island was now totally dominated by their activities, and in some districts the Mafia did form an unofficial local government. There was little room for manoeuvre, however, and no way at all for new Mafia groups to become established. This stale situation prompted many hundreds of ambitious mafiosi to follow the example of other Sicilians, especially Esposito, and sail to America. In the United States organized crime was almost unheard of, and the criminal opportunities awaiting the Mafia were vast.

Bootleggers and the Black Hand

Organized crime flourished among the Sicilian immigrant population for over 50 years with little interest from the US law enforcement agencies. Everyone knew that these gangs existed, that they exploited their own people, and were most productive wherever Sicilians and Italians settled. No one ever suspected that here, just as back in the old country, the Mafia crime syndicates were in communication with one another. The first two decades of the century were dominated by a mysterious group of extortioners calling themselves the Black Hand. Sometimes associated with or even identified with the Mafia, the Black Hand used that sombre symbol as a warning to its victims. It had no relation to the Serbian Black Hand cult active in the Balkans at this time, and by the 1920s had been eclipsed by more effective Mafia money-making schemes. The 1920s saw Prohibition.

Andrew Volstead, a congressman from Minnesota, sponsored the Eighteenth Amendment to the Constitution, and thus the amendment became known as the Volstead Act. It was more commonly known as Prohibition. The movement to ban the manufacture, sale and import of alcohol had been the culmination of a social reform movement that had its roots back in the nineteenth century. Patriotic fervour whipped up the moral crusade to new heights, and on 16 January 1920 the Volstead Act came into force. For crime gangs across America, including the Mafia outfits, Prohibition was a blessing. Even before the act came into force, normally law-abiding people were preparing to break it. America continued to drink as much as it ever had, and the demand was met by gangsters who transported home-brew or smuggled booze into the cities for sale at bars, clubs and speak-easies. In one fell swoop the entire drinks industry had been handed over to the underworld. Profits were incredible for those who could compete on equal terms with the toughest of the gangs. Murder rates in cities like Chicago and New York spiralled as the gangs fought for markets, suppliers, territory and the plethora of other 'entertainment' rackets that continued to flourish. Like drug gangs in any major city in any modern nation today, the incredible profits involved provoked violent jealousies in the dealers, all the more so because they were outside the law. On the street, power, profits and law were all the same.

Chicago became the most notorious city of the Prohibition decade because it was without doubt America's most corrupt city. Chicago's notorious gangster of the period was Al Capone, but although his family were Italian, Capone did not belong to the Mafia, the Black Hand or the Camorra. Like most other bootleggers, Al Capone organized a street gang that had no real racial or social ties. Business sense often dictated that gangs employed whoever was able to do the job, and the assimilation of small-time gangs by the bigger operations simply speeded this up.

The Chicago wars were violent and bloody, messily spilling from one vendetta to another in a complex web of changing rivalries: from O'Banion's North Siders, to the Genna brothers' West Siders and the powerful John Torrio faction. From 1923 to 1926 only two main players were left standing, Capone on one side and Bugs Moran on the other. This two-way stand-off did not last for long. Capone dominated the bootleg industry, and with his wealth and influence, he soon dominated every other kind of illegal activity as well. Gangsters up and down America were trying to do the same. Capone's empire was nicknamed the Outfit. The Outfit did not focus on just one or two types of crime; it covered the entire spectrum. This tactic of total dominance was a goal for which every gang aimed but that few could achieve. In New York today the power base still remains divided among five major Mafia factions. Capone led the way in neutralizing opposition.

His other ground-breaking tactic was the move into legitimate business. Of course, this had been a factor in criminal activities for many years because most illegitimate activities require some type of legitimate cover to hide behind. One of John Torrio's partners, Joseph Stenson, for example, produced real beer for Torrio from a quite legitimate non-alcoholic (and supposedly converted) 'near-beer' brewery. Capone moved not only into 'legit' business but also into the labour unions that went hand in hand with them. Control of the labour markets proved an incredible asset, and it was a tactic that the Mafia would not forget. In the 1960s, Jimmy Hoffa and the influential Teamsters' Union would be speedily recruited by the mob. Some of the gangsters played both ends, establishing legitimate businesses while controlling the labour unions alongside them. They had the market sewn up and brutally intimidated anyone who refused to come in or came in but then dropped out. One union in particular, the Unione Siciliana, could be controlled by Capone only through a Sicilian go-between. As a Neapolitan Capone could not join the union, and as a Neapolitan, Capone hated the Sicilians anyway. Good business sense, however, convinced him that it was better to have the Sicilian union working for him than against him.

Although he had insulated himself so carefully from prosecution, Capone was eventually jailed on tax evasion charges. With the god-father of Prohibition off the streets, the other crime syndicates breathed a sigh of relief. Capone had relentlessly sought media attention, and their own activities had come under scrutiny as a result. Now free from Capone's brief but omnipresent grip on the underworld, the gangs began to consolidate their business dealings. Prohibition was repealed in 1933, in part due to Capone's psychotic attacks but also to his total control of Chicago's local government. Those criminal gangs that had remained intact and prosperous until 1933 quickly realized that they didn't need Prohibition to sustain them any longer. Prohibition had made many gangs across America rich, and yet its demise did not necessarily signal the demise of the shadowy world of organized crime that had emerged to ruin it. Those gangs still in operation had moved to diversify, much as Al Capone had done, and they were now able to reap the profits from a host of illegal money-making operations. Bigger things were sure to follow.

Some conspiracy theorists have speculated that the Volstead Act was a sure-fire method of creating such powerful criminal syndicates. No one would introduce such an amendment, argued one such theorist, A. Ralph Epperson, without instantly understanding what would follow: people would continue to drink but would now be supplied by outlaw brewers and distributors. As the government, the police, the FBI and the Prohibition Bureau began a campaign of suppression against these bootleggers, the supply dwindled and the prices rose. Anyone who could remain in the business became phenomenally rich. The profits to be made enticed others to try their hand at supplying booze, which sparked off violent gang wars. The terrible violence that followed led the government to tighten the screw on the gangs, thus resulting in even higher prices and more profits. Epperson argued that this scenario could have easily been predicted and that Prohibition was designed specifically to help create the powerful criminal empires that we know today.

The engineers of this great conspiracy are thought to be Mafia masterminds or else a clique of international power-brokers *beyond* the Mafia. Such imaginative and cleverly composed theories remain just that. The idea has only ever had fringe support, mainly due to the fact that there has never been any evidence for such a complex and risky manoeuvre. The indisputable fact remains, however, that by the start of the Second World War, the American Mafia dominated the criminal underworld of the nation. Prohibition became just a bad memory after 1933, and the man on the street began to forget about the high profile crime syndicates run by Al Capone and his like. For many law enforcement agencies, it did seem as if the tidal wave had receded. In fact, the surviving crime bosses had dropped into intentional obscurity, away from the flashy press exposure, headlines and gossip columns that Capone had so eagerly sought.

A good deal of organized crime was now under the influence of Italian racketeers, who took over from the predominance of Irish and

Jewish crime gangs of the 1920s. Other ethnic groups were still plagued by criminal gangs, however. One of New York's most notorious gangs were the Westies, an Irish street gang that violently blossomed into a murderous criminal fraternity. The Westies followed the long-standing tradition of disposing of bodies quickly and neatly, cutting up corpses in the bathroom of a West Side apartment and flinging the carefully wrapped pieces into the Hudson River. But the Westies could never compete with the scale, sophistication and organization of the larger syndicates. This shifting control of the underworld, from non-Italian to the Italian Mafia, was pioneered by 'Lucky' Luciano, New York's leading gang boss of the mid-1930s. He did much more than just co-opt the business of organized crime, however. Luciano actually brought together the disparate Mafia operations ('families') across the United States, thus creating the Mafia as it exists today. As the nominal head of this octopus-like organization, Lucky Luciano could look forward to reaping the unprecedented profits from undoubtedly the greatest secret criminal brotherhood in human history. Unfortunately for the 'boss of bosses', Luciano's violent career suddenly came to an end when he was sentenced to a minimum of 30 years on charges of controlling prostitution. The fortunes of war came to Luciano's aid, however, for he enjoyed the confidence of tens of thousands of Italian immigrants, especially mafiosi fleeing torture and imprisonment under Mussolini in Italy.

At a period when the US Navy was rightly paranoid about sabotage on East Coast wharf fronts and docks, Luciano was able to guarantee the loyalty of Italian dock-workers. With military commanders planning the invasion of Sicily in 1943, the American Mafia was actually recruited to help with the operation. Luciano collaborated with the government and helped secure detailed intelligence of the island. The invasion was a great success, and the embryonic CIA (then the Office of Strategic Studies) released hoards of local mafiosi from Sicilian prisons. This rural army of violent gangsters vanished into the towns and villages, and despite brave but sporadic efforts by the post-war Italian government, would be almost impossible to put back in again.

Lucky Luciano's conduct during the war was grudgingly recognized. A quick release from his up-state prison was arranged provided that New York's 'boss of bosses' be immediately deported. He fled to Cuba, which had flourished under Mafia patronage during the pre-war decade. From this island retreat, Luciano masterminded the activities of the American Mafia for a short time. Gambling and heroin smuggling produced vast profits, and numerous Mafia heavy-weights flew out to Cuba to discuss business. Soon, however, even the government in Havana tired of him, and Luciano then set up his headquarters in Italy. Until his death at the age of 64 in 1962, Luciano continued to dominate the American Mafia, and thus the greater part of the sinister world of the country's criminal underworld.

'This Thing of Ours'

The fact of a nationwide Mafia crime conspiracy did not achieve any attention until 1957. In November of that year police accidentally stumbled across a high-rank meeting of Mafia bosses at a country estate in New York state. Although no one had committed any offence, their presence together stimulated a move to coordinate 'criminal intelligence' among the US police forces.

Until that point the FBI, realistically the only law enforcement agency able to crack cross-state organized crime, shunned the job. J. Edgar Hoover, the bureau's director, instead concentrated on chasing bandit gangs. Big-time criminals faded into obscurity in the 1930s, and Hoover, knowing that his agents would never be able to hold out against the bribery and corruption, decided to keep his men clean. They pursued Bonnie and Clyde, 'Machine Gun' Kelly, John Dillinger and Ma Barker's gang, among others. These were old-fashioned criminals with a gun and a car, evading the authorities in a pursuit that had only one inevitable conclusion. While these rural bandits grabbed the headlines, the heat was taken off the rapidly maturing Mafia. If Hoover knew about the rising national crime syndicate, he did not acknowledge it; if he did not know about it, he should have. The 1957 Mafia summit took the FBI by surprise and embarrassed them into the bargain. Still Hoover would not acknowledge the existence of the Mafia and prove right his opponents, who had insisted that there most definitely was such an organization.

The next big break came for the US authorities in 1963 when veteran mafioso Joseph Valachi decided to become a witness against the Mafia or, as he called it, *La Cosa Nostra* ('This Thing of Ours'). He believed his life was in danger and hoped he could stay alive under police protection by informing on the 'mob'. He opened up a whole new world for investigators, and his evidence supplied the FBI with the layout of a complexly structured organization, something of which they had, until then, no conception. Hoover could not now deny the fact of an American-Italian criminal empire, but rather than backtrack on three decades of denial, he announced the FBI's war on La Cosa Nostra (not on the Mafia). One could almost imagine that the bureau had uncovered the existence of some utterly new secret society, La Cosa Nostra (LCN), a deadly conspiracy that almost rivalled that of American Communism.

The American Mafia was divided up into between 25 and 30 powerful 'families', each of which had absolute control over the Mafia activities of a city or region. Only New York could boast more than one family – the city had five, led by the bosses Joe Bonanno, Carlo Gambino, Vito Genovese (Luciano's old partner), Tommy Lucchese and Joe Magliocco. Coordinating the activities of the Mafia families and attempting to smooth out territorial or succession disputes, was a National Commission, almost a board of directors for this vast money-making enterprise. Only the most powerful of the bosses sat on the National Commission, and this included all five of the New York families. Now with national coverage and a certain amount of uneasy unity, the Mafia could call itself La Cosa Nostra, a name that has become a euphemism for the (mostly) united American Mafia. Heading the organization in the 1960s was the 'boss of bosses' (*Capo di Tutti Capi*), who at that time was New York boss Vito Genovese.

Every boss (also known as a 'godfather' or 'don') had two advisors, an under-boss who deputized for him and a *consigliere* or counsellor. Beneath these, every boss had a number of lieutenants or *caporegimes*. Nik Gentile, Mafia boss of Pittsburgh, Cleveland and Kansas City, turned up in Sicily in 1963 after fleeing drugs charges in the US. In an Italian newspaper he revealed that the Mafia organization seemed to be 'very democratic', with elections being held quite regularly. Each *caporegime* handles one aspect of the family's business. It could be the criminal activities of an entire town, or it could be just one type of money-making activity, such as prostitution or gambling. In some cases the *caporegime*'s responsibilities might be a combination of these two. His men are called 'soldiers', and they make up the lieutenant's 'crew' with which he conducts his business. A crew might number anything from 30 to 300 individual soldiers.

What differentiates the Mafia from any other gang of profit-driven and highly violent criminals is not just the scale and sophistication of the syndicate but also its ritual. Mafia language is carefully codified. There are numerous words and phrases that are full of subtle meaning. A mafioso will introduce a friend to his comrades as 'a friend of ours' if he, too, is a mafioso; if he is not, he is introduced as 'a friend of mine'. This obviates the need for more graphic, and potentially incriminating, language.

La Cosa Nostra has numerous traditions and customs, many handed down from the early decades of this century. They form a 'code of honour', the Omerta. This is a binding blood-oath that demands that a newly 'made' member never reveal Mafia secrets – under pain of death. It is a code of respect, of loyalty and of duty. Some have even called this criminal brotherhood the 'Honoured Society'. The true mafioso follows the head of his family with as much devotion as the Japanese samurai followed his feudal lord, or *daimyo*. Everything is geared to this simple mechanism. Competence and loyalty are rewarded with responsibility and power. The moment a member becomes a liability, by breaking the Omerta or by 'going too far' in his application of violence, the family leaders will begin to have grave doubts about his future. He might be chastized; he might be ritually tortured and dumped in the boot of a car. The punishment is made to fit the crime. All have a place. No mafioso may get involved with the wife, girl-friend or daughter of another mafioso. This is not just good advice – it is a strictly enforced custom designed to allay potential friction among members. Other regulations included a prohibition on killings in the 'open cities' of Las Vegas and Miami (to promote tourism). To increase morale among Mafia soldiers, family bosses were told to allow a vote before they sanctioned the execution of a mafioso in their employ.

It is the threat of torture and death that haunts every mafioso, not fear of arrest by the police. When the father of mobster Joe Colombo was discovered having an affair with another mafioso's woman, the lovers were found dead in his car one morning. Both had been shot in the head, and his penis had been cut off and stuck in his mouth. In 1982 the body of Rocco Marinucci was discovered riddled with bullet-holes; his mouth had been stuffed with three unexploded firecrackers. The message for those within the mob was clear: his executors believed Marinucci responsible for a bomb that had killed a Philadelphia under-boss almost exactly one year before. Any instability, any liabil-ity is dealt with quickly and violently. A potential defector, a hot-blood drawing too much attention to himself and the family, an unpredictable wild card – all can be marked for execution by the boss. It happens every year across America. The doomed mafioso is set up and then shot in the head, strangled or otherwise dispatched and the body dumped.

Two Mafia hit-men, Campise and Gattuso, disappeared in 1983 just before they were to stand trial for murder. They had bungled an assas-sination and had to pay. Several days later their bloated and blood-soaked bodies were discovered in the back of a car parked in a nice Chicago neighbourhood. It had been the awful smell that had first attracted passers-by. The two mafiosi had been tortured and then stabbed to death. Gattuso had also been strangled, perhaps because he had managed to stay alive despite his wounds and had to be finished off. Their deaths were not the result of a Mafia feud but the calculated extermination of the Chicago mob's own people in order to save the organization. Such ruthlessness was sure to inspire terror in the sol-diers who went about their everyday business. Every Mafia execution carries a brutal message: either you are efficient or you are dead. There are no 'learning curves' and no such thing as 'trial and error' within La Cosa Nostra. The actions of every member have direct repercus-sions on everyone else – 'This Thing of *Ours*' – and ruthless pruning of the organization goes on almost routinely.

Harshly underlining the commitment to violence that the Mafia dis-plays, the fraternity created for its own uses the ominous group that called itself 'Murder Incorporated'. Murder Inc., as it was known, was reputed to have been responsible for 1000 executions during its short existence. This figure includes not only the many victims outside the criminal world, but also the killing of many of the society's own assassins. Originally established in 1936 by the New York mobster 'Lepke' Buchalter, the army of hit-men was recruited to wipe out any and every informer that threatened Lepke's safety. The terrible campaign of murder that followed thoroughly cleansed the underworld of Lepke's opponents. Once in business, Murder Inc. continued its trade in ruthless execution for some time. Staff on the payroll were all veteran murderers, hardened professionals who took the job deadly seriously and enjoyed it too.

The West Coast chapter of the execution squad was led by Benjamin 'Bugsy' Siegel, who carried out murders as efficiently as the rest of the mafiosi killers. Siegel achieved public notoriety because of his close relationship with the Hollywood set, and he died trying to turn Las Vegas into the Mafia-dominated gambling mecca that it later became. Albert Anastasia, one of New York's most powerful mafiosi, became heavily involved in the New York activities of Murder Inc. So ruthless was Anastasia that he was unofficially christened the 'Lord Executioner' of the society. Throughout the 1940s and 1950s veterans of the organization began to surface in Mafia families across the US. Albert Anastasia, for example, shot, stabbed and strangled his way to the leadership of a New York family after the war.

Murder Inc. seemed to fill a niche that straddled the old-style Prohibition gang wars and the more calculated assassinations of the post-war mob. Every Mafia family in America learned a valuable lesson from the Murder Inc. phenomenon. In essence, it paid to have a professional assassin on hand.

In the post-war years La Cosa Nostra has spread its many tentacles into almost every type of business, legal and illegal, that could be imagined. Industries ranging from the movies, to construction, gambling, transport, banking, law and the docks have all been inter-penetrated by the families. Wherever there is money, there is the Mafia. Legitimate business enterprises that turn a profit and seem quite respectable are the stock in trade of organized criminal syndicates and of the Mafia in particular. The concept was born out of necessity. The covert operations of a machine as vast as the Mafia remain covert only for as long as they remain shielded behind such a web of business 'fronts'. Al Capone discovered this too late and was jailed for tax evasion. He was unable adequately to explain the source of his vast wealth, and thus (at that time in Prohibition Chicago) openly advertised his criminal occupation.

The lesson has since been learned and mastered. Mafia fronts in New York are diverse, ranging from car sales to travel agents and drycleaners. *Caporegimes* may own (or part-own) these businesses, and soldiers may be on their employment rolls. As long as his soldiers receive a regular wage-cheque, they are free then to make money in more illegitimate enterprises without fear of having suddenly to explain how they are able to support themselves. Just as the rank-and-file mafiosi nominally work for these businesses, the bosses and under-bosses are often legitimate directors or shareholders in the bigger firms, a position roughly comparable with their 'official' Mafia rank. Fronts have many other uses, and although their use may have initially given individual mafioso a veneer of legitimacy, they have become a powerful money-making lever. Gone are the days of relying solely on the old-fashioned rackets of back-room gambling, prostitution, smuggling, loansharking, armed robbery and the protection game. They still exist and are as lucrative as ever for the Mafia machine, but the (almost) seamless fusion of legitimate and illegitimate companies has opened up an almost limitless vista of money-making potential.

Thousands of businesses used like this have been hit by a 'bust-out'. Mafiosi work together to ruin a legitimate business, playing off (perhaps Mafia-owned) suppliers against customers and frightening off anyone who has dealings with the firm, until the owner is ruined and *has* to sell to the mob. Now a soldier or a *capo* owns the firm and can start giving various legitimate jobs to his crew. Thousands more firms cannot pay off loans that they've secured (at often sky-high interest rates) with Mafia loansharks (or 'shylocks'). When these desperate individuals default on their payments the business they were trying to save usually ends up in the hands of the loanshark with whom they made the deal. The deal is: fail to pay – hand over the business. More subtly, an observant loanshark will waive a chunk of the debt if the business seems to be thriving, instead he demands to be 'cut in'.

Any criminal group can operate like this if it has the foresight. What makes the Mafia so different is its *scale*. Beyond the control of so many small businesses is the domination of entire industries within some US cities. This is usually coupled with the control of all the relevant unions. Dissent from within is crushed, and the Mafia is free to pilot the business in whatever direction it desires. Control of an industry also removes free-market competition and replaces it with an artificial 'arrangement' that best suits the money-making designs of the mafiosi in charge.

Along with numerous other enterprises similarly 'sewn up', the Genovese family in New York dominates a cartel of refuse companies. Customers, which include factories, schools, hospitals and restaurants, are forced to pay whatever rates are demanded for their refuse collection service. If they decide to try another company, the Mafia makes sure that the customer quickly changes his mind. Charges spiralled as the competition diminished, and the union representing the refuse workers, the Teamsters' Union, could do nothing about it. In fact that union, like so many others, is dominated by the Mafia. The Mafia-Teamster relationship goes back many decades and the organization, which is indisputably America's most powerful union, remains a powerful bastion of mafiosi and Mafia-controlled stooges.

During the early 1980s a children's hospital in New Jersey, dissatisfied with the mob-owned service it was receiving, tried unsuccessfully to change its collector. It soon found out that the Genovese 'owned' the garbage collection 'rights' to that hospital. There was no competition, no free choice – no freedom. As punishment, the hospital was forced to pay ever larger sums to the collection firm. Only when a Mafia accomplice stepped forwards as a Federal witness was the scam finally uncovered. He hated the grip that the syndicate had on his own garbage collection firm but was fatalistic about their power:

> Through the trade waste association the industry has been controlled
> by a select few. The cartel operators are scum. The independent just
> makes a living at the risk of having his trucks set on fire or even
> being murdered. The threat of violence is always there.

If control of businesses, industries and unions are the tactics of the Mafia campaign, then the ever-present threat of violence has proved to be their main weapon. Fear propels the nightmare empire along and drags in innocent victims who would desperately prefer to be free of it. When the Gambino family began a quite legitimate but second-rate knife-grinding business in the 1960s, butchers throughout the city of New York began to use the service. They stopped using their regular, non-Mafia grinders and switched to Gambino's operation purely out of fear – fear of retribution. As with other Mafia rackets of this nature, the butchers who held out would have been intimidated, beaten and fire-bombed. In an effort to rescue their doomed livelihoods, the legitimate knife-grinders were able to arrange a hefty cash settlement with Paul Gambino, and in return he closed down his grinding operation.

Securing this money sack is the unfathomable knot of political corruption. Bribery, coercion and a whole range of friendly kick-backs are the tools of the conspiracy. These tools were well-honed during the Prohibition period, when the gangsters virtually ran the city governments in which they operated. Mob ties with corrupt elements in Washington have waxed and waned over the past 60 years. A notable period of mob tension arose in the late 1950s and early 1960s, a period that involved some of the most famous individuals in modern America: Frank Sinatra, Jimmy Hoffa, Sam Giancanna and both John F. Kennedy and his brother Robert.

JFK and the Mob

As President John F. Kennedy waved to the Dallas crowds from the back seat of his Lincoln limousine, a series of shots suddenly echoed around the surrounding plaza. One of the shots hit Kennedy through the neck. As he began choking uncontrollably, his wife, Jackie, sitting next to him, tried desperately to help him. A third shot struck his head, killing the president instantly. The 35th president of the United States had been assassinated.

Almost immediately a suspect was apprehended and charged. Lee Harvey Oswald became the prime murder suspect – a lone gunman, acting on a politically motivated and highly personal vendetta. Soon, however, a dark cloud fell on the entire investigation. The suspect was himself the target of another 'lone' assassin, and questions began to be raised about almost every aspect of the orthodox evidence. From the single killer, 'lone gunman' hypothesis came a plethora of 'conspiracy theories', involving anyone and everyone from the CIA, the Secret Service, the KGB, anti-Castro Cubans, pro-Castro Cubans, the military-industrial complex and even his vice-president, Lyndon Baines Johnson.

No substantial evidence has ever come to light to confirm these theories, and they have hinged almost purely on the existence of *motive*. If motive is the measure by which the arch-suspects in the assassination can be judged, then the American Mafia had by far the greatest motive. Not only that, but it had dealings and double dealings with John F. Kennedy. There had been, in addition, an acrimonious falling out.

The killing of President Kennedy had taken place on 22 November 1963 following a bitter showdown between his brother, Robert, newly installed as Attorney General, and the Chicago mob. The Kennedys were committed to fight organized crime, and the Chicago family was as powerful and as violent as it had been in the 1920s when Al Capone created it. Although the Sicilians had long-since dominated the Chicago syndicate, it was essentially still the same organization that Capone's energy and ruthlessness had welded together, and it was still known in the trade as the Outfit. It dominated the crime world to the west and took a huge percentage of the profits from the gambling operations in Las Vegas. Only the New York bosses had more status and power. Chicago's boss from 1957 onwards was Sam 'Momo' Giancana.

Giancana hated the Kennedys. This hatred didn't stem merely from the fact that Robert Kennedy had publicly declared war on organized crime and on Chicago's Mafia in particular, but also from something far deeper. Allegations have surfaced during the past 30 years that

Giancana had actually been recruited to help *win* the 1960 election for John F. Kennedy. The bitterness and loathing for the Kennedys that Momo afterwards displayed stemmed from betrayal. Chicago's powerful mafioso had twisted arms and (so the rumours went) helped to force a Democrat victory in Illinois. With polling still in progress further west, a defeat in Illinois might have tipped the balance in Richard Nixon's favour and lost Kennedy the election. Even so, it was a close-run thing, and Illinois was won by only 9000 votes. It is not clear whether it was just the Mafia's iron grip over the city's politicians and labour bosses that secured the victory but whether also the elections themselves were rigged by mafiosi agents.

Senator Kennedy had met a woman called Judy Campbell (later Judith Exner) in early 1960, through the singer Frank Sinatra. Sinatra had known her for some time, and she would occasionally meet up with him and his Hollywood friends, the Rat-Pack. Through Sinatra, Campbell would be introduced to, and become involved with, two powerful yet diametrically opposed individuals: Senator John F. Kennedy and Sam Giancana. In this way both would-be president and mob boss came into contact. Their friends and associates overlapped in a subtle social interplay that resulted in Giancana's working to further Kennedy's election. Judy Campbell was sure that Kennedy and Giancana had met and were well acquainted with one another. Sinatra may even have acted as a go-between. Why? Did Sam Giancana hope to profit from a Democrat victory?

Whatever his hopes for the future, he was to be badly let down. Within months of the president's inauguration, Bobby Kennedy was given the task of crushing organized crime in America – and that meant the Mafia. Sam Giancana took the snub personally, and he was not a man to be double-crossed. His Outfit had a track record of terrifying brutality and sickening torture, and Giancana himself could easily lose his temper. He was as violent as he was unpredictable. In later years of FBI surveillance on the Armoury Lounge restaurant (Giancana's Chicago headquarters), these double-dealings were mentioned several times. Judith Campbell also provided evidence that Giancana had struck some kind of deal, and she told investigators how he had boasted that Kennedy's presidency couldn't have happened without Giancana's intervention.

As America prepared to go to the polls in late 1960, even the CIA was in league with various mafiosi from the Outfit. They knew that the Mafia-controlled casinos in Cuba had been hard hit by Fidel Castro, who had come to power in 1959, and they wanted to do a deal. If a Giancana-sponsored assassin were to kill Castro, the Outfit could look forward to an awful lot of favours from the US government. It was not to be. Kennedy scotched any plans to murder Castro after the abortive Bay of Pigs invasion by US-sponsored Cuban exiles, which ended so disastrously under his administration. Again Giancana had been betrayed.

There is no absolute proof that the Mafia killed JFK. There is, to be honest, no hard evidence even for a second gunman, on whose existence every conspiracy theory (including that of mafiosi-assassins) rests. But if a conspiracy theory is ever proved the Chicago Outfit will most likely be proved to be responsible for the shocking assassination and Sam Giancana (himself murdered by the mob in 1975) for its conception.

Frank Sinatra, the Mafia and murder have been reacquainted for a second time in a theory that links all three with the sudden death in 1982 of Princess Grace of Monaco. Speculation has grown that her death may have been a Mafia hit designed to stifle her influence over her husband Prince Rainier. The Sicilian Mafia are heavily involved in Monaco – wherever there exists wealth in abundance, the Mafia finds it profitable to skim off what it can. Although Princess Grace at first had no objections to the Mafia enterprises being run in Monaco, she is supposed to have turned against the mob and to have pressed Prince Rainier to have them driven out. Indeed, it may have been Frank Sinatra, a good friend of Grace Kelly's, who introduced her to his friends in the mob as 'a friend of mine'. We shall never know. But the speculation stems from a rumour that the car she drove over the edge of a Monaco cliff in 1981 zigzagged as if it were compensating for a lack of brakes. Had they failed? Engineers dispatched from the car manufacturers said 'no', and a French lorry driver trailing Princess Grace's car stated that no brake lights came on as it headed for the cliff edge.

The theory cannot (and may never) be adequately substantiated. The forces at work are too powerful and the gains to be made are too high to allow investigations to continue. The Sicilian Mafia continues to enjoy total control of the underworld of Europe, with business interests in every nation in the European Union as well as in their neighbours in the east. The recent capture of Sicily's godfather, Salvatore Riina, has only slowed down the organization's growth, not stopped it. In the USA, however, a recent government 'blitz' on the Mafia has produced more hopeful results. Is the American Mafia dead at last?

The Mafia is Dead – Long Live the Mafia!

The modern godfather of the American Mafia, John Gotti, is now in prison. He joins thousands of important Mafia leaders who have recently met a similar fate. At last the American government has been able to boast about its successes, and not lament its failures, in the war on organized crime. All the major Mafia bosses – and numerous 'would-be' bosses – have been arrested, and the highly secretive

National Commission has at last been broken up. The FBI is justly proud of its achievements – especially since it leaves the American mob with a dearth of experienced and talented criminal leaders. The replacements are greedy, over-eager, ill-disciplined and cut off from any sense of historical tradition. Unlike the Italian-American community of the 1930s, 1940s and 1950s, Italian-Americans are now almost fully integrated into American society. The ethnic hinterland that provided much of the loyalty and camouflage for Mafia activities is now almost wholly absent. These factors, and the fact that more and more of the mob's traditional rackets are being leased to other criminal groups, has meant a weakening of the Mafia grip on 1990s America. Unlike their international cousins, the mob families still prefer to kill each other than to unite against their biggest rivals, the members of the Sicilian La Cosa Nostra.

The Sicilians have always had ties with their cousins across the ocean. Lucky Luciano returned to Italy after the Second World War and virtually created the Italian Mafia as it stands today. It continued to flourish independently from the American Mafia and in the late 1960s began to cross the Atlantic for a second time in search of new rackets and new opportunities. The 1990s have seen an unhealthy resurgence in the Sicilian interest. The Sicilians have long been distrusted by their American counterparts, who consider them mysterious, secretive, predatory and uncooperative. Traditionally they stay clear of the American Mafia rackets and the cities in which they operate. Nevertheless their numbers are growing. Each time the FBI turns the ratchet on the mob, the Sicilians bring in more of their own men. One 1992 US estimate put the number of Sicilian mafiosi in the country at 'between 10,000 and 20,000 members and associates'. This is roughly equal to the current strength of the American Mafia.

The American Mafia might be close to death, but it is currently receiving a fresh infusion of new blood that is set totally to transform the flabby organization. The Sicilians have already integrated themselves into the fabric of the syndicate. The American bosses had banned any Mafia traffic in drugs but had cleverly side-skipped this self-limiting dictate by employing Sicilians. It was John Gambino (who is only distantly related to New York's all-powerful Carlo Gambino) who became the focus for heroin shipments into America from his operational base in New York. Gotti worked with him from the mid-1980s, but Gambino had masterminded the importation of tons of heroin since the 1970s. Until he was arrested in the 1990s, he worked directly for the Sicilian Cupola (the Sicilian version of the National Commission) and simultaneously liaised with America's 'boss of bosses'. Other Sicilian mafiosi have become 'made men' in the local syndicate, even taking up positions of power. Several have become *caporegimes* within powerful Mafia families.

These 'new bloods' are neither street thugs nor simple peasants. They are hardened terrorists, killers and torturers of the highest calibre, veterans of the so-called Great Mafia War. What they bring to the American Mafia is a dangerous willingness to carry murder to the police, to the law courts, to the FBI, to the government in Washington – anyone, in fact, who opposes them becomes a target for assassination. In the past the American bosses have perversely prided themselves on their restraint when it came to challenging authority. No boss, no *capo*, no soldier could be allowed to kill government officials or their families without a good reason and the approval of the National Commission. Sicilians, newly installed within America's most powerful operations, have made it clear they consider this a sign of weakness. 'You oughtta use Sicilian methods, like killing judges and cops,' one advised his American colleagues.

The evidence suggests that the Mafia in America is not out for the count, despite recent optimistic predictions. The take-over of the criminal underworld by the highly professional Sicilian syndicate could revolutionize the Mafia in the most terrible way. Gotti's empire always kept the ultra-violent, no-compromise soldiers of the Cupola out of America. With Gotti and the bosses imprisoned, with only their young and inexperienced followers left, La Cosa Nostra Sicilian-style may be on its way.

The Network: Masons, Moscow and the Mafia

Organized crime is a very real conspiracy that has links from the top of society to the bottom, and from the richest principality to the poorest Third World dictatorship. Its influence is subtle and awful, tightening selected victims in its coils and disposing of the bodies when it is through with them. Anyone searching for some 'global conspiracy' does not have to look far. It lies not in secret conference rooms attended by an unelected élite controlling the fate of governments through some subtle manipulation of policies and economies. It lies in the hands of the crime bosses, stretching out their blood-soaked hands to circle the world. Drugs, guns, nuclear materials, 'dirty' money, human organs and girls heading for sex slavery are the illicit cargoes of a vast covert business that defies comprehension. At one time working alone within a town, a city or a nation, the crime syndicate, like the multinational corporation that it now apes, continually forges new connections, 'networks', in order to eliminate competition. Nowhere is this network more fruitful than in the highest echelons of European government, particularly the governments of France and Italy.

Italy today has the unfortunate accolade of being home to four major Mafia organizations. Sicily is the traditional home of La Cosa Nostra; Calabria has the 'Ndrangheta; Naples has the Camorra; and the town of Puglia has the Sacre Corona. Not surprisingly, today's Mafia is strongest in Sicily, and its Italian cousins are but local sub-units, dependent on and beholden to Sicily. After being almost eradicated by Mussolini during the Second World War, the organization has re-established itself as the premier criminal brotherhood within Italy and throughout Europe. Sicilian Mafia families, relatively unconnected with the American mob these days, have their own 'National Commission', called a Cupola. The stranglehold that the organization has on various political parties and members of the government far surpasses the attempts of the Americans to co-opt Washington. In 1994 Italy elected media tycoon Silvio Berlusconi into government. That government quickly became tangled in a welter of bribery and corruption allegations, a situation in which the Italian Mafia could only prosper. Berlusconi denied charges that he was a member of an élite lodge of Freemasons known as Propaganda Due (or P2), despite evidence to the contrary.

Freemasonry in France, Belgium and Italy has a far more sinister side to it than its English and American counterparts. In fact, the English Grand Lodge has officially proscribed the so-called 'Orient' branches of Freemasonry, primarily because of the criminal influence that now predominates within them. These fraternal societies, appearing so acceptable and legitimate on the surface, have become almost a cover for Mafia influence through the 'back door'. With the newly installed liberal regimes throughout the Commonwealth of Independent States and eastern Europe now trying to mirror their Western counterparts, 'Oriental' Freemasonry and the criminals it hides flourish there, too. Most influential of these groups is the French Grand Orient, already discussed in relation with the French Revolution in Chapter 3.

Political power in Europe now indisputably rests with the European Union civil servants based in Brussels, and there is a considerable number of Grand Orient Freemasons among them. Italian politics, tangled by corruption, Mafia bastardization and the eternal war between communists and fascists, has also been the victim of Freemasonry. In 1981 it was revealed that the radical masonic lodge Propaganda Due had been planning to overthrow the government. The conspirators were politicians, members of the police, the secret service and the judiciary. They were all members of the breakaway French Grand Orient lodge. Although the group was officially disbanded, it continues to operate. Several terrorist bombings have recently been attributed to the banned lodge, one of which was even blamed on Propaganda Due's Grand Master Licio Gelli. Gelli is now connected with the Calabrian Mafia, the 'Ndrangheta, and is implicated in an extensive conspiracy of power and profit trading in illegal drugs and armaments.

Sicily's La Cosa Nostra and Naples's Camorra are still as active as ever. Freemasonry has provided the ever-expanding Mafia 'corporation' with a perfectly legitimate secret organization through which it creates ties, alliances and friendships away from public scrutiny. Thus, the legitimate and the illegitimate have been married together to create a pan-European monster. Who can ever know how far organized crime has penetrated into Europe's highest echelons?

Propaganda Due has in the past styled itself as a bulwark against communism, and in this way it has attracted the most right-wing of supporters and sects, in particular the American CIA. This ultra-secret intelligence organization has provided funds for the lodge, thereby financing European Mafia-inspired corruption at the highest level. It has further links with various military regimes in Latin America. Rumours have abounded since 1981 that one of these shadowy 'backers' actually controlled the lodge. One rumour-monger, a journalist and ex-lodge member named Mino Pecorelli, openly accused the CIA of pulling Propaganda Due's strings. Two months later he was murdered by unknown assailants. Other candidates have included the American Mafia. We have already seen how the CIA and the American Mafia have collaborated in the past. What webs are being woven between crime lords, governments and terrorists? Who controls whom?

Thoroughly dominating the Sicilian Mafia for the past 20 years, the ultimate 'boss of bosses', Salvatore 'Toto' Riina has made the Mafia everything that it is today. And it has certainly changed. Riina took over the leadership on the death of his predecessor, Luciano Leggio, in 1974. After establishing himself as a powerful new helmsman, he carved a name for himself in blood during the Great Mafia War that rocked Sicily from 1981 to 1983. Fighting for the survival of his own family, the Corleonesi, Riina waged a barbaric and terrifying campaign against his rivals. Thousands were murdered, many in the most sickening of ways. His style of leadership revolved around two primary attributes: force and terror. With his rivals eliminated, Riina initiated a similar war against the Italian state. Never had the Sicilian Mafia been so ruthless and so keen to carry violence into every echelon of the government apparatus. It was a struggle for survival against a growing tide of discontent and rebellion against the 'old system'. Riina ruled his new empire with deadly efficiency and the paranoia of a secret police chief. Over one hundred secret Riina agents were planted in the Cupola's most influential families, each one reporting back on individual family politics. Riina's empire was built on suspicion, fear and terror, not on old-style family loyalties, tradition and mutual agreement.

Mafia power in the 1980s seemed to make a mockery of the Italian judicial system. Hundreds of convicted mafiosi walked free after serving only fractions of their sentences in jail. Even the masterminds of the organization, the *capos* and the bosses, were able to subvert justice in one way or another. Typically, the organization would send representatives around to visit the judges presiding over a particular case. Any judge who refused to come to some kind of agreement with the Mafia wound up dead, either from a bullet or a bomb. A few brave and reckless judges and law enforcement officials were determined to hold out against these murders, of whom one of the best known was judge Giovanni Falcone. Falcone realized almost before anybody else that Italy's problem was also Europe's and the world's. He warned that the Sicilians were leading the way and that, in conjunction with the world's big crime syndicates, they had 'stipulated a sort of non-aggression pact, dividing up the world'. Such links were making it increasingly unlikely that the Mafia could be eradicated. Even more perplexing were the elaborate legitimate connections that the organization had cultivated. According to the Italian Ministry of Justice, something like one-half of all the Mafia's laundered capital is re-invested in numerous legitimate enterprises around the globe. Like a deadly cancer, the brotherhood feeds from and hides within the body of society.

Amid the complex and murky world of Mafia money-laundering, evidence has come to light in the last five years that 'dirty' money has actually passed through the Vatican. This alarming (though some would say predictable) revelation came about during a re-evaluation of the death of Roberto Calvi. Found hanged under London's Blackfriar's Bridge in 1982, Calvi was both a Mafia money-launderer and a member of Propaganda Due. His briefcase, which was never recovered, allegedly contained highly sensitive material linking Mafia money transfers through the Vatican's private bank. His close ties with the Vatican's financial dealings earned Calvi the nickname 'God's Banker'. Calvi is now believed to have been murdered.

From the very beginning of the 1990s the Italian Grand Lodge established several lodges in eastern Europe, and the Italian Mafia has been able to use these secret organizations to make contact with its east European criminal counterpart, the Russian 'mafia'. Shadowy meetings and business deals do take place on a regular basis between the thriving new Russian crime gangs and the Italian Mafia. These transactions have only one purpose: profit. Both criminal syndicates are able to profit from one another's existence, and both take the opportunity to do so. Heading the agendas at these 'summits' are the smuggling of drugs, of human organs, of girls and children, of Kalashnikov military rifles and of nuclear materials. As some measure of the size of this transshipment and resale industry, the gross income thought to derive from the trade in drugs and arms is estimated at around £300 billion each year – for the European Union alone. If the situation had been bad prior to the collapse of communism, it soon became even worse. The Italian Mafia wields frightening levels of influence and kills without hesitation. Yet the Russian crime gangs that have so explosively emerged onto the European scene go much further. Twinning poverty and desperation with military-grade firearms, they have proved to be even more ruthless than their Italian cousins.

A distinction should be made here between the Italian Mafia and the Russian network of gangs that are known by the same name. There are four main criminal brotherhoods operating within the former Soviet Union. All are based in Moscow and extend their reach out through Russia, into the former republics and across Europe. They are the *Dolgopruadnanskaya*, the Chechens, the Georgians and the Ukrainians. There are 40 other, less powerful clans, such as the Lubertsky and Ostankino, and at least 2000 other organized crime gangs operating on a smaller scale. Each one has a high proportion of trained soldiers within its ranks, men who can readily use the best Russian weaponry that the gangs now possess. Collectively, the organizations are known as *Vory V Zakone* ('Thieves Within the Code'), but those who do the killing, extorting, smuggling and trafficking simply refer to themselves as *mafiya*. The mystique of this now ancient and instantly understood word carries with it fear and terror.

That terror can stretch out to virtually every city in Europe, even to the innocuous British town of East Grinstead. Ten days before Christmas in 1996 the businessman Richard Watson was gunned down outside his house as he stepped out of his TVR Chimera sports car. Three weeks before, Watson had been attacked with an electric cattle-prod. His execution has been linked with the *mafiya* and the 'complicated' business interests that he had in eastern Europe. Bankers and businessmen have become quite tempting targets for the Russian crime gangs, but while their compliance can result in profits for the organization, their defiance always results in death. A number of individuals connected with the legitimate and illegitimate business world have recently met violent deaths at the hands of the *Vory V Zakone*. Oleg Kantor, the president of the Russian Yugorsky Bank, was found stabbed to death with his bodyguard in 1995. Within days the influential banker Sergei Parakhin was set upon by *mafiya* hit-men and beaten to death. But the shadowy spread of the Russian network is not frightening because of its simple brutality. First, the gangs have access to the weaponry normally reserved for battalions in the (now bankrupt) Russian army, and second, they have adopted all the 'trappings' of Western organized crime, creating ritual and custom out of thin air and a stereotype.

Always ostentatious in their displays of wealth, with BMWs, Mercedes and designer suits from Valentino and Calvin Klein, the *mafiya* soldiers play to a fictional concept of the 1920s gangster. Beneath their silk shirts they sport Yakuza-style tattoos: a spider web for drug traffickers, an eight-pointed star for robbers or a broken heart for the bosses. Across Europe their representatives make discreet enquiries about the availability of sumptuous mansions. In the minds of the *mafiya*, La Cosa Nostra is the criminal organization par excellence. The two organizations could not be more different, however. The Russian *mafiya* clans (termed 'brigades') are very loosely structured, bosses come and go, the family moves from one part of the former Soviet Union to another, and often the names are so vague as to be non-existent. In addition to the 'regional' *mafiya* families already mentioned, there is a gambling mafia, a currency mafia, a prostitution mafia and so on. The term 'family' is used here in its loosest sense. The Russian gangsters are rarely related by anything more than a passion for their work and a criminal ruthlessness without parallel. Indeed, the term 'brigade' does reflect the military background of many *mafiya* members as well as their ability and willingness to use military-grade weaponry, up to and including anti-tank mines and rocket launchers.

Unlike a handful of other powerful crime syndicates – the Chinese Triads, for example, the Sicilian Mafia or the Japanese Yakuza – the Russian *Vory V Zakone* has few historical traditions. It has no roots in some ancient feudal resistance organization or in a medieval bandit gang surviving down the ages. It developed piecemeal from the black-market economy that thrived under communist rule in the Soviet Union. Unshackled by the collapse of that now-defunct political system, the *mafiya* has expanded to fill the vacuum. Russia's many links with the global economy have also given the gangs free rein to shift their operations wherever they see a potential profit margin – to Germany, for example, or to Israel.

In its eagerness to take in Jews who were fleeing from the fracturing Soviet Union, Israel failed to spot the arrival of large numbers of Russian *mafiya* men among them. These gangsters immediately began to buy up key assets within the country. One intelligence chief told the Israeli parliament that 'the Russian mafia poses a strategic threat to Israel and is trying to infiltrate its political and economic system'. The Russian banking world is shot through with *mafiya* intrigue. Professor Lydia Krasfavina, head of Russia's institute for banking, has estimated that something like 80 per cent of private banks have been co-opted by the *mafiya*. That is a considerable degree of power, and power that is not easily curtailed. The USA also has a large immigrant population, and the main centres of Russian settlement have been in New York and Los Angeles. Agents for *Vory V Zakone* in California have aided and abetted illegal *mafiya* cash transactions that passed through businesses and banks in the state. Masterminding US affairs is the head of a major Russian crime family, Semion Mogilevitch. Mogilevitch is a Russian with a home in Tel Aviv, who happens to be a director on several British companies doing legitimate business in California. The FBI considers him to be head of one of the most influential (and therefore dangerous) of all the Russian factions operating within the USA. The chairman of Italy's Anti-Mafia Commission described the crime-sodden Russian Commonwealth as a 'kind of strategic capital of organized crime from where all the major operations are launched'.

Elsewhere the gangs continue to establish links with traditional criminals, from the big Italian mobs to violent criminals like the British Kenneth Noye and London's ghetto gangs. In the murky Russian underworld, £65 will secure a desperate buyer an army-issue Makarov handgun. For less than ten times that amount, the *mafiya* will sell the criminal a Russian RPG rocket launcher. According to some recent estimates, there are 1.5 million illegal firearms floating around the Russian underworld. European criminals large and small are queuing up to do business with these entrepreneurs. Some are after more than just handguns, Kalashnikovs and RPGs, however.

In late 1992 a Zurich clinic admitted a Polish man, Krysztof Adamski, who was suffering with symptoms that seemed to match those of radiation sickness. Adamski had received a fatal dose and was dying. His story, when he was forced to admit more in front of detectives, smacked of pure science-fiction thriller. He had been carrying a sample of highly radioactive Caesium-137 and Strontium-90 in his breast-pocket across Europe so that a potential buyer might first check out the merchandise. The two materials are prime ingredients for nuclear fission. Further investigation revealed that the nuclear materials were being shipped from Lithuania into Romania to Poland and then across the border into Germany. Acting on information given to them by a near-dead Adamski, the German police intercepted one of these shipments before it could reach its intended destination. Their discovery proved horrifying: inside a BMW driven by a Czech courier, the police found over 2 kilograms of high-grade uranium, perhaps 10 per cent of what was needed to complete an atomic bomb. It was being transported in a very poorly shielded container – the *mafiya* consider the lives of their couriers quite expendable. Information gleaned from this and other seizures led the German authorities to believe that a large cache of perhaps 9 kilograms or more of uranium was being stored somewhere in Germany.

The situation seemed critical. Polish police raided the home of a dying courier and discovered to their amazement and horror that 2 kilograms of badly shielded uranium were being stored in the man's bathroom. Like the other cargoes, this batch of nuclear material was leaking serious levels of radiation into the surrounding area. Sting operations set up to try and apprehend the *mafiya* dealers who were involved failed. Their preferred business arena for the exchange of 'hot-stuff' is post-war Croatia, a place of relative lawlessness and intrigue. *Mafiya* allies in the region are gangsters from the Serbian Ravna Gora crime syndicate. Another *mafiya* clan operating in neighbouring Italy was actually found in possession of nuclear stockpiles: over 30 kilograms of uranium and 10 kilograms of plutonium inside a Zurich bank vault! Confounding the situation in eastern Germany, from where the smuggling of nuclear material is masterminded, is the survival of the old communist secret police organization, the Stasi. Veterans of this organization have retained all their contacts and influence while moving into the criminal sector, pulling strings where they can and profiting from the Russian *mafiya* where possible. These indigenous gangs have become merely tools for the real power in eastern Germany, the *Vory V Zakone.*

Slavery still exists in Europe, despite the protestations of the history books. Prostitution is a growth industry in western Europe, and the *mafiya* are ready and able to supply an endless number of young women, girls and boys to feed it. The existence of this trade is truly heart-breaking. There *are* young women in the former Soviet Union and eastern Europe who are desperate to travel to the prostitution centres in Holland, Spain, France and Germany, and the *mafiya* takes every penny they have to smuggle them illegally across the border. These are the exceptions. Tens of thousands of prostitutes currently working in dire conditions for pimps in western Europe are there illegally against their will. Club owners in Amsterdam have told of being offered van-loads of kidnapped girls from Bosnia, Croatia, Romania, Poland, Russia and the Ukraine. None of the girls has official immigration papers, which (for the club owner) is all to the better. Sometimes they are starved and beaten until they agree to work for their new owner. They have little choice. Each girl is terrified of being reported to the authorities and jailed. She continues to work for the club owner despite the horrible life that this entails. If this involves making hard-core porn movies for consumption by Western males, she still has no choice.

The Serbian Ravna Gora and other Yugoslav crime gangs have earned themselves a sinister reputation for violence and terror in their scramble to control this lucrative sex-trade. But all the Russian *mafiya* are involved to one degree or another. The American Mafia is also involved in smuggling child pornography into Europe. This aspect of the sex trade is the most disturbing, but the atrocities committed by small, well-organized gangs of men cannot be recounted here. Supplied by the larger criminal outfits, they are left to their own psychologically twisted devices. One British gang, calling itself Lambs to the Slaughter, came to light during the trial of two of its members in 1989. Four years earlier the paedophile gang had lured a 14-year-old rent boy to a flat and drugged him. After abusing him in the most horrible manner, they killed him and dumped the body.

Paedophiles often meet each other while they are serving prison sentences, and their meetings and activities must always remain highly secret. Public hatred and loathing for these men is overwhelming. One such network is the Paedophile Information Exchange, a secret association of paedophiles who assist one another in obtaining videos, magazines and even young children. The media occasionally report on the existence of 'snuff' movies, in which the beatings and depravities carried out on children are filmed on video camera and are taken to the ultimate extreme – murder. Scotland Yard investigators claim never to have encountered a snuff movie, but that they exist is beyond doubt. It is believed that the Lambs to the Slaughter group actually filmed the murder for which they were convicted and that it is available on the Dutch black market. We are a long way from the gangster versus gangster killings that characterized the Chicago gang wars. Ruthless though Capone, Torrio and others were in the defence of 'business', there were limits. Not any more.

The Colombian Connection

By far the most lucrative business for the Russian crime syndicates is, and always has been, drugs. Europe has, according to some underestimates, around a million drug addicts who depend on shipments from South America and the former Soviet Union. Drugs are such a vital part of the criminal industry that the first major meeting of Italian mafiosi and their eastern imitators centred on drugs and the drugs trade. These 'summits' are now thought to be annual events. The three main centres of drug production are South America (supplying cocaine) and the Golden Triangle in Southeast Asia and the Golden Crescent in Afghanistan and Pakistan (both supplying heroin). A multitude of areas in Africa supplies the same drugs but at much reduced levels.

The drug barons of Colombia have blurred the tidy distinction between gangsters and terrorists. The cottage industry of drug manufacture that had existed in Colombia and the rest of Latin America for decades rapidly became the foundation for a multi-billion-dollar drug shipment industry that spans half the globe and employs hundreds of thousands of people. By the late 1970s the drug barons were in business. The expansion of the drug production industry, from cocoa plant to cocoa paste to cocaine base and finally to cocaine hydrochloride (cocaine proper), required immense efforts of organization. Efficiency and careful planning became the prerequisites for a vast earnings potential. The main players became incredibly wealthy, and the stakes higher than ever before. The event that fused Colombia's drug barons together to form the loose coalition that became known as the drugs cartel was a kidnapping carried out in November 1981.

Colombia is plagued not just with drug lords who control entire villages and areas of the countryside but also with radical terrorist groups that are dedicated to overthrowing the nation's government. One of the most flamboyant and sensational of these groups is M-19, named after the election of 19 April 1970, which the terrorists claim had been rigged. M-19 earned the deadly enmity of the various drug lords when they kidnapped Marta Ochoa Vasquez and also tried to snatch Carlos Lehrer Rivas in 1981. Carlos was a high-ranking drug smuggler, while Marta was the sister of Jorge Ochoa, one of the most powerful drug barons in Colombia. It seemed that M-19 wanted to prise some of the drug profits away from the cocaine kings and demanded that they pay a $1 million ransom. The town of Cali played host to a hastily held meeting of the drug barons; they agreed to work together and declared war on M-19. In a leaflet they publicly announced their intentions to create a 'mafia', and to use over 2000 killers to take their war out to the terrorists. There followed a brutal purging of the terror group, and both members and supporters were terrorized, beaten up and tortured. Within months M-19 had capitulated and the girl was released.

In the interests of profit, this temporary 'union' of drug lords soon became a permanent arrangement. Throughout the decade the cartel was dominated by three main powers: Pablo Escobar, Gonzalo Rodriguez and members of the powerful Ochoa family. The city of Medellín became the centre of the cartel's operations, and Escobar became its nominal leader. These three factions were known as *los duenos del cupo* ('the holders of the quota'), and between them they ran the most profitable drug production enterprise outside Southeast Asia. Escobar provided security and managed production of the finished cocaine; Rodriguez supervised the importation of cocoa paste from growers across the border in Bolivia and Peru; while the Ochoas handled the export (i.e., smuggling) operation.

From Medellín the cartel (or 'the Company' as it is sometimes called) was able to ship cocaine and crack cocaine across the globe using highly sophisticated smuggling techniques. Pablo Escobar somewhat resembled a 'boss of bosses' along the lines of La Cosa Nostra, and the Medellín chief sanctioned levels of violence that equalled or exceeded the atrocities of the Sicilian Mafia. In 1985 Escobar actually declared war on the Colombian government and initiated a bloody reign of terror that swept through the judiciary and government. About to debate the future of an extradition treaty with the US, Colombia's Supreme Court was stormed by 40 M-19 terrorists. Their previous differences forgotten, the cartel had grown so powerful that it now paid M-19 a reputed $5 million to carry out the raid. Colombia's president sent in the military, and almost all of the terrorists were killed in the shooting that followed, but by the time the commandos went in, 60 of the hostages had already been executed. If the purchase of a terrorist organization is remarkable, what is even more remarkable is that the cartel did it again. The communist terrorist group called the Revolutionary Armed Forces of Colombia (*Frente Actionista Revolucionaria Colombiana*, FARC) has in the past received payment in return for the use of its troops. FARC soldiers have guarded the largest of the cartel's production camps known as Tranquilandia, which was situated on an island in the River Yari.

With unprecedented fire-power at his disposal, Escobar resembled a feudal king. In Peru alone 300,000 people tended cocoa crops on his behalf, and within Colombia his M16-wielding troops were backed by guerrillas who had enough fire-power to challenge the government itself. Any military officer, police chief, judge or politician who dared to challenge the cartel became a target. They were shot and they were bombed. The assassinations were merciless. A Medellín judge, Carlos Mauro Hoyos Jimenez, suspected that a judicial conspiracy had led to the early release of a member of the Ochoa family. After he had ordered an investigation he was kidnapped by killers sent by the cartel. When he was found, Hoyos was handcuffed, gagged and blindfolded – he had been shot in the head ten times. The assassination of a newly installed minister of justice in 1984 resulted in a violent backlash from which the cartel's major bosses decided to flee. Manuel Noriega was happy to shelter the *los duenos del cupo* in Panama. Rather than exile themselves, the cartel leaders used the 'business trip' as an opportunity to establish drug distribution networks across the globe. Panama was already a considerable asset, and the cartel had the freedom to use its airports and banking systems with impunity (something George Bush would go to war about in December 1989). But the syndicate established links with military chiefs in Peru, Honduras, Cuba, Haiti, Brazil and Bolivia. At one stage in 1980, an army general who seized power in Bolivia actually worked for the cartel, appointing Bolivia's principal cocoa grower (and thus cartel ally) to the position of minister of the interior. Just a year under the control of the Colombian puppet-masters tied Bolivia inextricably into the cartel's carefully constructed web of conspiracy and clandestine recruitment. Meanwhile, a splinter drug syndicate, the Cali cartel, began to create a distribution network into Europe through Spain and Portugal.

Like a flourishing guerrilla army, the Medellín cartel gained a stranglehold on the local people. But rather than pushing to gain more territory or move on the capital, Bogota, as every revolutionary army aimed to do, the drug barons were content just to make money: somewhere in the region of £161 billion each year. This was guerrilla warfare with a unique twist. Government patrols, often assisted by the US Drug Enforcement Agency, penetrated the jungle retreats to track down the cocaine revolutionaries but were often beaten back or evaded by the able gangsters. On those occasions when their jungle hideouts were penetrated – Tranquilandia was raided in March 1984, for example – the cartel simply set up new refining and processing centres elsewhere.

As the American market became saturated in the mid-1980s, the Colombian cocaine lords began to compete for that highly lucrative market. Traditionally, the Medellín cartel had always controlled the cocaine trade in Florida while the Cali gang controlled New York. The rest of the decade saw a continuing battle for supremacy, one cartel killing members of the other through a chain of set-ups and tip-offs. The Cali drug lords even established a vigilante organization of hired killers who went under the name of Los Pepes (a name said to stand for 'People Persecuted by Pablo Escobar'). Escobar was eventually killed in 1993 at the hands of Cali gangsters, and by the early 1990s most of the leaders of the Medellín cartel were either in jail or dead, leaving the field wide open for the Cali syndicate. Cali has since eclipsed Medellín as the centre of worldwide cocaine manufacture and export. Cali mobsters, under the overall command of Miguel Orejuela, who ruled with his brother until he was captured in 1995, have taken over the Medellín operations wholesale.

Competing with the Cali cartel on an almost equal level in the late 1990s are the powerful Mexican drug lords. Power and profits shift uneasily around Latin America. Nevertheless, practically every major industrial nation has some sort of Cali presence to ensure the smooth supply of cocaine into that country. The USA and Europe form the two principal targets.

Jamaica has been a major conduit for Cali cocaine into both the USA and Britain. The battle-hardened street gangs of its capital, Kingston, are a major asset to the Colombians, and they have proved ready and able to help ship drugs into both countries – for a price, of course. The Jamaican gangs are known as 'Yardies' in Britain and as 'Posses' in the USA. By far the most infamous of America's posses is the New York Shower Posse, said to be under the immediate control of a Colombian drugs gangster. It was the Cali cartel that first created the bond between the Jamaican and Colombian underworlds, and it has proved exceptionally profitable for both the cartel and the Yardies. The difficult Jamaican patois, which interweaves English with the local dialect, has given the Yardie gangs an almost impenetrable street-slang. 'Yard' is a Jamaican term for home, and since the Yardies are almost exclusively expatriates, the word became an instant label for the gangs. Their activities range from shootings and stabbings to kidnapping, arson, armed robbery and, of course, drug dealing. Inter-gang wars fought for control of a local dealing 'patch' are also common. The profits derived from crack and cocaine are considered worth dying for. Yardie gangsters coming into the US and UK know what they want and exactly how to get it. There are few crime gangs more committed to violence and murder. Such is the casual regard for killing that US sources believe that the Posses are responsible for over 5000 murders during a five-year period. Killing is a duty, a job, a pleasure.

Heroin Kings – The Triads

Medellín was not the first major drugs empire; nor was it the most productive. Those doubtful accolades go to the Golden Triangle, dominated by General Khun Sa for over 30 years. Heroin pours out of the border region between Thailand, Burma and Laos, and the warlord Khun Sa directs it all from his safe-haven in the town of Chiang Mai in northwest Thailand. With his own mercenary army of local Meo tribesmen and renegade soldiers, the drug lord was given every assistance possible by the CIA following the end of the Vietnam War. The full story is beyond the scope of this book, but a brief précis will serve as an illustration of the twisted ways in which governments, secret societies and criminal syndicates cooperate. (The interested reader is directed to *Kiss the Boys Goodbye*, by Monika Jensen-Stevenson and W. Stevenson.)

When the USA pulled out of Vietnam in 1972 the CIA desired to continue to have some sort of covert capacity against its former enemies. Khun Sa was to be the new ally – never mind that he was responsible for producing practically every ounce of heroin that was beginning to flood the streets of the US. Khun Sa provided a wide-ranging network of routes and agents, and he could strike effectively and anonymously against Vietnamese-backed forces in Laos. It was the use of Khun Sa's network that uncovered the existence of US servicemen still being held prisoner by forces loyal to Vietnam within Laos. This information had to be suppressed, of course, because it would have been impossible to explain to the American public that the CIA had hired the resources and expertise of the world's most prolific drug manufacturer in its war against communism. Today the heroin that is produced there ends up in the hands of Triad gangs in Southeast Asia. From there it is smuggled into Europe and the United States.

During the earliest days of the Vietnam War the criminal underworld of the country – and the heroin trade with which it soon became synonymous – were in the hands of the Binh Xuyen, a Saigon crime family that had ruled the Vietnamese underworld during the 1940s and 1950s. After a brief flirtation with the Vietnamese revolutionaries, the Viet Minh, the Chinese Triad gang formed an alliance with the puppet-regime in Saigon, led by emperor Bao Dai. Leading the Binh Xuyen during this pre-American phase of the war was Le Van Vien (alias Bay Vien), a former chauffeur for the French occupation forces.

The biggest gambling house in Cholon, the Chinese suburb of Saigon, was the Grande Monde, and Bay Vien was installed as its manager. The alliance of Bao Dai and Bay Vien paid dividends for both sides. In return for a percentage of the heroin trade, the emperor gave the Triad boss freedom to build up his empire. By the early 1950s, the Binh Xuyen controlled Saigon's largest department store, 100 other shops, Asia's largest brothel (called the Hall of Mirrors), 20 large houses and a fleet of river boats. The alliance climaxed when Bay Vien was given the position of Vietnam's chief of police!

When South Vietnam was created as a bulwark against communist incursion from the north, the newly installed premier, Ngo Dinh Diem, was soon forced to fight for his life. The Binh Xuyen rose up to challenge his position on 29 March 1955. More than 6000 gangsters had taken up arms under Bay Vien's leadership and marched on the presidential palace. The fierce street fighting ended in stalemate, only to be resumed days later with audacious mortar attacks. President Diem ordered his own mortar and artillery teams to retaliate and sent his best military units out to retake the streets. There were more than 500 dead and 2000 injured by the time the Triads had been forced to flee from the city. The Rung Sat swamps, for a long time the perfect stronghold for the mobsters, were overwhelmed with troop patrols, and the stunned Binh Xuyen were successfully eradicated. From 1955 onwards the crime syndicate failed to reappear, but the heroin trade never went away, as other, less organized and less ambitious, criminal groups simply picked up where the Binh Xuyen had left off. Today, despite the strong communist intolerance of organized crime, the Saigon drug trade has been controlled by gangs like the Saigon Cowboys and the Young Turks. They are Triads, following a tradition that goes back to the Binh Xuyen and earlier, back to the rise of the Triad movement in nineteenth-century China.

Triad crime families are the chief producers and distributors of heroin throughout the world, and their presence is felt wherever there is a Chinese population. Chinatowns have sprung up in every big city, as the hard-working and entrepreneurial Chinese have emigrated to new shores and new continents in search of freedom and the opportunity to make an honest living. But the Triads are always there, feeding off the desperate and the prosperous alike. Extortion is by far the greatest earner after drugs, and the community-orientated Chinese have always been reticent to turn to the police for help. In London's Chinatown, which is relatively small, a restaurateur who refused to pay the local Triad collectors was soon made to pay the price. One evening, unexpectedly, thugs from the organization came into the busy restaurant and viciously attacked one of his customers at random. Inevitably the owner was forced to pay off the gang to prevent a recurrence.

The largest Chinatowns in cities like Singapore, Manchester, New York and San Francisco are home to large numbers of Triad gangsters, each affiliated to rival Triad families. Where a mutually beneficial understanding cannot be reached about the division of criminal activities within the city, newsworthy 'Triad wars' break out, with bloody vendettas being settled in a frenzy of shootings, stabbings and horrific machete attacks. The large populations of refugee Vietnamese, who have settled among the Chinese and established their own crime gangs, have been the cause of even more bloodshed. Even among themselves the Vietnamese squabble, the Northerners retaining deep-seated grudges against the Southerners and vice versa.

The Triad Society began as a single secret society in southern China that was dedicated to overthrowing the foreign dynasty that was at that time in control of the country. It is first heard of in a government prescription of 1662, under the name of the Hung Society, but the sect had other names, one of which was the Three United (or Triad) Society. It was not just a revolutionary organization, however. It formed a covert regional government to look after the interests of local people against the oppressive regime of the central government. At times the cult attempted to overthrow the rule of the emperor, but every attempt met with failure, and the survivors often fled abroad with other refugees to the growing Chinatowns of Southeast Asia. Cholon, in Saigon, became one of these Chinatowns. However, the lack of positive results in its struggle against the Beijing government eventually forced the Triad Society into the realm of crime. Being the strongest and most widespread secret society in southern China, the society did not just dominate the underworld, it was the underworld. It had always required some sort of income to survive, and income from gambling, prostitution, extortion, heroin and robbery would do as well as any.

In 1911 Sun Yat-sen, an influential member of a Hong Kong Triad called the Chung Wo Tong Society, was able to lead a revolution that at last overthrew the imperial dynasty in Beijing. In its place he established China's first ever republican government, but the Triads demanded their cut in return for their assistance during the uprising. For the next 40 years the Triads were firmly ensconced within the Chinese government and corruption was rife. Membership of the Society became a prerequisite to a position in the civil service or government, while in the more lawless cities of the republic, Triad gangs fought openly for control of the lucrative profits that were now available.

In 1949 another revolution, led this time by the Chinese communists, swept away the corrupt republic and established in its place the Peoples' Republic with Chairman Mao Zedong at its head. The former government fled, with its Triad supporters and controllers, to the island of Taiwan (Formosa), where it still rules today and offers jobs in its secret service to members of Taiwan's experienced Triad gangs. Elsewhere, Triads grow rich on the profits from heroin and the rackets practised to perfection for a century and more. When they need to expand their operations beyond the rather limiting Chinese community, the Triad leaders liaise with the Mafia, who have the potential to reach a much larger population of potential victims. Although the Triads still initiate members using ancient rituals full of symbolism and meaning, such rituals now rarely last longer than an hour – the original took three days to complete. One aspect of the initiation has stayed the same, however: a candidate must drink from a bowl that contains his own blood, the blood of a cockerel and the ashes of a yellow paper that bears his name. He must swear by the 36 oaths of the organization and must adhere to them or be killed.

Most of the offices of a Triad society possess ritual names, such as Dragon Head, Incense Master and White Paper Fan, which hark back to its pseudo-religious heritage. The hierarchy of each Triad headquarters is often rigidly defined and full of ritual. The Shan Chu presides as the society's overall leader. His deputy and stand-in is the Fu Shan Chu, a position similar in many ways to the Mafia office of under-boss. Two officials, the Heung Chu (Incense Master) and Sin Fung (Vanguard), are responsible for the ceremony and religion still practised by the organization, but as time passes these titles are becoming just that – titles that are essentially divorced from their ancient responsibilities. A council of department heads comes next in the hierarchy, and these chiefs deal with the day-to-day running of the Triad group.

There are other titles and offices, but two are of particular interest: the Pak Tsz Sin (White Paper Fan) and the Hung Kwan (Red Pole). The White Paper Fan fulfils a similar position within the Triad hierarchy as does the Mafia *consigliere* within his family. He discusses strategies and policy and is invariably an educated man of high status and influence. The Red Pole is usually also a department head, but he has additional duties to perform. Red Poles are the enforcers, the disciplinarians and hit-men of the Triad societies; they will plan and lead raids on rival Triads or on victims of the Triad's enterprises. Formerly, Red Poles were always martial artists of some skill, but today's Red Pole enforcers will more than likely be familiar with firearms and blades – anything that will maim and kill. Other Triad lodges within the main organization are led by the Chu Chi, an official who leads the rank-and-file Triad gangsters, the Sze Kau, in the criminal business of the organization. A Triad who runs petty street gangs of 'wanna-be' kids as extra 'muscle' or as drug couriers is called a Dai Lo. Operating from London's Chinatown are Dai Los who hire white and black kids, equipping them with cell-phones and knives and using them to perform the most menial, deniable jobs the Triads have to offer.

Across the East China Sea the Japanese have also had more than their fair share of criminal activity. Like the Triads, the Yakuza originated in the dim and distant days of feudalism, but they have weathered the storms of change to establish themselves as influential members of the global criminal community. They are totally unrelated to today's Triad gangs, although there is a similarity in the historical origins of the two groups. Like the Triad Society, the Yakuza gangs were originally folk heroes called *Machiyokko* (Servants of the Town), who fought the tyrannical depredations of evil landlords (*daimyos*), and they are first attested in records surviving from the early 1600s. A century or so later, the Yakuza gangs were operating on Japan's highways as robbers and wandering gamblers. Street peddlers became known as *tekiya*, and traditional gamblers became known as *bakuto*. A third group, *gurentai* (hoodlums), became established only after the Second World War. It is said that the Yakuza name is derived from a losing card combination (8, 9 and 3, translated as 'ya–ku–sa'). Gambling provided a jumping-off point for the entrepreneurial gangsters, and they were able to turn a profit from drugs and prostitution as well as from various protection rackets.

Self-preservation demanded that the criminals adopt the organization and code of silence that has bound together many other crime syndicates. In the initiation ceremony, the candidate swears unswerving obedience to his crime family, and an exchange of sake cups is made in front of a Shinto altar. The amount of sake in the cup is determined by the candidate's status and relationship to the master of ceremonies. The secretive families owed allegiance to their family head, the *oyabun*, and this man had the power of life and death over any member of the group. He was almost a sinister mirror image of the *daimyo* who commanded an army of utterly loyal and obedient samurai warriors. The Yakuza gangsters were the *oyabun*'s samurai, and they owed him as much loyalty. Any member who fouled up a mission or who was otherwise disgraced cut off the joint of a finger (a practice known as *yubitsume*). This mirrored the samurai's willingness to commit suicide to atone for his mistake. The Yakuza would then offer the finger joint to his master. If it were refused, he had no choice but to commit suicide himself, a practice that has survived into the twentieth century. Another survival, less painful and more popular among modern gangsters, is the Yakuza penchant for tattoos – the greater the coverage of the body, the higher the rank. Obviously in keeping with the organization's secrecy, these tattoos are always concealed beneath clothing.

These customs may sound like the extreme practices of a tiny minority, but the Yakuza are a national institution, an integral part of Japanese consciousness. When the British Broadcasting Corporation tried to market the children's TV show *Postman Pat* to the Japanese, it was dismayed at the result. Postman Pat was a puppet with three fingers, and the Japanese executives could not allow such a figure to be portrayed on Japanese television – with missing fingers he would be taken for Yakuza!

As already noted, the *oyabun* (also known as a *kumicho* or supreme boss) sits at the head of a Yakuza crime family. Often he will have a *consigliere*-style senior advisor or *saiko komon* with whom to discuss strategy. This advisor will himself control a number of sub-gangs. Deputizing for the *oyabun*, is a number-two man or *wakagashira*. He will have control over a large number of gangs and some important aspect of the Yakuza operation, as will the number three under-boss (or *shateigashira*). Of less importance is the headquarters chief (*so honbucho*), a man who still retains some status and control over his own body of gang-members. Assisting the *oyabun* is an entire entourage of accountants (*kaikei*), advisors (*komon*), personal secretaries (*kumicho hisho*) and counsellors (*shingiin*). Both the second- and third-in-command have a number of lieutenants (*wakagashira hosa* and *shateigashira hosa*). Real power devolves to the massed army of senior bosses (*shatei*, younger brothers), who control the syndicate's gangs. Along with their juniors, the *wakashu*, the gang bosses can number over 100.

With the growth of business in modern Japan, the Yakuza have grown too. Their traditional rackets have continued unabated (and unchallenged) in cities throughout Japan. Centre of the Yakuza gambling, prostitution and pornography industries is the Kabukicho section of the Shinjuku suburb in Tokyo, but as Japanese corporate fortunes soared, so did the Yakuza's. No other crime organization has ever matched the depth of penetration into the corporate world, and no other crime syndicate has enjoyed such immunity from prosecution. The country's largest Yakuza family, Yamaguchigumi, which is based in Kobe, has established its own company, Yamaki, through which it conducts its legitimate business, and there are also business consultancies, art galleries and estate agencies, totalling over 2000 different business concerns. The Yamaguchigumi has a total of 750 separate gangs with a total manpower of 31,000 members. A recent gang war with the rival Yakuza Ichiwakai proved to be immensely bloody and assets in the US were tapped in order to fund the war. From the US side of their operations, the Yamaguchigumi obtained a formidable arsenal of illegal weaponry, including machine-guns and rocket launchers.

Until 1992 the syndicate was largely ignored by the government, despite its stranglehold on the underworld and, increasingly, on the business world. There can be few official money-making schemes left in Japan that do not yet feel the influence of Yakuza extortion, ownership or money laundering. The National Diet, the country's parliament, is heavily involved with Yakuza scams, and 130 of its members were, in 1992, found to be taking money from the syndicate. Control of the Japanese multinationals is usually effected through extortion. Yakuza, called *sokaiya*, become legitimate shareholders and are then entitled to attend the company's annual shareholder meetings. If a company has refused to cooperate and to pay off the gang involved, the *sokaiya* turn up to the meeting and cause havoc, shouting, tipping over furniture and causing a scene. For the Japanese this constitutes a serious loss of 'face' in the eyes of the other shareholders, the media and the business community, and the company often resolves to pay up next time rather than suffer the indignity again. Interestingly, this tactic has been put to use by more ecologically minded groups in Britain. By legitimately buying up shares in large oil companies such as Shell, these protesters are able to use the annual general meeting of the company as an opportunity to display their outrage and to demand answers from the chairman.

Wherever business flourished, the Yakuza followed: Taiwan, Singapore, Hong Kong, the Philippines and much of the rest of Southeast Asia. More recently the families have established themselves within the cities of the West, throughout Europe and North America. Financial investment, money laundering, corporate extortion and the running of drugs and guns have proved profitable enterprises in the West. But the Yakuza do not entirely divorce themselves from their roots. The expatriate Japanese community will always remain a sanctuary for the Yakuza abroad – not only is it a hiding place, but it is also a well-established well of revenue extracted from a poor immigrant population. Having fled their homeland to escape such injustices, they can only have felt despair when they found the criminals once again in their midst.

Such has been the fortunes of the immigrant across the world in ghettos from London to New York, Kowloon to Manila. The weakest members of society are universally preyed upon by the strongest and most ruthless. This is the essence of the syndicate story, and provides a clue to the most frightening aspect of modern criminal organizations. Like playground bullies torturing the smallest school children, the vast multinational criminal empires are happy to unite, to refrain from petty bickering and infighting, lest the victims see their chance and run. Imagine this scenario on a global scale.

The Ultimate Conspiracy

Time and again there is evidence that the large criminal syndicates cooperate. Anyone brought up solely on a diet of gangster movies may find this hard to believe. Gangsters are supposed to be violently competitive and fiercely jealous of their business empires and their rackets. This is the 1990s, however, and the age of international co-operation has reached even the criminal empires. Rather than fight for territories and rackets, the global syndicates have carved up the world into vast territories, each worked by a different organization. The *Vory V Zakone*, the Yakuza, the Triads, the American Mafia, the Cali cartel, the Yardies and Sicily's La Cosa Nostra work together in a giant global conspiracy. This is not speculation derived from rumour. It is fact, accepted (uneasily) by all the Western governments. Leonardo Messina, Riina's turn-coat under-boss, testified to an Italian commission that the Mafia 'belonged to a worldwide structure'. Not only that, but until Riina's capture in 1993, it seemed that the Sicilian Mafia (and thus the Corleonesi and 'Totto' Riina) were the default leaders of this conspiracy. There are practically no inter-syndicate killings and no international crime wars. Opportunities for expansion are deemed so prolific that the criminal organizations have formed an unshakeable alliance, by which they cooperate for mutual benefit where they can. Otherwise, their business interests are studiously compartmentalized – there is no overlap, only cooperation.

Judge Falcone noted that these diverse criminal brotherhoods all had humble, even glorious beginnings, as rebels, freedom fighters and folk heroes. Created in times of social conflict, they originally banded together with codes of silence and secrecy to fight an oppressive government or a hated occupying power. With the fight won (or abandoned), the brotherhoods were left only with their secret codes and propensity for violence. Today the huge international criminal conglomerates are violent, flexible, formally structured, incredibly wealthy and insulated from the 'powers that be'. Together they form one of the greatest threats ever posed to humanity. At no other period in human history has such an invisible, invincible covert world government ever existed. And this cooperative conspiracy has really existed only since the beginning of the 1990s.

Violence and Anarchy

Other organized gangs also find perverse pleasures in the act of violence, terror and intimidation. Now stereotyped and perhaps more lightly treated than they deserve, the Hell's Angels have at times functioned as a particularly nasty criminal association in the USA and Europe. This organization was first established in San Bernadino, California, in 1947. Initially a local gang of bike fanatics, the movement actually began to take shape under Sonny Barger, who founded the Oakland Chapter of the Hell's Angels. Since then, it has gone from strength to strength and has many of the trappings of a cult. Barger himself is still alive and regarded as a figure of awe and reverence by today's members. An initiation ritual separates the members from the outside world, but honorary membership can also now be extended to professionals who are able to manage the increasingly sophisticated affairs of the brotherhood. Rumours abound that some lawless chapters employ an initiation that involves a candidate committing his first murder, primarily to prevent infiltration by the authorities. It has been alleged by a former American Hell's Angel that candidates must also prove themselves in front of their chapter by having sex with, first, an under-age girl, then with a woman over 65 years of age and, finally, with a corpse. This allegation was given under oath to a Congressional committee, but it is unknown to what extent this is true (if at all).

Biker gangs can go under other names – the Outlaws, for example – but the highly distinctive imagery remains. Nazi helmets and regalia, a plethora of swastikas and SS runes and uniquely painted leather jackets serve to identify a biker as a member of this cult. Much of the movement's activities are crime free and orientated to flamboyant displays and participation in public shows. But there is a darker side, perpetrated by an inner core of bikers. Drug running forms a large proportion of this minority's criminal activities, and less conspicuous vehicles, such as BMWs and Mercedes, are used for trips abroad. Scotland Yard has recently claimed that the biker gang phenomenon is one of the fastest growing areas of the drug smuggling business.

Investigators have discovered hard evidence of links between the Cali drugs cartel and these biker gangs, and the entry point into Europe for much of the cartel's cocaine is through Spain and Portugal. In Britain the Hell's Angels are fiercely protective of their name and go to great lengths to protect the 'Hell's Angels' image in the law courts. Chapters in Europe and eastern Europe have sprung up over past decades, and they have pushed the boundaries of crime to new heights with the formation of a legitimate 'front' business enterprise, called Hell's Angels Europe Incorporated. It acts to bind the chapters together in a legal framework and to help coordinate their activities. Murder Inc. was always a sick joke among those who knew it existed. But could we soon be seeing 'La Cosa Nostra Incorporated' or the 'Cali Corporation' for real?

Like all modern criminal organizations, whatever their origins, the bikers have attempted to shield some of their nefarious activities under the cloak of respectability, merging illegal and legal, legitimate and illegitimate activities. On the street Nazi-bikers brutalize rivals and ship drugs, public relations experts smooth over bad press, and accountants and bankers invest the ill-gotten gains, turning 'dirty money' into 'clean'. Hasan-i-Sabbah, Grand Master of the medieval sect called the Assassins, would have appreciated this vital strategy. Working from within and on a day-by-day, side-by-side basis with the intended victims, the Arab killers were able to achieve an unprecedented number of high-level assassinations. No one knew where the next dagger would fall or from where it would emerge. That deadly conspiracy lasted hundreds of years and was essentially fuelled by the assassins' intense faith in their Grand Master and their schismatic religion. How much easier today for a criminal brotherhood, the Mafia, for example, to achieve a similar level of efficiency of devotion and of interpenetration into the daily lives of millions of oblivious citizens. This is a conspiracy fuelled not by blind faith in a religious system, but the personal desires of its members.

Is it purely greed that motivates the Hell's Angels, the endless numbers of would-be mafiosi queuing to join the mob or the *Vory V Zakone*? Or is it something deeper – a question of power? A street soldier for the American Mafia may earn a substantial wage, but before he can join the mob a candidate often has to prove his earning potential. He must bring to the Mafia money of his own. Many newly 'made men' are seasoned criminals even before they swear the Omerta. So why do they join? Wealth or the prospect of it goes some way to explaining the attraction of organized crime, but the true appeal of these brotherhoods of fear lies in their true power over others.

Organized crime rules by fear, both internally and externally. Not only are the victims of extortion compelled to hand over money to placate the violence and terror of the gangsters, but the lives of the Mafia's own soldiers are utterly dominated by the *caporegimes* above them. Respect is given to those who have the power to direct violence, whether he is a Colombian drug lord or a Yardie gang leader, he commands the fate of his followers and can demand their execution for real (or even suspected) slights. Torture and the use of brutal and sadistic beatings are commonly employed as routine punishments. Humiliation in front of other members or loved ones can also serve as a painful reminder of the power of the group over the individual. Chicago boss Sam Giancana once had the mother, father, wife and children of a mafioso urinate on his naked body in order to discipline him. It worked. To be under this kind of threat on a day-to-day basis hardens the lowly member and gives him only one option: rise through the ranks to become one of the élite. Put the boot on the other foot.

Few such organizations allow members to leave the society – alive that is – but however hard pressed the lowest mob hit-man or money collector is, he knows he is a step up from the poor wretches who are the victims of organized crime. Within the criminal society he is a brother. The mafiosi, for example, carry out a ritual at a candidate's initiation that binds him, through blood, to the other members. The American mafiosi like to refer to themselves not as 'gangsters' (a bare and socially devoid term) but as 'wiseguys'. They are part of an élite brotherhood sworn to defend one another, even while they are under interrogation by the police. It may be called a 'thieves' code' or some-thing else entirely, but the majority of criminal societies have also adopted some sort of similar social mechanism. An organization that operates outside the established laws and social norms *must* establish its own set of 'honour among thieves' rules to which its members will adhere. A lone burglar may act as he wishes, but the actions of a single New York mafioso can have repercussions that affect not only mem-bers of his own 'family' but also fellow mafiosi across the country. In this way, the ruthlessness and willingness to use physical violence in pursuit of the organization's aims must be tempered by the knowledge that the use of excessive force could result in summary execution. True sadists have their uses to the bosses of the criminal brotherhoods, but they are rarely tolerated for long. Mimi Sciala was a lieutenant with the Colombo family in New York. After getting drunk he once had the misfortune to insult the 'boss of bosses', Carlo Gambino. He was quickly killed for his disrespect. When a couple of Mimi's loyal soldiers started talking about revenge in a bar a few days later, they, too, were murdered.

Organized crime is not an open democracy but neither is it anarchy. The criminal empires stretching across Russia and eastern Europe, across western Europe and across North America and Latin America are a modern form of dictatorship. As a totalitarian leader, ruling by force, fear and with little legitimacy, the crime bosses are Roman emperors, parcelling off vast provinces of their empires to subordinate dictators who rule in their stead. Everything flows upwards to this figure, and as time begins to run out the succession must be ad-dressed. Does it go to a loyal lieutenant or to the under-boss? Mob wars are usually a violent result of problems in the legitimacy of any succession.

Because the criminal underworld is so huge, almost all illegitimate activity must often go through it, despite the ideals and identities of those involved. Terrorists are a perfect example. Where terrorism is a powerful force within a community, often it is the only underworld force. The Irish Republican Army, waging a terrorist campaign against the Protestant communities in Northern Ireland, is just such a group. In areas where they wield the greatest power their members patrol the streets and regularly kidnap petty criminals and joy-riders. Many are 'knee-capped' with handguns – street justice meted out by a would-be government. The IRA has other trappings of a crime syn-dicate. It extorts money from local businesses, it smuggles drugs into the province, and it controls a whole range of black-market rackets, from video piracy to armed robbery. In January 1995 IRA terrorists teamed up with Irish gangsters to snatch £3 million in Dublin – it was Ireland's biggest armed robbery to date. Estimates put the annual turnover of IRA profits from their criminal empire at £9 million.

According to the Royal Ulster Constabulary, 'gangsters are told: oppose us and you die'.

Where does terrorism end and organized crime begin? The definitions become blurred as the organizations themselves shift their emphasis from their stated objectives and to survival. The Baader-Meinhof gang originally hit the headlines with a series of bank raids designed to swell their purse. The need to make money afflicts every terror group, and if there are no foreign nations willing to bank-roll it, the organization has to turn to other methods. Many guerrilla armies are initially forced to alternate their attacks between military targets and banks. For anarchist or revolutionary groups such as the RAF, which claimed to be fighting against the 'capitalist system', this need for ready cash has to be uncomfortably squared with its cherished philosophies. With a clandestine network already in place to organize safe houses, weapon shipments, forged documents and training, the basic framework for criminal activity exists. From smuggling guns to smuggling drugs is only a small step, and one that reaps incredible financial rewards. Those guns, when not used to kill civilians or policemen, can be readily employed in post office and bank raids.

Likewise, when a criminal syndicate with enough power and influence to challenge a government is threatened, it may turn to the tactics of the terrorist in order to get its own way. Sicilian judge Giovanni Falcone had pioneered the use of so-called 'Maxi-Trials', which allowed the swift and safe prosecution of hundreds of mafiosi. On 23 May 1992, despite the elaborate security precautions that are a way of life for the Sicilian judiciary, Falcone, his wife and all of their bodyguards were murdered. The tactic used was one that had already been perfected by the IRA in Northern Ireland – a massive culvert bomb, placed beneath the road that was to be used by the judge's entourage. As the motorcade passed over that point in the road, the operational leader, watching through binoculars from a nearby hill, depressed the radio detonator. The bomb obliterated the road, the cars and their occupants. Only a huge rubble-filled crater remained. Falcone was one of only a few officials in the late 1980s who had the dark vision of a global criminal conspiracy. When the Medellín cartel and the Sicilian Mafia agreed to join forces in the drug trade in October 1987 (on the Mafia's own private island, Aruba), Falcone declared it a 'shattering and terrifying portent'.

This selective assassination of government officials (such murders have occurred before and since) smacks more of terrorism than organized crime. The cartel has murdered government officials time after time to secure its position in Colombia. In retaliation for government successes against its operations, the Medellín cartel planted a bomb on an Avianca airliner and exploded it in mid-air, killing 107 people.

The two types of organization use the same tactics and often have the same objectives and concerns for survival. How they broadly differ is in emphasis. A terrorist group seeks to achieve political goals and turns to organized crime in order to do this. The crime syndicate generally pursues organized crime for the profits that it reaps, and resorts to terrorism to secure the safety of those profits. As we have seen, it is easy for one type of group to lose sight of its main objective and become involved in a disorganized welter of connections and activities. Today the labels applied by journalists, governments and law enforcement agencies to these secret underworld organizations are but guidelines. As many-headed creatures, they are capable of a wide and frightening range of activities that break all traditional barriers. Powerful beyond the comprehension of even Capone, organized crime syndicates can take on the attributes of whatever suits the occasion: crime syndicate, terrorist group, multinational corporation, guerrilla army, fraternal society or even shadow government. How do you kill a creature like that?

CHAPTER SIX

Tribal Magics

Secret societies established with sinister intent are not just the pre-
serve of industrialized nations. The phenomenon of sects, cults and
brotherhoods is also present within some of the most primitive cultures on earth. Most secret gangs within these tribes are harmless –
even beneficial – organizations, which help to create tribal identity, to
separate the initiated 'adults' from the non-initiated and to wield
tribal power. Others, however, have had a far darker purpose, con-
cealing intrigue, terror and murder beneath a shell of tribal ritual and
magic. Some of the most savage are explored here.

Leopards and Jackals

It was night, and the local villagers were gathering in the wilderness
under Africa's skies. They were preparing to watch and participate in
the Jackal Dance. Among them, hanging back so that he would not be
noticed, was the British writer and traveller, Frederick Kaigh. With the
aid of his servant, Kaigh had 'blacked up', donned the skimpy local
costume and joined the throng heading into the countryside. He knew
full well that he was to be the only Westerner to see the full and unex-
purgated version of this highly secretive and potently magical ritual
dance.

Only after a great deal of persuasion had Kaigh's servant agreed to
smuggle him into the ceremony and then only when his other servants
were fooled into believing he was bed-ridden with the fever. Every
attempt was made to allay the suspicions of the native people, for they
would never reveal the horrible secrets of the dance to outside eyes.
The actual ritual was to take place at the dead of night in the old pro-
tectorate of Northern Rhodesia (modern Zambia), close to a thick
swamp in which the natives believed that pterodactyls still thrived.

While everyone assembled and found places to sit (some in the surrounding trees), Kaigh made sure he did not utter a word. Although he
spoke the local dialects, he had been warned that a secret language
was employed at ceremonies such as this. Soon the *nyanga*, the witch-
doctor, arrived and the ritual began. Wearing a coat of jackal skins and

topped off with a jackal's head, he was totally covered in ceremonial body paint. With the constant accompaniment of thunderous drums, the assembled natives alternated ritual chanting with the consumption of vast amounts of beer.

Suddenly there was silence. A lone howl, the cry of a jackal, pierced the humid night air. Throwing back his head, the *nyanga* howled a perfect response and was answered by other jackals. He then began the Dance of the Jackal. So bizarre, so inhuman, was this dance, that the enthralled Kaigh suspected the use of drugs. So frantic was the witch-doctor's dancing, that he passed out, and the dancing was immediately taken up by a nubile young couple who leapt into position over seated spectators. Their erotic, animal dance shocked Kaigh, and 'the horror of it brought the acid of vomit to the throat'. Finally, the astounded traveller witnessed the horrifying climax of the Jackal Dance. In the book describing his experiences, *Witchcraft and Magic in Africa*, he sets down with disbelieving eyes, what he saw: 'In a twinkling, with loathing unbounded, and incredulous amazement, I saw these two *turn into jackals before my eyes*. The rest of their act must be rather imagined than described.'

With the frenzied mating of the two jackals complete, they disappeared into the bush, whereupon the assembled crowd began to emulate the beasts, copulating until all were thoroughly exhausted. So ran Frederick Kaigh's testimony. It was not written in the murky depths of the nineteenth century, when belief in such matters might still be expected, but in 1947. Kaigh knew that what he had witnessed was impossible, yet he resolutely stuck to his testimony. In his words: 'that awful lycanthropic thing: did it take place?'

Caught up in the ecstatic mood of the ceremony, amid the dancing and the rhythmic drumming, perhaps Kaigh was fooled by trickery designed to do just that. This book does not attempt to explain away the supernatural feats of certain primitive cults and dark religions, but it will explore these cults.

Despite the march of technology and the advance of modern civilization, the developing world seems remarkably resilient in many ways. One such is the way in which the developing cultures have nurtured their native tribal religions. Some of these religions have focused on the veneration and control of local spirits as well as on the spirits of the tribe's long-dead ancestors. Intrinsically caught up within this spirit magic are the darker, more sinister magics that lie below the normal fabric of everyday tribal life. Often buried within a secret sect or within some sort of brotherhood that requires formal initiation, these mystical effects are supposed to remain secret and part of an unpublicized cult.

Such brotherhoods merit attention here because they are real societies with real memberships and rituals. Those that follow retain a deadly grip over their members and their families, for these people truly believe in the dreadful magical powers of the cult. Some readers may believe, too, that certain tribal magic can turn a man into a jackal – others may not. Whether or not the magic actually works or not is irrelevant. For those involved in its operations, the magic exists and is effective. It is a power to be feared, if not venerated, and the witch-doctors who control it are the most powerful individuals of all. As with all the organizations discussed in this book, the only important fact to remember is that the believers believe in the cult and its power. This fact motivates all the 'brotherhoods of fear'.

While the cult bravely penetrated by Frederick Kaigh centred around the worship of jackals and lycanthropy-like jackal-transformation powers, there was a more evil and more widely known cult in Africa, the West African Society of the Leopard. This savage group of men worshipped that particular animal and were initiated into the society only when they were considered to meet certain standards. Initiation was costly, but conferred great privileges. The cost was not financial, however, but human. A prospective candidate was required to produce for sacrifice at his initiation ritual a teenage girl, either his sister or his daughter. On the night before the sacrifice, all members of the group ate a meal of human flesh and sent the candidate, accompanied by four leopard-men, out into the jungle. There they acted out the part of wild leopards. At night, the leopard-men would wear the skins of leopards and would fasten wickedly sharp claws over their hands. Thus equipped, they vanished into the night to terrify, maim, rape and murder.

The following evening, as the sacrificial victim was walking alone to a predetermined rendezvous, one of the cult members leapt out to attack her. With his leopard's claws he cut her throat and returned to the initiation ceremony with her body. There the corpse was ritually dismembered, each cult member receiving a piece. Even the family of the dead girl was presented with a part of her, a gift apparently made to forestall any acts of retribution. Orgiastic dancing and the accompanying consumption of drugs had always preceded the night-time sorties, and it was related by some that the killers also venerated and drank human blood.

Fear both preceded and followed the nocturnal activities of the dreaded Society of the Leopard. The main victims of the cult members were travellers in Sierra Leone – the cult's home territory – and it was thought that they ate their victims during the cannibal feast that followed. Rumours also abounded of young boys being purchased by the influential leaders of the society, to be fattened up, killed, cooked and then eaten. How much of this is true and how much speculation, rumour or just pure fabrication is now difficult to judge.

The Society of the Leopard was not an overly sophisticated or widespread organization. It was a primal religious cult, a movement that had sprung quite logically from the tribal custom of adopting an animal totem. Such totems became a religious focus for several African tribes, and the tribesmen and women would, in one way or another, adopt the attributes of their totem creature. In addition, tribal ceremonies would always include some reference to the animal. Amid much speculation, it is believed that the leopard-men performed their abhorrent acts in order to strengthen the magical power of the entire tribe. Like members of some other violent cults, the leopard-men had higher goals than mere blood-letting.

How widespread the cult was, when it first became established and how many members the society had are relatively unknown. In many ways it resembled the practice of Thuggee in medieval India. Suppressed by British colonial forces, the Thugs were devotees of the Indian goddess Kali, goddess of destruction. Their acts of devotion included roaming the highways of the country in secretive bands, murdering travellers and burying the bodies. Like the leopard-men, the Thugs lived an otherwise normal existence and were sworn to absolute secrecy about their nocturnal killing sprees. British authorities also tried to eradicate the Society of the Leopard. Little was actually achieved, although three leopard-men were executed in 1895 for their part in the murder of a traveller, and it is unclear what became of the Society of the Leopard. It, or a later incarnation, may well still exist in some form or other.

Other tribal societies venerated totem animals in this way. The Westerner John R. Jewitt, stranded among the native North Americans of Nootka Sound, was witness to a wolf ceremony among the tribe, and he reported the existence of a wolf cult. Called Tlokoala, this cult required that its members first undergo a process of initiation, thus setting themselves apart from the other members of the tribe. When Jewitt was able to observe such a Tlokoala ceremony, it was the chief's son who was about to be initiated. After pretending to be shot, the youth (wearing a wolf mask) fell to the floor while the tribe's women began weeping and wailing in distress. The villagers would then rush in to investigate the noise. They were accompanied by two members of Tlokoala, dressed in the skins of wolves and wearing wolf masks. Acting out their roles in the smallest detail, the cult members came in on all fours and, after lifting up the body of the 'dead' candidate, went out of the hut in the same way.

It is likely that these secret society members had adopted the wolf as their totem, venerated its power and attributes and imitated its behaviour. All would have been initiated by feigning death. Such a procedure was a common method of initiation into a number of tribal societies. The next day, the wolf-men of Tlokoala returned the 'dead' initiate to the village for resurrection. A magic stone was hidden on his body, and he could return to life only when this stone was found. When the tribe's witch-doctors removed the stone, the boy came to life and was reborn into the society of the Tlokoala. This group had few of the sinister overtones of the Society of the Leopard, which Frederick Kaigh actually compared to both the Mafia and the sinister Black Hand society.

Another North American secret society employing mock violence was the Olala, a cult among the Niska people of British Columbia. During the initiation ceremony, the candidate's friends pretended to murder him with knives. While he slipped away for the next stage in the proceedings, the murderers hacked off the head of a dummy and allowed the tribe's women to mourn over the effigy. A funeral followed, while the candidate was taken away by members of Olala. For an entire year the boy lived with his prospective comrades and was not allowed to come into contact with any other members of the tribe. When he returned at the end of his 'death', he arrived on the back of the Olala animal totem (represented by members in costume), whatever animal that might be. The tribe had four distinct Olala cults, each venerating its own totem animal – eagle, wolf, raven and bear.

In the same area the Kwakiutl people also employed a mock-death ritual during the initiation of young men into one of several mutually exclusive 'shaman's societies'. Each society or 'house' had its own ritualistic dances that were never revealed to outsiders, even of the same tribe. The dances were passed down from father to son, and were associated with the ancestor spirits of the society's membership. Each member was supposedly able, during his initiation, to contact and adopt one of his family's ancestor spirits.

Much as the Tlokoala candidate was kidnapped by wolf-men, the Kwakiutl initiate was kidnapped by one of these guardian spirits and held at some distance from the village, while the spirit taught him the secrets of the society. When he returned to the village, the initiate had to have his guardian spirit exorcised from his body before he could be reborn into the tribe. During this ritual, the boy would use his newly acquired knowledge to summon up the spirit. This, and other magical skills, were achieved by the highly ingenious use of stage magic employed by the society's shamans. Articulated puppets, cleverly disguised speaking tubes, trap doors and complex moving masks were used to enhance the ceremonies and to create the illusion of real magical effects.

During the Kwakiutl initiation ceremonies, one man, the cannibal-dancer, a high-ranking shaman, moved in a frenzied dance from spectator to spectator. He simulated the devouring of human flesh, pretending to eat the dead and bite the bodies of the onlookers. This cannibalism was all for show, however, and was never anything more than part of the drama of the initiation story.

Cannibal Cults

Cannibalism actually existed in some of the world's tribal societies and survived into modern times for Westerners to observe and record. Again, such a practice had deeply rooted ceremonial and magical meanings that went far beyond a simple lust for human flesh. It is doubtful that any human being could knowingly eat the flesh of another without the impetus of some incredible psychological drive: survival, in the case of some modern examples, and religious and magical belief, in the case of certain cannibal tribes. Cannibalism, contrary to some of the more fanciful tales of Western explorers and sailors, has been rare. Today it is an extinct practice, revived only briefly in the most desperate of survival circumstances, such as the terrible plight of the Andean plane crash survivors in the 1970s.

Some archaeologists believe that early man may sometimes have eaten the remains of his fellows. The fact that certain skulls of Peking and Java Man (some of humanity's earliest ancestors) have holes in their bases suggests to some the extraction and consumption of the brain. If other parts of the body were untouched (which is unknown), ritual cannibalism is therefore likely. Cannibalism as a form of dietary preference has never been known – at least in the level-headed studies of anthropologists and archaeologists – but travellers' tales told of the Batak people in the East Indies who made a living from the sale of human meat at market. These were preposterous stories, which tried to illustrate just how savage the savages were (especially in comparison with the superior 'whites'). Few tribal cultures actually sanctioned the eating of human flesh, even for ceremonial purposes. The North American Ojibwa people considered that any man who turned to human flesh in order to avoid starvation had been possessed. The possessing spirit was named Wendigo, an evil and deadly monster, which roamed the wild woods, preying on the living and devouring human flesh.

In the Pacific, the chieftains of the island of Fiji were said to eat the flesh of humans and to keep a careful count of the number they had eaten, an indication of some definite ritual purpose. Much of what is known about early Fijian practices has come to us from the reports of Christian missionaries sent there to convert the islanders. Naturally these ministers vividly coloured their accounts and portrayed the Fijians in the worst possible light. According to the Reverend John Hunt, not only were the Fijians cannibals, but they rounded up shipwrecked sailors and roasted them alive over cooking fires.

The details of the cannibalistic practices hint at some deeper meaning beneath the gory descriptions. Victims weren't simply killed, cooked and eaten. Sometimes they were first insulted or tortured;

sometimes the victim would have a piece of his body cut off – his tongue or an arm – cooked and eaten in front of him. It is even reported that such cooked body parts could be offered to the victim. Skulls of the devoured victims were kept as trophies and used in subsequent rituals, indicating an unknown magical connection. Anthropologists have discovered that the huntsmen of certain tribes are eager to consume the hearts, brains or livers of strong and powerful animals they have killed. In this way they take on the strength, courage and power of the dead beast. From this, anthropologists believe that the cannibalistic practices of warrior societies like Fiji were derived from a similar tradition. By ritually eating the organs or flesh of a powerful enemy, that enemy's power and strength passes into the body of his killer. In addition, the victim's spirit cannot avenge the murder.

Typical of the head-hunting cannibals that seem to match the stereotype were the Central African Bangala people. In raids and wars, the Bangala warriors brought back both live captives and also dismembered human bodies, either of which would form part of a cannibal feast. The missionary John Weeks was witness to just such a raiding party when it returned home. On the following day he was offered what he considered to be human flesh, one of the limbs he had seen the day before, prepared and cooked, ready for eating.

Other tribes have given this gruesome reasoning a more personal slant. The Yanomamo of Brazil, the Amahuaca in Peru and the Birhori people in India all ate the cremated remains of their own dead. Rather than consign the body to the ground, these people believed that to eat a dead relative returned his or her life-essence back to the tribe. In Peru, for example, the deceased person's ashes were powdered and mixed with gruel. The Yanomamo used this opportunity to forge alliances, by offering to share the remains with a neighbouring family or clan. Most peculiar of all, some Australian Aboriginal tribes were known to smoke the remains of their relatives on a bonfire and drink the juices that oozed out of the super-heated body. There were magical benefits to be gained from such a custom. By drinking the juices of a dead relative, their wisdom and knowledge could be absorbed and passed on.

West African Cults: Poro and Oro

Crossing several of today's political boundaries, including those of Guinea, Sierra Leone and Liberia, the Poro Society of West Africa was, until recently, a remarkably widespread and influential secret society that initiated young men into the tribe, while excluding the women. In their turn, the young girls were initiated into an associated cult called the Sande. Poro is a term that doubles for the name of the secret inter-tribal society as well as its initiation ritual. Through the Poro, the various tribal groups educated and indoctrinated their young men into the roles that were expected of them.

The Poro was first mentioned in European literature, mainly Spanish and Portuguese, from the sixteenth century. Although industrial development has seriously affected its role, the Poro Society survived intact well into the twentieth century. Thus the society might possibly be 500 *or more* years old. Poro initiations always began with a 'bush school', a long house built deep in the jungle away from prying eyes, which served as an educational establishment. Boys ready for membership into the Poro were taken there and, as their families looked on, were tossed over the reed screen into the enclosure. Like many such rituals, the theme revolved around death and rebirth, and in this case the boys were supposed to have been devoured by demons. Bizarre screams and whistles – the supposed sound of spirits and demons – could be heard, and a bloody spear was thrust out of the hut's roof, terrifying the onlookers who believed their children had been murdered by the demons.

During the next few weeks, the boys would learn the skills they would need in manhood and be introduced into the 'mysteries' of the tribe. This short regime was brutal. First, the candidates were circumcised. Many tribes also ritually scarred their charges, a symbolic sign of the struggle they had put up against the crocodile spirit that had supposedly 'devoured' them. Any youth who became infected during either of these procedures is reported to have been killed in order to stop the infection spreading. Before the medicines of the twentieth century, this must have been a common occurrence. Poro priests claimed that these unfortunates remained forever in the belly of the great crocodile spirit and would never emerge.

While being educated in the doctrines of tribal life and Poro beliefs, the young men were threatened with summary execution should they reveal certain Poro secrets or attempt to imitate aspects of the rituals. To reinforce the threats, the boys were sometimes shown a wooden tray that contained row upon row of human toes, fingers and thumbs. Obedience, as any drill sergeant knows, comes from rigorous use of threatening behaviour and the inspiration, in the victim, of fear of retribution. For the Poro initiates severe beatings could be administered at any time, day or night, which demoralized the candidate and took away his self-respect. He became obedient, afraid and compliant. Part of their ritual initiation included eating the products of the female circumcisions, which were carried out by the Sande, the women's society. In turn, the girls were forced to eat the remains of the boys' circumcision ritual.

Some of the young initiates were groomed as priests of their tribe, and as such were to learn certain secret signs of recognition. Wherever the priest went and to whichever tribe he travelled, he was always sure to be given a warm welcome by other Poro members. It was claimed that there were as many as 99 grades of initiation within the Poro priesthood and that the very highest of these ranks were always filled by members of certain influential families.

The Poro could not fail to be caught up within the tribal politics of the region. Tribal chiefs were Poro members but were nevertheless subject to the commands of the Poro members above them. While tribal matters were resolved by the chief and his elders, matters of greater importance, perhaps those affecting two or more tribal groups, were discussed by Poro priests who met with the chiefs to find a solution. These councils were highly secret. At the very highest level, a group of elderly Poro members masterminded the broad sweep of the secret society's activities. After death, many of these élite councillors were represented by masks, which were worn by their replacements. This council often ruled according to the wishes of the Poro ancestors, and so ruled the land of the living by the dictates of the dead. This 'government from the spirit world' has its parallels in other African secret societies.

Another West African society, the Ogboni of the Nigerian Yoruba tribe, once carried significant political weight. Resembling a political organization, with lodges established across the tribal territories, the Ogboni often challenged the authority of individual chiefs. And there were also periods when the society abused its preferential position among the Yoruba. Part of its power depended on the upholding of religious traditions on which the tribe depended. One of these traditions was rumoured to be the sacrifice of human prisoners on the initiation of new members. If this practice ever existed at all, it stopped long ago. One of the most secret aspects of the cult was its religious images – metal statuettes of the earth deity, Edan. The coming of colonial governments quickly eroded the importance of the cult, and eventually it did little more than organize funerary rites. In 1914 the Ogboni transformed itself into the Reformed Ogboni Fraternity, in which Christians were able to participate fully. Much of the secrecy had been shed, and it was the group's fraternal beliefs that attracted the new and more 'enlightened' breed of initiates.

During its heyday, the Ogboni was served by an executive arm, a sub-cult, called the Oro. Typical of many West African cults, the Oro initiated only males, and strict secrecy was employed to shield its activities from prying eyes. Wrong-doers condemned by the Ogboni were apprehended by members of the Oro and executed in a specially marked cult grove. Victims who were killed in this way often had their skulls displayed alongside scraps of their clothing in a tree at the local market. In addition, they pursued witches and harassed various types of 'undesirable'. With the masculine domination of the group and the tangible aura of fear that pervaded the local area when members were abroad, the cult somewhat resembled the Ku Klux Klan. What official justice could not accomplish, the Oro almost certainly could.

When the cult members emerged from their cult grove, the women of the village were forbidden to look on them. This usually took place in the evening, and it was heralded by the use of the 'bull-roarer', a shaped wooden weight whirled at speed on the end of a cord. The sound signalled to the women of the village the imminent arrival of the Oro. In previous years the Oro held an annual festival lasting a full week. For the entire period the women of the tribe were forced to remain locked in their huts, day and night, except for certain periods to fetch water and food. It was during this week of Oro domination that some of the younger cultists strode around naked, and stories have survived of unfortunate girls caught peering out at the young men. The penalty for such curiosity was execution.

Initiation was open to any male of the tribe who could provide the statutory payment of one sheep. The new member was then able to attend the Oro meetings in the grove and join the cult on its night-time forays. All meetings were held in the secret Oro grove, a selected site with a palm frond marking the entrance. Meetings in progress were guarded by Oro sentries, who stood on the path into the grove and demanded the secret passwords of the organization before allowing entrance.

Witch and Witch-doctor

Although we have observed that the phenomenon of witchcraft reached all parts of medieval Europe, it was not peculiar to that time and space. African tribes have long recognized the existence of a shadowy group of people who have mastered the black art of causing illness and calamity to their members. These witches have been hunted by the tribal leaders, but, predictably, few witches have ever openly admitted to practising their magical skills. Have African tribes-people been deluding themselves, just as seventeenth- and eighteenth-century magistrates had done? Is the myth of the witch truly universal?

Within pre-industrial societies devoid of science and scientific explanations the unseen realm of magic is able to provide all the answers. An obvious cause and effect can usually be observed in most situations, but occasionally some ill may affect a tribesman and he can think of no known cause. Illness was perhaps the main unexplained phenomenon, but there were many others. An accidental drowning or a catastrophic event, such as a hut burning down, prompted the tribesman to suspect foul play: the unwanted intervention of a witch. The greatest and most widely feared power of the witch was the ability to cause death at a distance, without there being any physical contact between the witch and the victim. The resulting death was often unusual, unexpected and seemingly without justification. In Central Africa, the Azande people believed that virtually every misfortune that struck the tribe without an obvious explanation was induced by the evil powers of local witches.

It is easy to see how these beliefs took hold. An isolated social group battered by the winds of fate, by disease, famine or drought, would rather suspect that a lone magician was responsible than blind chance. Identifying some human element is a far more positive step for the tribesmen than acknowledging that they are, in fact, utterly powerless.

Initiation into the practice of witchcraft was thought to occur in different ways, depending on the tribal beliefs. The Azande people believed that prospective witches carried an innate witch substance within their belly. Activated by the intense emotions of greed or envy, the witch substance could act independently of its host and would often lie in wait for years before beginning its life of misfortune and death. Other cultures had more conventional visions of the witch, and it was most common for a student of the black arts to be initiated into the practice by another witch or to undergo some sort of ritual in order to gain the powers of a witch. An explanation should be given of the connection between medieval satanic witches and the African witches: there is none. African witches resemble their European counterparts only superficially, and perhaps the only thing they have in common at all is that they use magic to bring harm to other people. Often there are no covens, no satanic pacts – no Satan. The label 'sorcerer' is perhaps more apt and freer from prejudice, but the term 'witch' has been used throughout history and has stuck.

The 'evilness' of a witch was not based on his or her destination in the afterlife and whether or not their soul would be saved, but by their acts in the present. In a world where the tribesmen and women depended on each other for their well-being, if not their survival, the fact that one individual should turn against the tribe and work towards its destruction was seen as illogical, spiteful and evil. Naturally, such a witch was considered to be totally abnormal when it came to morality and custom. He or she would flout the conventions of the tribe, living with lions and hyenas and journeying naked during the night. Most of the Ghanaian tribes, including the Ashanti and the Fanti, took this belief quite literally and were disposed to think of a witch walking upside down. Although he could create the illusion that he was walking upright in the normal fashion, a clever witch-doctor believed that he could kick dust at the ankles of a suspected witch and actually blind him!

When the tribal elders, with the aid of a skilled witch-doctor, hunted for a witch, it was often the physically different or the socially retarded who seemed to fall under suspicion. In the first category were the disabled or blind, in the second, the gossip-mongers and the unusually greedy. Anyone who did not conform could fall under suspicion as a witch. Wherever tensions existed within a community, witchcraft, or the fear of witchcraft, seemed to thrive. The food-sharing people of the southern African Nyakusa tribe believed that the evil acts of the witches were driven by greed for roast meat, which put them directly in conflict with their fellows. For the Pondo people (also of southern Africa) the tribe's complex social interactions were often among blood relatives. Pondo witches were believed to ignore social niceties and break whatever sexual taboos they wished, even coupling with their animal familiars. Many of the Pondo witches were squabbling wives, believed by the men to resort to black magic in order to get their way. Pondo society was polygamous.

Although witches were often thought to be secretly living within the tribe, there *were* tried and tested methods for the detection of a witch. By far the most common was the use of a poisonous bark: a suspect who failed to vomit up the dangerous brew formulated from the bark was judged to be a witch. Only one who matched poison with poison would not reject the deadly drink. The past half century has seen an unexpected rise in the number of witch-finding cults, each dedicated to investigating accusations of black magic and to the identification of the witches believed responsible. Such anti-witch cults have existed across post-colonial Africa, from Nigeria and Ghana through to Zambia and Uganda. These cults mainly take the form of expert witch-finders, who roam across the land, visiting tribes and attempting to identify local witches. Strangely, many of those accused spontaneously confess to their previous evil actions. This suggests that they are not charlatans but devout believers in the efficacy of their own sorcerous powers.

Witch-finder cults prospered, perhaps, because the old authoritarian methods of witch detection and prosecution were frowned upon by the colonial regimes. Harsh poison ordeals, trials and royal oracles were curtailed, as were the methods by which most tribes punished their witches. The exile, mutilation or execution of a suspected witch was not thought to be worthy of a civilized race, and the colonial administrations soon put a stop to such barbaric practices. The spread of such witch-finding cults has accompanied social disruption and tribal tensions, riding a wave of discontent and frustration. Change, often associated with the arrival of western capitalism, could be linked with witchcraft and the breakdown of the old morals. Witch-finding cults have gained a whole new impetus in the last century, and thinly scattered across the developing world they have acted as sporadic and uneven brakes on the development of pre-industrial societies.

Almost without exception, all pre-industrial societies have supported an activity that has traditionally been reserved for the specialist witch-doctor. Half-healer, half-magician, the witch-doctor (or his equivalent) is socially distinct from the rest of his or her tribe. He is special – his training will have been extensive, his selection rigorous (or hereditary) and his position within the tribe second only perhaps to the chief. The fact that these magical-healers mix the supernatural with the natural so easily should come as no surprise. In a universe based purely on observation, the causes of illnesses and their cures are more readily explained by the intervention of spirits than the activities of micro-organisms. In the nature-rich environment of tribal life, however, it was only logical that any natural remedies would be fully exploited. Illnesses that could be treated with herbal medicines were addressed physically; those that could not were addressed magically. The witch-doctors did not differentiate between these two methods. For them the spirit world and the physical world blended together imperceptibly.

Driven by logic and not wild fantasy, members of these tribes attempted to rationalize the motives of the attacking spirit. Was it an angry ancestor? Was it the spirit of a taboo tree that has just been cut down or of a stream or spring that has been polluted? Of course, as we have seen, it is not just the malign influence of spirits that may cause a patient to sicken. Evil witches may target their enemies with magic that must also be countered. Thus the witch-doctor became exorcist, witch-finder and physician all in one. Diagnosis of the patient's illness was often done via the spirit world. The witch-doctor could employ a variety of methods, depending on the traditions of his tribe. He could send himself into a trance (often with the aid of locally cultivated drugs) and then converse with the spirit world, or he could separate his spirit from his body (discorporate) and personally visit this realm. By interrogating the ancestors of the tribe and of the natural world, he was able to determine the 'cause' of the sickness.

Since the evil spirit had menaced the victim for a specific reason, the witch-doctor was quite logically able to address this reason. Perhaps the tree- or river-spirit would be placated with offerings, the opinions of the ancestor-spirit would be heeded and so on. In many cases the possession of the human body by a malign spirit was reversed by the removal of a hidden 'foreign object'. It could be a dart, a thorn or some other object that the witch-doctor 'removes' from the patient's body at the end of a public exorcism. Singing, dancing and elaborate ritual were all universally employed by the witch-doctor in order to assure success. When the witch-doctor removed the dart or thorn from his patient, he was not wilfully engaging in deceitful fakery, but symbolically acting out the more spiritual event taking place. Does the Christian minister engage in fakery each time he dispenses bread and wine to his congregation? Are the participants really partaking of Christ's blood and flesh or is the entire ritual simply a metaphor for a more spiritual event that is taking place?

If the patient were a victim of tribal witchcraft, the cure became more complicated. First, various amulets and spells could be used to ward off the evil magics being directed towards him. Then the business of trying to identify the witch would begin. Since a good many 'witch-inspired illnesses' would be nothing of the sort, the chances of locating the supposed offender were slight. If the witch could not be caught, the substance used as a channel for the deadly magic had to be located and destroyed. The whole approach revolved around the idea of 'sympathetic magic'. To bring harm against an enemy, a small effigy of that person could be harmed instead, or his hair, nail-clippings or excrement could be used in some magical rite designed to weaken and ultimately kill him.

Some tribal witch-doctors involve the entire tribe in the healing process, rightly identifying a definite therapeutic value in this. The Ndembo people of Zambia, in Central Africa, for example, often gathered around a patient and had a public airing of grudges against him, which resolved tensions and cleared the air. The Ndembo also believed that a powerful man who held a grudge against another could cause an unhealthy 'tooth' to become lodged within his enemy's body. To remove this 'foreign object' the Ndembo witch-doctor required the assistance of the entire community in a collective ceremony of healing. Caught up in the emotion and energy of the ceremony, several participants would confess their personal grudges against the patient. Only after the perpetrator's public confession could the 'tooth' be successfully removed. Such a public ritual, although with apparently little actual medical value, did seem to have an effect. This can be put down to the great psychological benefit that can be gained from such a display of group solidarity.

Ndembo rituals of healing are usually termed 'drums of affliction', after the drum accompaniment to the ceremony. The members of the tribe who come out to aid an afflicted fellow were those who had themselves suffered a similar affliction. These 'cults of affliction' crossed family and clan barriers, forming loose intra-tribal links that would not otherwise exist. Participation in such a ritual as a patient qualifies the man to participate in the cult's activities. Closing the circle, it was often believed that the ancestor spirit who had possessed the victim and caused the affliction had itself been a member of the cult in life. Most Ndembo belong to one of these cults of affliction, and many are members of more than one.

By the late 1960s there were 16 different cults of affliction in existence among the Ndembo. For hunters having trouble finding animals there was the Wubinda cult; for patients with breathing problems there was the Kayong'u cult; for sudden illness there was the Kaneng'a; and for crop failures and assorted sicknesses there was the cult of

Chihamba. In this last secret organization, the patient dreamed of the ghost (and former Chihamba cult member) who was responsible for afflicting him. To drive away the spirit, other members of the cult would pursue the patient and after they had caught up with him, would perform a ritual interrogation. At a secret location, hidden from the other members of the tribe, the cult would carry out the symbolic murder of the spirit. Most of these cults divided up their rituals into three definite stages. First, an introductory ritual called Ku-lembeka. This was often followed by some sort of seclusion of the patient. The final and most elaborate ritual was usually called the Ku-tumbuka. It was common for the majority of the tribe to attend the first ritual, with only cult members able to attend the second.

A good example of a cult of affliction was the secret society known as Nkula. Patients were women who suffered from infertility, and they usually had a male assistant who could attend them throughout the various phases of the purification. The first of these phases consisted of a public ceremony that lasted for an evening. The second involved the patient being secluded from the other cult members and attended by the cult doctors (the ayimbuki). Finally, a long and involved ritual was performed throughout one night and continued until the following midday. Blood (more specifically menstrual blood) and the colour red played a large part in Nkula ritual. Women doctors involved in Nkula had at one time been patients themselves, and, similarly, the male doctors must have served as male assistants to female Nkula patients. If successfully cured, the patient was entitled to join the cult as a chimbuki wanyanya (little doctor). Her rank, responsibility and medical knowledge could develop as she became involved in the cult's ceremonial activities.

Very real and potentially deadly diseases have been known to be successfully resisted by the most stubborn and optimistic of patients – the power of the mind does have the capacity to resist illness and fight off death. Unfortunately, the reverse is also true. There have been several reported cases of tribesmen, convinced that an evil spell has been cast on them, dying from no known illness. Belief in the power of black magic was so strong that individuals could be said to have 'willed their own death'.

Among the Australian Aborigines the method of killing a person without recourse to physical contact was called 'bone-pointing'. The secret society of witch-doctors practising this black art was called the Kurdaitcha, and its members were responsible for tracking down and executing condemned tribesmen. Only initiated men were allowed within the society, and its rituals and traditions were kept strictly secret. Most secret of all was the method used to fashion the kundela, the deadly 'pointer'. Ostensibly a sharpened wand made from a human or kangaroo bone, the kundela had formidable powers, if only in the minds of those against whom it was used. The wands, usually between 15 and 20 centimetres (6–8 inches) long, were tied with a braid of hair that was held by a natural resin. After being charged with the spiritual energy of its maker, the wand was handed over to the Kurdaitcha member who had been given the task of killing the unfortunate victim.

These executions have continued into modern times. An Aborigine called Kinjika, from the Mailli tribe in Australia's Northern Territory, was flown to a Darwin hospital in 1953. He was in an extremely critical state and barely held on to life as doctors tried desperately to save him. After four days wracked by pain, Kinjika died, the victim of a tribal execution through *kundela*. Doctors had been unable to identify the unusually rapid and deadly illness. After breaking one of his tribe's more serious sexual taboos, the Aborigine had fled his homeland for fear of retribution. In his absence the elders of the tribe condemned him to death, a *kundela* was quickly prepared, and an executioner was dispatched to carry out the sentence.

The Kurdaitcha assassination attempt was not simply carried out by a lone witch-doctor travelling the countryside searching for his man. Several (usually two or three) cult members went out together as a group, well motivated and prepared, to carry out the killing. The society had gained its name from the magical shoes that each member wore while hunting the human prey. The shoes were carefully made from human hair and cockatoo feathers. Their wearers believed them to leave no footprints. To complete the macabre preparations, the killers stuck kangaroo hair to their bodies with human blood, and then donned emu-feather masks.

Use of the charged *kundela* in the hands of the Kurdaitcha was highly dramatic. The two or three cult members would track down their victim and address him face-to-face. Holding the *kundela* almost as if it were a gun, the wielder of the wand dropped to one knee and directed the magical weapon at his victim. With a short, powerful chant the magical energy that was supposed to be pent up within the bone was released. According to Dr Herbert Basedon, the victim 'attempts to shriek, but usually the sound chokes in his throat, and all one might see is froth at his mouth. His body begins to tremble and the muscles twist involuntarily.' Unable to move and too terrified to flee, the victim was left alone, and the hunters returned successful to the tribe. Within days the condemned man would grow sick and begin to die. His friends and family often shunned him since they believed (like the victim himself) that he was already dead. This must have reinforced the victim's own belief in his doom, and a psychosomatic death soon followed. The exact cause of *kundela*-inspired deaths have perplexed those Australian doctors who have come into contact with these bizarre cases. Various theories have been fielded, often revolving around the inter-linking effects of adrenaline production on blood pressure and red blood count, but the results of such tests have varied from case to case, and none of the theories has been adequately confirmed.

In 1976 the writer John Godwin included a recent account of an Aborigine fleeing the Kurdaitcha in his book, *Unsolved: The World of the Unknown*. According to Godwin, the Aborigine, who was named Alan Webb, had accidentally shot another member of his tribe in a struggle over a hunting rifle. The Australian authorities in Alice Springs ruled in Webb's favour, and declared that the death had been accidental. But Webb's tribe, the Arunta, were not to be so forgiving. As the court proceedings came to an end, a number of elders from the Arunta met with Webb to inform him that the tribal elders were going to try him themselves. He knew that they would not rule in his favour but instead condemn him to death, the traditional penalty for murder or manslaughter.

At the earliest opportunity, therefore, Webb fled from Alice Springs. As he had rightly predicted, the tribe sentenced him to death in his absence. From the time of the court case in April 1969 until 1976, he continued to keep one step ahead of the dreaded Kurdaitcha. Modern methods of transportation complicated the chase somewhat. Webb drove a camper van in which his family and dogs travelled across Australia. While his dogs guarded the van at night, Webb slept with a loaded rifle at his side. His belief in the powers of the *kundela* and of its wielders, the Kurdaitcha, fuelled his terror and paranoia. It is clear that Webb, driving his van from town to town in the search for odd-jobs, believed in the reality of the death that awaited him if he abandoned his flight. With the executioners constantly on his trail for seven years he continued to travel, always moving on when he heard that the Kurdaitcha might be getting close. No one knows what happened after 1976 when Godwin published his account. Is Alan Webb still on the fringes of Australian society, living in nomadic anonymity? Or did the tribal death squad finally catch up with him and unleash the – imagined – power of the *kundela*?

Voodoo

Few tribal belief systems are too complex or overly elaborate. Most are based on the veneration of personified natural forces in conjunction with the varied inhabitants of the spirit world. Voodoo, however, is different. A blend of Black African tribal religion and orthodox Christianity, which is, without doubt, one of the most ordered religions on earth, voodoo is utterly unique. To the Western mind, it also incorporates certain unsettling aspects that merge the distinction between religion and sorcery.

The cult of voodoo developed on the island of Haiti. It incorporated the beliefs of West African slaves who had been transported there to the plantations into the Christian tradition that was forced on them when they got there. Complicating this development were a number of influences from Amerindian, Spanish and French folklore. As a religion of slaves, voodoo was from its earliest incarnations, a religion shrouded in secrecy: a cult. The word 'voodoo' is probably derived from the word *vodu*, meaning 'powerful spirit-god', as used by the Fon tribe in Benin, West Africa, but it has also been connected with the name of the heretical French cult, the Vaudois.

A Fon tribesman traditionally gave himself up for possession by a particular ancestor spirit and joined the cult that venerated the spirit. Later in life he could call on this spirit for help in almost all matters, and the tribesman was free to join any number of cults and call on any number of similar spirits. Although each powerful spirit-god had its own temple and priesthood, the religion proved highly personal and was easily able to survive the shocking transition to slavery in the Caribbean. There the religion took root, and its fundamental belief rests on the assumption that 'god' is everywhere represented by spirits, in the animate and inanimate, even beyond the grave. A good deal of voodoo ritual, therefore, centres on the summoning, control and exorcism of such spirits. Other spirits are venerated and propitiated with sacrifices that are designed to win a spirit's favour.

Today, voodoo is followed by people across the globe, with some estimates claiming that the religion has something like 40 million active participants. It flourishes mainly among the black communities that were founded as slave colonies by the Western plantation owners. In this way voodoo is a religion of salvation and protection against the dark and brutal forces of social injustice. It relies not on an organized chain of churches or an established and ordered hierarchy but is simple and personal, reflecting the dire background from which it sprang. Haiti possibly saw some of the worst injustices against black slaves in the seventeenth and eighteenth centuries, and it was the growth of the voodoo cult that resulted. Secrecy was always an important part of the faith, as much as it was for the early Christians in the days of the Roman Empire. Voodoo was feared by the white owners, and anyone caught in possession of the cult's ritual paraphernalia faced imprisonment, torture and execution.

The cult has had a colourful life. During the earliest days of Caribbean slavery, a group of voodoo initiates escaped from the plantations and established a resistance movement in the remote wilderness of the island. With Haiti in black hands, voodoo flourished and developed into a fully fledged religion besides the 'official' religion of Roman Catholicism. Known as maroons, these fighters loyally followed their leader François Macandal in the slave rebellion of 1758.

Macandal's successor, Bookman, was the man responsible for drawing up a bizarre 'voodoo declaration of independence'. This explained who the voodoo gods were and what they did; and it specifically stated that the voodoo gods 'order us to avenge our wrongs'. Haiti was eventually liberated from the crushing imperialism of France, although the leader of the revolt, Toussaint L'Ouverture, was eventually apprehended by the authorities and sent to France, where he died in prison in 1803.

Because it was so informal in structure, voodoo was easily able to incorporate many aspects of orthodox Christianity. Even today, practitioners of voodoo revere certain aspects of Christianity, especially Roman Catholicism. Certain items, such as candles and holy water, are thought to be so magically powerful that they are regularly stolen from churches for use in voodoo ceremonies. Christian festivals are also recognized and celebrated by voodoo congregations, and some Christian figures are revered by the Haitians. John the Baptist, for example, is given full honours in the voodoo cult as the great spirit called Ogoun. The Christian vision of its saints does, in fact, closely resemble the voodoo perception of spirits (*loa*). There are saints of war, of travel, of love and of almost everything between. In the same way, voodoo populates the natural and human world with *loa*, many of which preside over a single well-defined area of the universe. The actual power of the church is not in dispute, but the priests of voodoo are able to provide a less authoritarian religion, amalgamating the remote power of the Christian Church with the more immediate benefits of spirit worship.

This synthesis is perfectly illustrated by the July feast of the Virgin of the Palms in the Haitian town of Saut d'Eau. Here the congregation prays not only to the Virgin Mary but also to the well-established *loa* community. Greatest of these spirits is the enigmatic figure of Baron Samedi, who is worshipped with great ceremony on Christian All Souls' Day. Atop his altar, effigies of Baron Samedi more nearly resemble eighteenth-century plantation owners than spirit gods. He is often depicted as dressed all in black, wearing a tall hat and black coat, and his title, Baron, is a hold-over from the days of wealthy European despots ruling the Haitian slave communities. A roadside shrine to Samedi might consist of nothing more than a black cross, with the macabre addition of human bones at its feet. Life and death have very indistinct (and overlapping) boundaries within the voodoo philosophy.

Alien to the Christian system is the notion of the voodoo priest as magical practitioner, able to harm or to heal. Evil sorcerers are priests using their powers for ill, while the practitioners of white magic to counter these evil sorcerers are merely voodoo priests using their powers for good. Thus a voodoo priest is knowledgeable in both the positive and negative aspects of the cult. In the same way, medicine can be used either to prevent or cure an illness or to inflict that same illness. Voodoo, in this way, is a system of belief that is capable of being used for either good or bad. Of course, most voodoo priests are considered to be using their powers for good, through medicine and exorcism. A priest who has no real congregation, who uses his powers for selfish reasons and personal gain, is known as a *bocor*. Such individuals have accepted a position on the fringes of the voodoo religion, and because of the ill-will that exists will rarely admit that they are *bocor*.

Most harmful voodoo magic works on the human soul, or *gros bon ange* (great good angel), which is supposed to be located in the nape of the neck and is a vital part of every human being. Also part of the spirit is the *'til bon ange* (little good angel), which acts as the conscience – a bodiless spirit, which evil sorcerers are able to control. The *gros bon ange* is continually at risk because of its susceptibility to strong emotion – loss, love, bitterness, anger, shock and so on. Voodoo is supposed to be of great benefit to this spirit because it is able to manipulate the emotional state through the drumming and music that is played during ceremonies. At certain climaxes in these ceremonies the worshippers may be overcome by spiritual fervour. Taken to be the possession of the human body by a spirit, the *saisissement* (seizure) is often a central part in the voodoo ritual. It in some ways resembles an epileptic fit, with the body being wracked by uncontrollable contortions, followed by collapse and muscle spasm. The whites of his eyes roll up and the affected person may foam at the mouth. The spirit that manifests and possesses or 'rides' the victim will remain on hand to help cure any sickness with which he may be afflicted. As with African religions, the voodoo priest may also help the process by discovering some 'foreign object' on the patient, such as a needle or lizard. Several *loa* may be summoned in a single ceremony, and the individuals who are 'ridden' by these well-known folk-spirits assume their personalities for the rest of the evening. Beginning with the lesser ranked spirits, the participants will move on to more and more powerful *loa* as the night progresses.

Possession is not desired for the purposes of self-help alone but also in order to initiate new members into the voodoo cult. A priest is on hand to control the *saisissement* procedure as well as to administer the ritual of initiation that symbolizes both death and rebirth. On initiation, the new member will have to make a choice about the specific 'nation' of *loa* that he wishes to follow, although for most initiates this will be the *loa* of their parents. The most powerful of these 'nations' are the Rada of Benin, the Siniga of Senegal and the Wangol of Angola. Otherwise, the local Haitian Petro-*loa* are available for the candidate to choose. The voodoo priests are always ready to help new recruits make the best choice of spirits. Initiates must purchase all the ritual paraphernalia that is required for the ceremonies to come and have to spend two weeks in preparation and seclusion before they are deemed ready to join the voodoo cult. At this time, the candidates will have been taught all the relevant passwords, secret signs, prayers and gestures needed and will have been fed only white (that is, 'dead') food. As they emerge from their seclusion, the candidates will be dressed all in white, again symbolizing 'death'.

Before the initiation ceremony proper, each candidate's *gros bon ange* is removed to a small pot by a priest in order to facilitate the possession of the body by the *loa*. The *loa* are now free to enter the initiates' bodies, and they travel down a specially constructed post to reach the participants in the ceremony. This post symbolizes both the human backbone as well as the sacred tree of Legba, Messenger of the Gods. He is *Legba Grand Bois Chemin* (Legba, the Path of the Great Tree).

Many of the practical benefits to be gained from membership in this cult revolve around sex and sexual power over others. Sexual passions are an integral part of voodoo culture, and some of the new initiates may actually be local prostitutes (*bousins*) or women living off the gratuities of their lovers (*jeunesses*). Because of this element within the voodoo ritual, it has been relatively easy for an unscrupulous priest to take advantage of his position and force female candidates to sleep with him. However, voodoo is not male dominated, and there are priestesses as well as priests. The priests are known as *houngans*, the priestesses as *mambos*.

Phallic dances often accompany voodoo ritual. Women dressed in the black of Baron Samedi assemble in the cemeteries of local villages on the ritually significant All Souls' Day. Clutching phallic symbols, the women perform an outrageously erotic dance that seems to describe the cult's general attitude to Baron Samedi. It is one of defence and control. Samedi embodies the dark passions of the old slave masters and landholders, with a grasping, ever-hungry, sexually demanding and brutal personality.

Voodoo priests organize and orchestrate the complex rituals of the cult. They straddle two worlds, the physical and the spiritual, the living and the dead. Unlike the newly initiated voodoo cultists, the priests are able to remain conscious while the *loa* converse with them yet refrain from full possession. Their central role is as mediators, organizing the summoning of the *loa* and the possessions that follow. The priests' mastery of both black and white magic is necessary so that they can control the powerful and contrary forces of the *loa*, and they are, as a result, commonly believed to live extremely precarious, even dangerous lives. The status of priests in Haitian society reflects this. Both male and female practitioners of voodoo train for years, sometimes decades, in order to become priests. Responsibility for the time-consuming and complex ceremonies is the main reason for this. Any mistake, however small and seemingly insignificant, will not just wreck the ritual but could summon an unwanted and potentially dangerous spirit.

The cult does not just have theological connections with Christianity, but physical ones. A number of *houngans* live a double life as both voodoo magician and practising Catholic priests. *Mambos* may, although rarely, be Catholic nuns. Often, the priest's voodoo alter-ego will be kept secret from his Christian congregation, for although some may not care, there may well be some who do. Secrecy colours various aspects of the cult's activities. Small towns in Jamaica and Haiti will make no secret of their affiliations to the cult, but communities in larger towns, such as Kingston, Port-au-Prince and New Orleans, prefer to keep the cult out of sight. There are quite large voodoo 'underworlds' in these cities, and the general climate of toleration for the religion is high. Public ceremonies in cities are rare, but in rural settlements such meetings occur on Saturdays if possible, although the ceremonies are not organized according to a strict schedule. The participants usually slip off out of town one by one until the entire community is gathered together for the summoning ritual.

More recent Haitian history has witnessed a truly horrific side to voodoo. Used as an instrument of state terror by the regime of postwar dictator 'Papa Doc' Duvalier, voodoo crossed the line. *Houngans* and *mambos* became tangled up in the machinery of government and cynically used their knowledge of the people's religion against those same people. Beyond the spiritual, the very physical and very ruthless secret police, the Tonton Macoutes, enforced Duvalier's rule on Haiti's streets and in its ghettos. Among its ranks were fully fledged voodoo *houngans*.

Zombies

The fear that Haitians have for the magical powers of voodoo sorcerers is immense. Much of that fear stems from the belief in zombies. Long considered by the West to be no more than superstition or at best religious metaphor, the existence of zombies has recently been given much more serious attention. The fear is not of the zombie itself (his or her plight is rather to be pitied) but of 'zombification' itself. Voodoo is a religion in which the role of spirits is crucial; death is seen as part of a bigger picture that is concerned with the evolution of the spirit's existence. Zombification represents the power of an evil sorcerer to halt this natural process by preventing the human spirit from taking up its rightful position and by turning the still-living body into a mindless slave.

Not every *houngan* and *mambo* can create a zombie, the knowledge is severely restricted and is the most secret aspect of voodoo. If the

religion itself can be termed a secret cult, those few experts who practise zombification can be described as forming a cult within a cult.
Spoken of in whispers, this sub-sect is known as the Sect Rouge (Red
Group). Information about the cult is often conflicting, and to account
for these discrepancies, some observers have suggested that there may
be more than one Sect Rouge. Practitioners within the organization are
feared and respected, and few in the voodoo community will talk
openly of them. It is known, however, that they specialize in summoning the older, more dangerous *loa* (known as the *Petro-loa*), which
further increases the respect that people have for them and earns them
a reputation for dark dealings and destruction.

The process of creating a zombie seems to involve the use of a rare
nerve toxin, perhaps taken, as some accounts have suggested, from
certain fish. There have been reports of a powder-like substance being
blown into a person's face and that person dying suddenly soon after.
In these cases the cause of death resembles sudden heart failure. What
follows still remains speculation, but speculation based on the numerous testimonies of survivors. Those who have inhaled this powder
and have been pronounced dead by the medical authorities are placed
in a coffin and buried. But they remain alive, paralysed by the mysterious poison. Within hours, the *houngan* responsible for their 'death'
has them disinterred and marches them off to his estate. In a half-
dead, drug-induced stupor the survivors claim to have been subjected
to a hideous life of brutal slavery, working the fields along with others
similarly afflicted. All willpower, memory and active consciousness
are gone.

One victim of zombification told his story in the American press in
1982. Clairvus Narcisse had died suddenly and mysteriously in 1962
in his hometown of L'Estère on Haiti. Two decades later he returned
to the town with his incredible story. For two years, Narcisse had
lived the living death of a zombie, bound in the service of an evil
houngan.

With a hundred others like him, Narcisse had worked on the
houngan's fields as a mindless slave, until one day the supervisor
failed to administer the zombies' regular dose of drugs. Without it,
some of the zombies regained their senses and realized what had
become of them. Like Narcisse, they rebelled and fled the estate they
had worked on after killing their overseer. Rather than face the
brother he believed had been responsible for organizing his 'mock
death', Narcisse stayed away from the village of L'Estère for another
16 years. Only on receiving news that his brother had died did he
dare to venture back to his home town. His return in 1980 shocked
and astounded his relatives who had seen Narcisse buried almost two
decades previously. Closing the macabre cycle of events, Narcisse
returned to the graveyard in which his body was initially interred and

was able to identify the grave from which he supposedly emerged.

There are numerous stories of zombification practised by some evil *houngan* that was intent on securing for himself an army of pliant and silent farm workers. Whether they are well-rehearsed folk-tales or amazing-but-true accounts, the stories told by zombie victims are *believed* to be true by voodoo initiates. This gives the men and women responsible – the Sect Rouge, *bocor* or simply renegade *houngans* and *mambos* – an incredible aura of mystery and power. Few will question the authority of someone who can turn an innocent victim into a pale shadow, a member of the walking dead. No one knows for certain what is actually happening here, and no one knows who is responsible.

The stories of zombies are not restricted to the voodoo cult, but are also found among the African beliefs, in which voodoo originated. The word 'zombie' is probably derived from the Bantu word *zumbi* or *zombi*, meaning 'enslaved spirit'. In original African lore, a powerful enough sorcerer was able to capture the spirit of a human being or an animal, alive or dead, and force it to work on his behalf. Today the term 'zombie' is used only to describe humans who have had their spirits (or their souls) stolen by an evil sorcerer. Without their soul, without willpower, the victim becomes a mindless servant.

On the lower reaches of the River Congo in Central Africa, the Ndembo also institutionalized a form of symbolic zombification. The society's beliefs centred on death and resurrection. Initiation into the cult involved ritual death followed by a rebirth and reawakening, a common theme in religions around the world. The initiates were prompted by the witch-doctors who ministered the secret society, and they entered into a fit. This trance was called 'dying Ndembo', and in it the candidates were picked up and carried away from the tribe. For many months, sometimes years, the 'dead' individuals were kept separate from the other tribe members and were sent food and supplies by their families.

When the time was right for re-animation, and the witch-doctor had received his payment and a feast had been prepared, the initiates were returned and brought back to life. But the new members of Ndembo were not fully human – they were zombies, half-alive and half-dead. As Sir James Frazer put it:

> At first they pretend to know no one and nothing; they do not even know how to masticate food, and friends have to perform that office for them. They want everything nice that any one uninitiated may have, and beat them if it is not granted, or even struggle and kill people ... Sometimes they carry on the pretence of talking gibberish, and behaving as if they had returned from the spirit-world. After this they are known by another name, peculiar to those who have 'died Ndembo'.

Kenya's Killer Uprising

Relatively few tribal secret societies have had the power to challenge the heavily armed military force of a colonial regime. In Haiti the religion of voodoo helped to inspire the slave rebellion of 1758, which led eventually to the successful achievement of Haitian independence. The Indian Thuggee cult continued to murder travellers under the noses of the British in the nineteenth century and was eventually suppressed. Finally, in 1900 the Chinese secret society calling itself the Righteous Fists of Harmony (or the Boxers), helped to orchestrate a general uprising that aimed to push the colonial powers out of China. The cult and the empress dowager who supported it only just failed in that attempt and were roundly chastised by the combined military forces of the major colonial powers.

These distant events belong to another era of colonial repression, exploitation and injustice. Now a part of history, it was envisaged that the tribal sects that secretly helped to foment and organize such uprisings were also long gone, but events in the post-war period have proved these assumptions wrong. Colonies across the globe were pushing for independence throughout the 1950s and 1960s, either through peaceful channels, or through guerrilla warfare. The way forwards had been lit by the fires of resistance, and a ruthless East African cult called the Mau Mau emerged into this light.

The Mau Mau uprising, known by the British as the Kenyan Emergency, began in 1952 and lasted until 1960. The uprising involved a secret tribal society from the native Kikuyu tribe. Kenya was at that time in the hands of Britain, and the rebellion that the cult attempted was unique in the British experience. Today the details of the movement are still shrouded in mystery, and no satisfactory answers have been forthcoming as to the real origins of the Mau Mau. No one, for example, has been able to provide an adequate explanation of the organization's bizarre title. One theory suggests that it derives from a warning shout, 'Uma! Uma!' (Out! Out!), given by lookouts when government soldiers were seen approaching the meeting hut. This shout could have became almost a password, then an informal title for the society, Mau Mau.

Providing the impulse for the revolt were a number of important factors that seemed to affect the Kikuyu tribe more than any other in Kenya. The working conditions for black farmers had worsened after the Second World War, and their living standards had declined too. At this time, the late 1940s, the minority white population was, however, enjoying a renewed prosperity. Even more significant was a new political and anti-colonial awareness that recognized the injustice of Kenyan society. Blacks were treated as second-class citizens in their own country, and black soldiers who had fought for democracy in foreign lands returned home, adding to this sense of frustration. Unrest broke out around the capital, Nairobi, in 1952, and the situation became serious following the murder of the Kikuyu Senior Chief Waruhiu, a well-respected tribesman who was on very good terms with the British.

A mysterious group of black veterans, calling itself the Forty Group, was active at the time, and these men may have had more influence in the origins of the revolt than has been previously thought. This group of men had joined the British Army in 1940 and sailed off to fight to save the Empire. They returned home with a vision for change.

The Mau Mau movement was established in the late 1940s as an anti-white secret society, which bound its members together with an oath – the Oath of Unity. It exhorted its newly initiated members to kill any opponent of the cult. Oaths had always played a significant part in the tribe's life, but the Mau Mau oath was considered to be unclean, since it was sworn at night, in secret, and was administered by force. Although a traditional *githathi* stone was used for the ceremony, no respectable witch-doctor (known among the Kikuyu as a *mundu mugo*) would administer an oath sworn in this way. Only a sorcerer (*murogi*) would dare to violate the Kikuyu taboos. The ceremony involved anointing the candidate with goat's blood and the ritual biting of a goat's lung. A fee of five shillings had to be paid, and when the oath had been made, the initiate was instructed in the Mau Mau response for identifying another member. 'Where were you circumcised?' a cult member would ask. If the answer was 'I was circumcised at Karimania's with Karimania,' he knew he was talking to a fellow Mau Mau. The Oath of Unity was the first of several oaths that a new member could aspire to take. Other oaths were used by leaders in the field to initiate trusted men into higher and more secret degrees. It seems these were improvised as the local commanders saw fit and that they would sometimes take the form of degrading or perverted acts. One of these oaths ended:

> I shall abide until my death by all the promises I have made this day, I
> shall never disclose our secrets to our enemy nor to anybody who does
> not belong to the movement and if I transgress against any of the vows
> … may this oath kill me.

Although it came to operate under the 'cover' organization of the Kenyan African Union (KAU), in practice the Mau Mau proved to be relatively disorganized. A Nairobi-based central committee and war office functioned as a headquarters and attempted to orchestrate logistics and large-scale strategy. When the Mau Mau command structure failed to live up to expectations, its local leaders were forced to rely on their own initiatives. They often relied on sheer loyalty rather than on any formally assigned rank. Of course, fear played an important part in instilling this loyalty. Deadly oaths and a system of ad hoc punishments, including mutilation and death, were enough to inspire a certain amount of discipline among the Mau Mau foot soldiers. These commanders operated according to their own view of the 'struggle'.

Mau Mau attacks were rarely directed against the security forces, which always out-gunned them. Firearms were rarely used, and they were, in fact, so difficult to obtain that Mau Mau workshops turned out hundreds of homemade shotguns. Fashioned from door bolts and metal pipework, these crude guns were more of a danger to the operator than to a target. Bullets and grenades were also manufactured, and these were of an equally poor quality. This factor may have led the Mau Mau to attack only civilian targets, and that usually meant women and children – with sickening results.

Mau Mau leaders tried to appeal to the whole of the Kikuyu population, but this attempt was doomed to failure. Not only were there Christians among the tribe who would resist any oath-swearing ceremony, there were also those who were loyal to the incumbent government. Many others were appalled by the barbaric acts of violence that the Mau Mau were so casually carrying out. With the tribe split, a great deal of Mau Mau hostility came to be directed against the uninitiated Kikuyu. At the start of 1952 the village of Nyeri in central Kenya suffered an arson attack, and two loyalists were shot and dumped into the River Kirichwa. In only six months 59 blacks loyal to the government had been murdered by the Mau Mau, and white settlers were being harassed and their farms attacked on a regular basis. The movement continued to grow.

Rumours soon reached Nairobi of mass oathing-ceremonies at which up to 800 new Mau Mau were initiated at a time. What really disturbed the authorities, however, were the methods used by the cult. Few of their murders were carried out swiftly and 'cleanly'. Mutilation enhanced the fearful mystique of the brotherhood, but it also alienated many potential recruits. A victim was usually attacked with the favoured Mau Mau blade, the *panga* . Limbs and genitals were customarily severed, and the victim would be finished off by slitting the throat or during the agonies of further mutilation. Soldiers, children, women – none were spared, not even animals. Farms at Timau were raided by the movement in 1952, and the livestock there was brutally attacked with *pangas*. Around 120 cattle and 240 sheep were disembowelled or dismembered and left to die.

In the following year the greatest atrocity of the uprising took place. It grimly illustrated the fanatical and ruthless obsession of the Mau Mau in their struggle. More than a thousand Mau Mau descended on Lari, a village that was home to many Kikuyu who were members of the Home Guard. Again, women and children were the chief victims of the atrocity. Initially cables were hastily thrown around huts and securely tied to prevent the doors from opening. These huts were doused in petrol and set alight. Villagers escaping the individual infernos were caught by armed Mau Mau and hacked to death. In all, 200 huts were burned down killing an untold number of innocent victims, and over a thousand head of cattle were mutilated. While 30 or so villagers survived the ordeal despite terrible wounds, more than 80 were butchered with *pangas*. One woman had seen her own baby decapitated in front of her, and watched a Mau Mau drink its blood; she survived even though her own arm had been cut off at the joint. The chief's eight wives were not spared, and the chief himself was hacked in half by the blood-crazed cultists. As the Lari massacre horrified the world, it also illustrated the futility of the cult's fight. Wavering Kikuyu were now more than ever inclined to join the loyalist cause rather than side with a movement that seemed to discredit itself at every opportunity.

The uprising flourished in the jungles of the Aberdare Mountains and around Mount Kenya, but it could not resist the power of the British authorities. Police, military and civil agencies cooperated to isolate the movement. Identity cards were issued, and Home Guard defence forces, which had previously been armed only with clubs, spears or *panga* machetes, were issued with rifles. Regarded as the overall commander of the Mau Mau society, the activist Jomo Kenyatta was convicted of that charge in 1953. His punishment for masterminding the bloody uprising was seven years' hard labour.

Nairobi had always been a central supply depot for the Mau Mau operating in the wilderness, and a concerted search of the city was able to round up thousands of Mau Mau suspects in 1954. More unorthodox methods of reducing the manpower of the secret society were already in use. Great efforts were made to reverse the oaths set on members, and witch-doctors were employed by the security forces to carry out these 'de-oathing' rituals. Just as *githathi* stones were used by the sorcerers to initiate Kikuyu into the Mau Mau, they were used by the government witch-doctors. Good magic fought evil in the battle for men's loyalties. By reversing the oath, many Mau Mau who had been forced to join the cult could be freed from that solemn vow and could shun the movement.

Mau Mau 'generals' enjoyed a variety of different fates, depending on their conduct during the uprising. General China, for example, the famous Mau Mau leader on Mount Kenya, attempted to help the authorities with planned peace proposals. Following Kenyan independence in 1963, he was given a commission in the Kenyan army. At the other end of the scale was General Kimathi, a psychotic and murderous individual with delusions of grandeur. Convinced that it was his destiny to one day lead the Kikuyu people, Kimathi seized on every opportunity for bloodshed that the Mau Mau struggle presented. Deep in the Aberdare Mountains he organized a despotic guerrilla army, murdering any man who failed to comply with his strict directives. Possible rivals were sent away or killed, and all links with the outside world steadily dwindled away. Kimathi, who proclaimed himself Prime Minister Sir Dedan Kimathi, KCAE, by God Knight Commander of the African Empire, eventually presided over a band of forest fighters who swapped their murderous attacks on civilians for a life of harsh survival in the wilderness. Hunted relentlessly by the police officer Ian Henderson, Kimathi was eventually caught in October 1956, sentenced to death and executed.

Although the state of emergency that had been declared in 1952 was not lifted until 1960, the Mau Mau had been virtually suppressed by the end of 1956. More than 11,000 Mau Mau insurgents had been killed in action, while another 1000 were formally executed. In its turn, the secret society had murdered around 2000 black and 32 white civilians, and been responsible for the deaths of approximately 600 members of the security forces. Many of these had been native Home Guard volunteers, and a few – 63 – were white soldiers and policemen. Since 1963 and independence, Kenya has enjoyed relative peace and stability, although a recent movement has put itself in direct opposition to the government. It seems, however, that Kenya has permanently exorcised the terrible spectre of the Mau Mau society. Jomo Kenyatta, nominal leader of the resistance movement, became the first prime minister of Kenya and was joined in government by hardened Mau Mau veterans who were able to win seats in the country's National Assembly.

Unfortunately, the fever that gripped Kenya during the terrible years of the Mau Mau uprising could and did strike again. In 1995, across Lake Victoria, the nations of Rwanda and Burundi were devastated by a series of genocidal massacres that defied human comprehension. There had been massacres in 1972 and 1988, but not on such a vast scale. No sinister cult or society was to blame for the beatings, beheadings, mutilations and mass-murders; nor was a single tribal group or revolutionary organization responsible. The senseless massacres were driven by a chaotic frenzy of jealousy, fear and power. Both Tutsi and Hutu tribes – the two dominant ethnic divisions in the more seriously afflicted nation, Rwanda – were involved. But the killings constituted neither a war nor a revolution. Civilians picked up machetes, just as the Mau Mau had done 40 years previously, and murdered their neighbours.

CHAPTER SEVEN

Horsemen of the Apocalypse

> And I looked, and behold a pale horse: and his name that sat on him
> was Death, and Hell followed with him. And power was given unto
> them over the fourth part of the earth, to kill with sword, and with
> hunger, and with death, and with the beasts of the earth.

BOOK OF REVELATION 6:8

Across the night skies of the world a bright comet plunged majesti-
cally. Each evening the celestial wanderer appeared to have shifted
further over in the sky. Eventually it would disappear altogether, to
return thousands of years hence. It was the spring of 1997 and the
comet Hale-Bopp was making news. This was one of the brightest and
most visible comets to have appeared in the heavens for a long time.
Traditionally, comets have been regarded as omens of bad fortune and
of catastrophe. To the ancients, who had learned to follow the ordered
rhythms of the night sky, the comet seemed to appear from nowhere
and cut right through the constellations and alignments that meant so
much to the earlier astronomers. Strangely, Hale-Bopp, emerging from
the darkness of the stellar void at the brink of the second millennium,
was to be no different.

Salvation through Suicide

On 27 March 1997 the bodies of 39 men and women were discovered
in an opulent mansion in San Diego, California. In three shifts, these
people had killed themselves with a mix of vodka, barbiturates and
suffocation. As stunned investigators moved through the building,
corpses could be seen at peace laying on beds. All were middle-class,
educated followers of a tall, balding man called Marshall H. Applewhite. All wore dark clothing and had Nike sports trainers on their
feet. Each lay in peace with a purple shroud folded into a triangle
across their chests. Police attempting to discover who these people
were and why they had killed themselves were amazed to find extensive material on their suicidal beliefs not just in print, but also on
video tape and on the Internet.

It transpired that the victims were the members of an exotic religious group, which combined *Star Trek*-like science fiction with a fundamental belief in ufology and the afterlife. Each committed member believed that he or she – 21 of the corpses were women – was on a mission to abandon the earthly 'vehicles' or 'containers' for the next stage in their life, which was to be found out there in the cosmos. Death would be the trigger that would metamorphose the followers from mundane, earth-bound caterpillars into cosmic butterflies. The group became convinced that the appearance of the Hale-Bopp comet was the marker for which they had long been waiting. According to their beliefs, a UFO was trailing the comet, and it was to that alien spacecraft that they believed they would go when they died.

The cult ran an Internet web-site, *Higher Source*, which explained their beliefs: 'Our 22 years of classroom here on planet Earth is finally coming to conclusion – "graduation" from the Human Evolutionary Level. We are happily prepared to go with [the spaceship's] crew.' One of the Internet pages proudly declared, over a star-filled background, that 'Hale-Bopp Brings Closure to Heaven's Gate. As was promised – the keys to Heaven's Gate are here again'. The cult thus became known as Heaven's Gate, although it had previously gone by several other names in its nomadic, 20-year history.

Such was the scale of the mass-suicide that President Clinton publicly described the deaths as sickening, heartbreaking and shocking. Like many others, including the bewildered families of the victims, Clinton vowed to find out every scrap of information about Heaven's Gate and to discover exactly what had motivated its adherents to commit suicide. Psychologists have long been aware that suicide is the last retreat for the desperate, riven by depression brought on by loneliness, guilt, fear or other emotions – but religious fervour? To kill oneself in order to reach an afterlife that exists only on the evidence of one man's – Applewhite's – say-so, must have required the most intense faith and devotion. Heaven's Gate is not alone in the tragedy of its demise – there have been other death-obsessed cults – but it is notable for the peculiar reasoning behind it. For the first time the UFO-cult, which began in the 1960s, matured in the 1970s and received media attention in the late 1980s and early 1990s, has come of age. Heaven's Gate has taken ufology into the murky realm of apocalyptic religion, alongside the Christian Branch Davidian sect, the Japanese cult Aum Supreme Truth, the People's Temple of Reverend Jim Jones and the Swiss Order of the Solar Temple. These particular religious cults have become notorious for the deaths that they have inspired. Other cults have been in the media limelight at infrequent intervals. Both the Children of God (which has been accused of engaging in child abuse) and the Church of Scientology are cults. Many ex-members and relatives of current members would categorize them, and others of that ilk, as 'mind-control cults'. Although these organizations occasionally engage in questionable activities, we are concerned here with those groups that break even those boundaries – that go beyond, into realms of human terror and mass death.

How can a religion inspire such devotion? Some would answer that misguided faith in the beliefs of such an 'alternative' religion is the only factor. Others warily declare that there is often a more sinister force at work. The parents of one Heaven's Gate member grimly described the deaths as 'one suicide and 38 murders'. Ian Haworth of the London-based Cult Information Centre believes that any suicide inspired by a cult is 'best described as murder'. But what is a 'cult'? And how can suicide be described as murder? Are these groups really religions or are they something else entirely?

To find out what kind of powerful force grips these followers, it is necessary to look below the all-too deceptive surface of the cult. Many of those who were acquainted with the Heaven's Gate members saw them as a polite and well-educated group of computer enthusiasts. Their web-site advertised the cult and its message to people across the globe, and they were actively involved in designing web-sites for other organizations. In addition, the group had recently completed a screenplay entitled *Beyond Human: Return to the Next Level*, which was pitched at several leading movie studios. NBC television showed some initial interest in the science fiction tale of evil reptilian aliens that were in conflict with good aliens for the control of Earth and the 'mother-ship'. They later lost interest. Underneath the veneer of computer-literate, business-minded extroverts, the group smacked of an antiseptic and well-disciplined regime with Applewhite at its head.

An atmosphere had been cultivated of 'personal development and concerted effort', and the work they were doing on the Internet became obsessive. Neither smoking nor drinking was allowed, and there was a conscious repression of gender, sex and sexuality. For this their leader was responsible. Applewhite's psychological inadequacies became the religious doctrine of his followers. A repressed homosexual, Applewhite could never come to terms with his sexuality, and in the 1970s he checked into a clinic begging to be 'cured'. When his problem became acute, the cult leader castrated himself, later persuading several of his male devotees to do likewise. He reasoned that castration was an essential step to the 'Next Level'. His persuasive powers were put to an even more sickening task: to convince the men and women who hung on his every word to kill themselves on his word alone. One of the group, in a pre-suicide video tape, expressed trepidation, if not outright fear, at the pact that the 39 men and women had made: 'Maybe they're crazy for all I know. But I don't have any choice but to go for it, because I've been on this planet for 31 years and there's nothing here for me.'

Applewhite's charisma was the force that drove the Heaven's Gate group, not team spirit or a true belief in the Next Level. Without 'King Do' (as he styled himself), the cult would have fallen apart. In this it resembled many other fringe religions that have spectacularly made the headlines in the past few decades. In an isolated, monastic setting, where the norms of society are replaced by the dictates of the leader, the word of that charismatic leader becomes law. With few exceptions, he is privy to the ear of God, or to other mystical secrets that set him apart from the rest of humanity. Because he has elevated himself to a semi-divine position, his followers will often obey any command, however repellent to their nature. Suicide ranks as one of the most extreme of these commands.

Mass-suicides are not a common occurrence, and have involved a large number of Americans only twice – the Heaven's Gate suicide on 27 March 1997 and the horrific demise of 383 Americans in the People's Temple of Jim Jones on 19 November 1978. The People's Temple episode shocked the world. No cult, before or since, has ever perpetrated such a fantastic and deadly crime against its own members. In all, 917 people of various nationalities died for the Reverend James Thurman Jones in a single day. Not all had committed suicide. The disturbing evidence gathered by the investigators on the scene at a site called 'Jonestown' in Guyana suggested that perhaps as few as 200 members of the People's Temple had killed themselves voluntarily, while the rest were executed or forced at gun-point to drink cyanide-laced Kool Aid. The scale of the event is difficult to comprehend, even as a massacre of innocent victims, which it certainly was not. That it was a religious act and had all the overtones of an unearthly suicide pact, made it all the more incomprehensible.

Jim Jones was not an ordained priest and had not even received any formal ecclesiastical training. Marxism was his single obsession, and he had joined the American Communist Party back in the 1950s. With the help of his wife, Marcie, Jones raised a multi-racial family of seven adopted children, and they accompanied him into the mountains of northern California in 1961. His apocalyptic visions of a coming holocaust coincided with the publication of a minor article that named several 'safe-haven' locations that would provide shelter from the effects of a nuclear holocaust. The mountain town of Ukiah, in a supposedly 'apocalypse-proof' corner of the state, became Jim Jones' first secure retreat. His successes there, preaching racial equality and social fairness through the vehicle of Christianity, persuaded him to return to the big cities and to continue recruiting from the poorest and most disaffected minorities.

In San Francisco Jones established his People's Temple, a church that recruited mainly people from the non-white minorities who were attracted to its false promise of a Christian paradise. Jones's divine pledge to elevate his followers to the side of Jesus Christ proved to be a twisted deception – he was never a devout Christian; he was a devout Marxist. The People's Temple was to be an adventurous experiment in Marxist philosophy masquerading as apocalyptic Christianity. For this cruel demagogue, Christianity was nothing more than an effective method of recruitment, hooking in society's poorest and most desperate souls and slowly eroding their Christian beliefs, while feeding them a carefully prepared diet of Marxist doctrine.

His church in San Francisco and a second that was established in Los Angeles prospered and were well received by the local authorities, who commended the attention he paid to the poverty-stricken minorities. Politicians were not embarrassed to be seen with the Reverend Jones, and the then vice-president, Walter Mondale, even entertained the proselytizing preacher on board his private jet. In order to gain favours from the politicians of San Francisco, Jones got his followers out on the streets soliciting votes for whoever would help him. At one point, he was even able to secure the chairmanship of the city's housing authority. His public involvement in politics reached a crescendo in 1976 when he joined Rosalyn Carter on stage at the opening of the San Francisco Democratic Party headquarters. The media were not taken in by this short, slightly overweight and ever-smiling preacher, however, and he never enjoyed the public acclaim he sought.

In keeping with other religious cult leaders, Jones had a very powerful charismatic personality, and the poor members of his church willingly gave up all they had. Jones became very wealthy from these donations, a situation that made a mockery of his position as the head of a church of struggling, poverty-stricken followers. Wearing sunglasses and accompanied at all times by a bodyguard a dozen strong, Jones started to isolate himself from his loyal congregation. It was estimated that his annual income at this time was over £150,000. Jones's charismatic leadership went hand in hand with a strict, authoritarian regime that including beatings, demanding and tiring work schedules and the bizarre use of boxing matches as punishment. Despite a healthy membership of several thousand, the People's Temple eventually became entangled in financial shenanigans, and Jones was forced to relocate abroad. He chose a sprawling estate at Kaituma in the South American country of Guyana and named it 'Jonestown'.

Today that name is associated with the images of slaughter on a massive scale, slaughter calmly directed by one tyrannical man. The strict lifestyle that had begun in California intensified in the jungle encampment, and actions deemed to be 'non-positive' were rewarded with physical abuse. Access out of Jonestown was strictly controlled. The nuclear catastrophe that Jones was now predicting led him to initiate this harsh regime of pain and punishment. Jones believed that only through strict conditioning could his followers survive the end of the world. Cut off from the checks and balances of civilization, Jones stumbled along the road to insanity, often adopting a thick Russian accent, accusing the CIA of poisoning his food and declaring over the camp's loudspeaker system that attacks were imminent. More than once Jones believed himself to be Lenin, the revered figurehead of the communist Soviet Union. Later Jones styled himself a messiah of Lenin-like proportions, and his commitment and belief in the imminent nuclear destruction fuelled his paranoia and his rigid domination of the Jonestown cult members.

At its height, the Jonestown camp was home to around 1200 cult members, but how many of these wanted to leave and were forcibly held there against their will is uncertain. Certainly, the United States became very alarmed at reports reaching Washington from Guyana. The Jonestown massacre was actually sparked off by the arrival of an American congressman, Leo Ryan, who had travelled to Guyana, together with four journalists, to investigate for himself the allegations that US citizens were being held there. Jones could not allow them to leave the camp alive, and all five were gunned down as they tried to escape. He had to prevent them from telling the outside world what they had seen at Jonestown. That was on 18 November 1978.

When soldiers from the Guyana national army and other American agents flew into Jonestown the next day, the sight that greeted them numbed the senses. Hundreds upon hundreds of corpses lay piled in gardens and lanes in row after row, some on top of others. Those that hadn't been poisoned had been shot. Unbelievably, though, there *were* survivors. The harrowing accounts they were able to give painted a terrifying picture of chaos, fear and death. Following the murder of Leo Ryan, Jim Jones had suddenly initiated his unholy campaign of ritual murder. Poisons (a mixture of cyanide and tranquillizers) were mixed with Kool Aid by the commune doctor and his assistant and handed over to the willing cult members. Jones spoke on the loudspeakers to encourage mothers to serve the deadly cocktail to their children, and other announcements earnestly proclaimed the dignity of the coming death and resurrection. Everywhere the faithful were following their prophet's commands, dressing up in their best clothes and committing suicide. They blindly did as the fanatical and desperate Reverend Jones demanded. Others were not convinced. All along they had nurtured reservations about, if not open hostility to, the living hell that the People's Temple had become. They tried to flee into the jungle that Jones had told everyone was a death-trap, filled with snakes and other deadly beasts. Only a handful managed to evade Jones's security guards. Those that were caught were forced at gun point to drink the cyanide poison or they were simply shot to death as they ran. Loyal to the end, Jones's guards finally shot themselves in the head.

The Reverend James Thurman Jones, who had himself taken a fatal dose of the poison, thus became known as one of the world's most twisted cult leaders, a sadistic megalomaniac, commanding the loyalty of hundreds of followers. Many followed him into death, while a tiny élite massacred the hundreds remaining. It was done in the name of religion – and it became a shocking spectre of things to come. Cults were proliferating throughout America and other nations of the industrialized West in the 1970s. Would there be more Jonestowns? Thankfully, no (at least not on such a horrific scale). Would there be more James Thurmans? Sadly, yes.

One such fanatical and charismatic leader was Joseph Di Mambro, the head of the Order of the Solar Temple. This bizarre group of French-speakers worshipped Di Mambro as the actual reincarnation of a Knight Templar, one of the mystical warrior-monks who fought in the crusades. Dressed in the imposing regalia of a medieval knight, Di Mambro wielded not just *any* sword, but Excalibur, the sword of Arthur Pendragon, King Arthur of the Celtic romances. A French-Canadian, who was born in France during the 1920s, Di Mambro had had a prosperous career as a jeweller and businessman until charges of fraud brought the enterprise crashing down around him. Throughout the late 1970s he was responsible for establishing not one but two religious cults. In 1974 the Centre for the Study of the New Age was formed in Switzerland and was relocated to Collonges-sous-Saleve, where its headquarters, known as The Pyramid, were eventually burned down in mysterious circumstances. Five years after founding his first spiritual group, Di Mambro founded another, the Golden Way, a mystical, sun-orientated cult, which owed its name to the nineteenth-century cult of magicians and spiritualists called the Order of the Golden Dawn. Di Mambro's group, the Golden Way, prospered in the small town of Annemasse in Switzerland. In 1982 the cult was reorganized into individual cells called Club Amenta, which consisted of both initiates and the higher grade adepts. Other cells established in Canada were called Club Archedia, and these, as well as those in Switzerland were managed by Di Mambro's wife, Jocelyn.

It was at Annemasse that Di Mambro first met the veteran paratrooper and medical doctor Luc Jouret. Jouret had long been fascinated with homeopathic medicine and New Age thinking. An interest in Eastern mysticism led Jouret to join the Golden Circle, and he proved to be an able orator, who, an authority on his subject, gave many talks at both the Swiss and Canadian clubs. The two men joined forces in 1984 to create a new group, an occult order combining solar mysticism with all the occult heritage ascribed to the medieval Knights Templar. This secret cult was the *Ordre International Chevaleresque Tradition Solaire* (Order of the International Knights of the Sun, OICTS). It was from this short-lived organization that *Le Temple de*

Soleil, the more popularly known Order of the Solar Temple, was created and finally destroyed itself in two headline-grabbing mass-suicides in the mid-1990s. The new obsession was with the Knights Templars, the warrior order that fought so valiantly in the crusades. The Templars were not ordinary knights, but knights who had taken vows of monasticism. They lived in seclusion, in the harsh lifestyle that was rarely seen outside a monastery, and had a fierce reputation as warriors of god. The history of the Knights Templar ended ignominiously, with the vast wealth and extensive holdings of the order being seized by the French king. Witchcraft, satanism, black magic and Eastern mystical practices were ascribed to the Order, and although many of these allegations were untrue, they proved to be sufficiently damning to legitimize the destruction of the order. Just how 'mystical' the Knights Templar actually were remains a mystery, and numerous books have been written in recent years to try to locate the source of these wild rumours. Certainly the Templars earned for themselves a reputation that long outlived their earthly existence.

Occult groups throughout history have taken on board the name and mystique of the Knights Templars. Freemasonry has not hesitated to continue this tradition – in English Freemasonry, for example, a branch called the Knights Templar is reserved solely for practising Christians – but occult groups of all shapes and sizes have adopted Templar attributes. From Chapter 2 we have seen how Adolf Lanz created his own Aryan religion that went under the name of the *Ordo Novi Templi* (Order of the New Templars), even though there was no connection whatsoever between his racist cult and the Christian warrior brotherhood he so admired.

Like Adolf Lanz, Jouret claimed that his Solar Temple was a lineal descendant from the Knights Templar and that both past and present incarnations recognized the same charter. Unlike the medieval Order, however, Luc Jouret's theories included a great deal of fire and sun worship. In particular, he believed that the imminent apocalypse would engulf the entire population of mankind in fire, just as the leaders of the Knights Templars had been burned at the stake on an island in the middle of the River Seine. Recordings of his lectures in Switzerland and Canada were offered for sale in the cult's journal, a magazine entitled *Excalibur*. Fundamental to Jouret's theories was a belief in regeneration through fire. Fire was to be the final salvation of the cult's membership, freeing them for the onward journey into the afterlife that awaited them. Just as the Heaven's Gate cultists were destined for some far distant world in the cosmos, Jouret claimed that he was, in fact, a time traveller capable of leading the Solar Temple worshippers across the void to a planet orbiting the star Sirius. It was there that they would eventually be reborn as perfect beings. 'Liberation is not where human beings think it is,' declared Luc Jouret. 'Death can represent an essential stage of life.'

The Solar Temple recruits were from France, from Canada and from Switzerland, and they were generally affluent individuals who willingly handed over their property and finances to the cult. They constituted a membership numbering at least 500 and, according to some estimates, as many as 3000, including affiliated members. All the funds that had been donated were reinvested by Di Mambro and amounted in the end to a considerable fortune. The willing members, entranced by Jouret's persuasiveness, were not innocent youths, but level-headed businessmen, journalists and even government officials. What they made of his apocalyptic prophesies and astral journeys is not known, but they were certainly as attracted to the cult's ritual as any Freemason is to his ceremonies. The idea of being knighted by Jouret in the full regalia of a medieval Templar, with a sword named Excalibur and a sacred chalice, did not faze the candidates in the least.

Like several cult leaders, including Jim Jones, Joseph Di Mambro was heavily involved in financial mismanagement. Money made from his illegal activities was laundered through the Solar Temple, and these 'activities' included gun-running. Although Di Mambro remained the brains behind the Solar Temple and its lucrative business dealings in particular, Luc Jouret masterminded much of the cult's theological doctrine. Part of this doctrine advocated mass-suicide. The apocalyptic bent to the religion almost demanded some kind of forthcoming 'ordeal' for the 'faithful', and, as for the Heaven's Gate believers, that ordeal was death, followed by resurrection and a new life among the stars. Jouret's attempt to orchestrate his first cult suicide in the spring of 1993 failed when he was arrested in Canada on firearms charges. But the momentum of the cult, its leaders and devotees could not be stopped by so insignificant an obstacle. The murders began just over a year later, in September 1994.

Di Mambro sincerely believed that his 12-year-old daughter, whom he had named Emanuelle, was not an ordinary mortal but was born of divine conception. Great things were expected of her: she was to have an important role in the cult, thereby ensuring its spiritual future. Because Emanuelle was the unique child of God, Di Mambro was outraged when two Canadian members of the order named their newborn son Emanuelle. Di Mambro decreed that this boy was the Antichrist and must be destroyed. The couple, Toni and Nikki Dutoit, were approached by fanatical members of the order at their home near Montreal and stabbed to death. Three-month-old Emanuelle Dutoit was ritually murdered – the attackers drove a stake through his heart. This horrific murder provided Jouret and Di Mambro with the catalyst to initiate Armageddon. The cult was doomed by its actions and damned by its leaders.

The Dutoits' killers, Joel Egger and Dominique Bellaton, were discovered several days later. Both had taken an overdose of drugs and activated one of Jouret's delayed-action fire-bombs. At around the same time almost all of the Solar Temple's membership committed ritual suicide. On 5 October 1994, at the cult's headquarters in the Swiss town of Chiery, 23 cultists, including one child, were found dead. All were wearing elaborate ceremonial robes in the order's colours of white, red, gold and black, and their bodies arranged on the ground as if imitating the radial points of an occult star. They had been either shot or drugged, and although Jouret had provided a fire-bomb for this occasion, too, it failed to detonate, leaving the Swiss police with a perplexing amount of evidence to examine.

Meanwhile, another mass-suicide was taking place further south at Granges-sur-Salvan. Two buildings owned by the Solar Temple were thoroughly burned to the ground, but police were able to determine that 25 people had perished in or before the fire. Using dental records the investigators were able to identify the charred corpses of both Joseph Di Mambro and Luc Jouret among the dead. Di Mambro and 12 of his close disciples had attended a 'Last Supper' together the day before the killings. The intentions of the dead had been mailed to French and Swiss authorities by a cult member named Patrick Vuarnet. In line with the order's astral doctrine, they were bound for a planet orbiting Sirius. The cult was dead and the apocalypse so long pre-dicted by it had come at last.

Just as at Jonestown 14 years earlier, the suicides proved, under closer scrutiny, to be nothing of the kind. Drugs seem to have been forcibly administered in some cases, and reluctant members were shot. One can only imagine those last terror-stricken moments. The bravest and most devout willingly accepting death, others perhaps bullied or persuaded, but the majority refusing to the end, with fierce shouting and panic. The ugly reality of the situation perhaps dawned on them for the first time. Silence would have followed the gunfire as the last few arranged the bodies in a star shape and triggered the delayed fire-bomb. Then they blew out their own brains. The ferocity of the mur-ders perplexed the local authorities. Those gunned down at Chiery had been repeatedly shot in the head, and then hooded with plastic bags. One investigator believed that one of the victims had first been smothered and his body then peppered with bullets.

Near Grenoble in the French Alps a chilling epilogue to the cult sur-faced in a forest clearing only two days before Christmas 1995. A total of 16 corpses was discovered. All had been drugged and then burned almost beyond recognition; some had been shot. As at Chiery, the corpses had been arranged in the shape of a star, and one newspaper article claimed that two of the cultists, both police officers, had orga-nized the mass-murder. The authorities believed that two men shot the drugged cult members and, after laying out the bodies, doused them in petrol and set them alight. Finally, they shot themselves. With members of the cult still alive in Canada, France and Switzerland, we can expect to hear of further such incidents from time to time. The suicide strategy was not an overwhelming blitz, as it first appeared, but a long-term campaign. As recently as 23 March 1997 five cult members committed suicide at a house in Quebec. A Jouret-style incendiary device then detonated, setting it alight. Fortunately, there were survivors this time. A girl and two boys, both heavily drugged, were found behind the house. A suicide note discovered at the scene spoke of a 'departure', confirming the theory that the Solar Temple still has loyal devotees committed to following their dead comrades.

Suicide merges with slaughter to confound the investigating authorities. Only the tiniest minority of fringe religions have resorted to ritual suicide in order to achieve notoriety, but the term 'suicide' may be a highly inappropriate term. One definition of suicide is 'the act of killing oneself intentionally', and the so-called suicides of Heaven's Gate, Jonestown and the Solar Temple lie uneasily within this definition. In most cases the deaths are 'assisted' with drugs and/or guns supplied by the cult. The facts that the victim is both isolated from society and surrounded by individuals fanatically propounding suicide also complicates the matter. Peer pressure may escalate to bullying, threats and murder. How many were shot voluntarily? How many participated in the ceremonies knowing that it would end in mass-suicide? Cult 'suicide' is now generally considered to be a form of murder.

Waco

In recent years one cult massacre has become a beacon for all sides in the debate about cults. Circumstances surrounding the deaths of 80 members of the Branch Davidian sect at Waco in Texas are still shrouded in controversy. A war of words has raged between the Federal authorities on one side and the survivors of the siege and their many supporters on the other in a long running argument over what actually took place on 19 April 1993. The fire that engulfed the compound at Waco and ended the lives of the 80 inhabitants has been blamed on the FBI by the survivors. The FBI have vigorously denied this allegation and insist that the Branch Davidians set fire to their own compound in order to bring about their own destruction – that it was, in fact, a case of mass-suicide. The Waco incident highlights many of the problems confronting a law enforcement authority that has to deal with a 'cult'.

Most importantly, it raises the questions 'What is a cult?' and 'Why are only those organizations mentioned in this chapter labelled as such?' The word 'cult' has inherent connotations of evil, of illegality and of fakery, connotations for which the media must take at least some of the blame. The media has perpetuated a great deal of misunderstanding about the existence of cults in the modern world, but minority religions themselves have seriously failed to address their own public image. Some of these groups are catching up quickly. Both the Children of God movement and the Church of Scientology have learned the hard way that public opinion must be considered – even by a religious organization.

There are many conflicting meanings attributed to the word 'cult', although they usually associate the relevant group with a minority or alternative religion or with a religious schism. The term is used more specifically in *Brotherhoods of Fear* to describe small religious groups that are dominated by a charismatic leadership. This leadership enjoys extreme mental, physical and emotional control over its membership. Key words here are 'extreme' and 'control'. All religions in some way modify – or hope to modify – a person's behaviour, but the cult specifically manipulates its members in order to alter their behaviour. The force for change comes from without not from within. The spiritual element of more traditional religions, that inner part of the worshipper that connects him with God and provides the thrust of his motivation, is often noticeably absent. In its place is often a subtle (or not so subtle) set of manipulatory techniques. These techniques include:

1 Restricted access to the mundane world outside the cult.

2 Restricted access to information about the mundane world outside the cult.

3 Freedom to quit the cult is curtailed through:
* Portrayal of the mundane world as evil;
* Cultivation of belief that God will punish those who quit the cult;
* Cultivation of belief that only cult members will survive the coming Armageddon.

4 Control of behaviour through:
* Humiliation and public embarrassment;
* Use of confessions;
* Portrayal of family and friends as hostile (or even evil);
* Elimination of privacy and of private ownership of property.

5 Control of emotion, thought and belief through:
* Tiring work schedules;
* Endless repetition of prayers/sayings/mantras;
* Auto-hypnotic exercises;
* Restricted sleep periods;
* Creation of a mood of fear, uncertainty and tension;
* Cultivation of loyalty and worship of the leadership.

Note that some legitimate religious communities may, on the surface at least, resemble such a cult. A Christian monastery demands a very rigorous lifestyle from those who decide to join, and hard physical work is alternated with frequent attendance at prayer, long and monotonous chanting, the abandonment of the trappings of the mundane world and isolation from that mundane world. But a monastery is not a cult. Its leadership does not require fanatical loyalty nor does it try to prevent a disillusioned member from leaving or pit the community against the mundane world. Not all minority religions are cults by virtue of their size, and not all religious communities are cult headquarters. Our definition hinges on the control wielded by the leadership – and specifically on *mind* control. We could easily qualify our working definition of these cults by terming them 'mind-control cults', as opposed to New Age religious cults or Christian sects.

The Branch Davidian cult was an off-shoot of Christian Seventh Day Adventism, and in the 1980s, under the domination of David Koresh, it took on all the trappings of a mind-control cult. It began life in 1929 as an innocuous and quite harmless Christian movement, however, and no one could have foreseen the controversy and pain that the organization would cause some 64 years later. Its founder, a Bulgarian-born immigrant to the United States named Victor Houteff, had decided that the half a million Seventh Day Adventists had become too complacent. Houteff claimed that he was the 'prophet from the east' (eastern Europe, at any rate), who would oversee the selection of 144,000 Servants of God. These core believers would form his new religion and carry it back to Israel. In the Holy Land the members of his new religion would await the coming of Judgement Day, when they would enter into Paradise. Because the Jewish religion asserted that the Kingdom of David would be returned to Israel, Houteff named his new movement the Davidians. From a biblical quote, 'Behold I will bring forth my servant, the Branch,' he created the name Branch Davidians that has remained with the group until the present.

In 1935 Houteff established the Branch Davidian community near Waco, Texas, and named it Mount Carmel. After his death in 1955 the community became disillusioned, and many members decided to quit. During the 1960s and 1970s, however, under the leadership of Ben and Lois Roden, the fortunes of the group began to pick up. Three years after Ben died in 1978 an eager young disciple of the Branch Davidian movement joined the community and began to build a close relationship with the ageing Lois Roden. When she died in her late sixties in 1986, this young man, Vernon Howell, became her designated successor, much to the chagrin of her son, George. Vernon had actually attacked George Roden's ranch with an armed gang and in the ensuing fight had shot him. Roden survived but was committed to a mental hospital, leaving the leadership of the Waco community open to Howell. Vernon Howell changed his name to David Koresh and began radically to remodel the small community.

He took a wife, Rachel Jones, the 14-year-old daughter of a Branch Davidian member, and they soon had a child. He then married his wife's 12-year-old sister, Michelle, as well as three adult women. Koresh claimed to be receiving 'messages from God', which legitimized any decree he cared to make. His momentous declaration proved to be the beginning of the end for Mount Carmel and its 80 inhabitants. The cult leader proclaimed that he was the Lamb of God and the recipient of the Seventh Seal, the final message from God before the Apocalypse. He was an angel to whom God spoke directly, and his word was the word of God. Devoutly religious people who believed themselves to be on a divine mission, the Waco worshippers comfortably accepted Koresh's statements as truth. According to the Branch Davidian belief, Koresh was only reinforcing what Victor Houteff had originally set out in 1929.

According to a number of former cult members who had left the Branch Davidians through fear and disillusionment, Koresh was actually a ruthless and paranoid egomaniac who was relentlessly pushing the commune to destruction. Two subjects were fundamental to the prophet's fanatical paranoia: the right to bear arms and the wrath of an evil, unsympathetic and dangerous government. It was Koresh's obsession with firearms that first put agents from the Bureau of Alcohol, Tobacco and Firearms (ATF) onto the trail of the Waco cultists. It would cause the bloody slaughter of 80 of his followers, and became an article of faith permeating all other aspects of life at Mount Carmel.

His élite guard was known as the Mighty Men, named after the *gibborim* (mighty men) of the Old Testament, a warrior brotherhood that fought in the service of King David. They continually carried out combat exercises, weapons drills and physical training. Constantly under construction was a network of tunnels, which were intended to be used for escape or retreat during the Apocalypse. At night the 20 Mighty Men slept with loaded weapons by their beds. Other items of paramilitary equipment were being stockpiled for some future 'military-type operation'. Tactical vests, gas masks, radios and police-band scanners, binoculars and night-vision goggles all featured in Koresh's procurement lists.

The Branch Davidian commune at Waco would never have come to public attention had not the FBI stumbled on Koresh's massive arms procurement operation in 1992. Not only had the group amassed a couple of dozen handguns and rifles, but they had stockpiled over a hundred M16 assault rifles, hand grenade casings and explosives for the grenades as well as the manufacture of homemade bombs. Neighbours regularly heard gunfire from the Mount Carmel firing range, and one witness even saw a test bomb being detonated. The question that the FBI and ATF wanted answered was: What did Koresh plan to *do* with this fire-power?

Investigators did not have to look too far for an explanation. Koresh himself openly explained to a Waco social worker that the world was about to come to an end and that when he 'revealed' himself the LA riots of that year would pale into insignificance in comparison with what would happen at Waco. In his prophesied 'military-type opera- tion' all the 'non-believers' would suffer. The cult worshipped guns. Most of the men bore arms for 24 hours a day, and Koresh was no exception – he always carried an Austrian-made Glock 9mm handgun around with him. Movies about the Vietnam War were played over and over again as a way of conditioning the cult members. David Koresh had a fascination with the Vietnam War as portrayed by popu- lar Hollywood movies – he likened the Mount Carmel camp to a US Marine outpost deep in enemy territory. The men were all eligible for guard duty, and slits in the walls provided effective fields of fire if they were ever needed. The four-storey-high water-tower in the centre of the complex provided the commune with an excellent guard post. Intruders were to be shot.

The male members of the sect were usually separated from the females and were forced to remain celibate. Koresh, however, did not follow any such restriction. His sexual appetite was regularly sated on the women and girls of the cult. Since the marriages of all new mem- bers were annulled by Koresh when they entered the community, he was free to sleep with whomever he chose. His attentions ranged from one woman to another and, according to ex-members of the cult, from the teenagers in the group to even younger girls. One witness claimed that Koresh had fathered at least 15 children by different women and girls, one of whom was 12 years old when she gave birth. The leader did not have to force himself onto the female membership – they adored him and felt that his attentions were flattering. Claiming to be the Messiah, Koresh was able to demand anything and be sure of total compliance. Husbands watched their wives go to him; mothers saw their young daughters go to him. In one disturbing instance a mother had willingly left her ten-year-old daughter alone with the cult leader in a Waco motel room. He sexually molested her. The families that moved to Mount Carmel were consciously split up by the leader, and their loyalties and love for one another were redirected towards him- self alone. He was the father figure of the cult's children and the self- appointed husband of the women. The 'House of David' was a term used in the cult to describe his 'harem' of women and girls, and according to Koresh's unfathomable biblical interpretations, he was entitled to take up to 140 wives.

His absolute power over his faithful followers turned into abuse – sexual, psychological and physical. Primitive living conditions at the camp meant that on any given day, someone was always sick. There was no running water, hot or cold; there was no well, no flushing toilets and no established system for preparing food. The kinds of food allowed for meals varied from chicken or stew to popcorn or fruit. However, Koresh's unstable personality led him constantly to vary the diet, banning some foods one day and allowing them the next. Denial of food became a useful method of discipline for the cult leader. He, of course, never went without. Malnutrition for the inhabitants was inevitable, and anyone who suggested visiting the Waco doctor was severely reprimanded by Koresh. He did not want his worshippers to expose his mistreatment or transfer their need to another person. Punishments for children included severe beatings on children as young as eight months old, and these beatings were sometimes so severe that bruises and bloody cuts were inflicted. Koresh's own son, Cyrus, was systematically and brutally beaten for the smallest thing – he was to receive no special treatment. Sometimes a child that had broken some cult directive was forced into the camp sewage pit to think about the offence.

Further investigations made by the local authority convinced it to act on the information that it had been receiving. Koresh believed himself to be Jesus Christ, the Lamb of God, the long-awaited Saviour of mankind. In truth, he was a monstrous paedophile, who exploited the children of people who believed his outrageous claims and who surrounded himself with a paramilitary bodyguard. He had set himself up as god of Mount Carmel and had insulated himself from the outside world. He despised the democratic government of the United States, refused to pay taxes, flouted gun laws and committed sex crimes against innocent under-age girls. Koresh knew that he would have to come to account for his crimes sooner or later. He expected a fight and was prepared for one. He created a situation of *them* and *us*, with the *us* represented by a tiny band of loyal followers, the armed bodyguard of Christ, reborn into a hostile and uncaring world. They would defend their messiah to the bitter end, not just the Mighty Men but the rest of the men, too, and even the women. Koresh inspired an unswerving loyalty in those Branch Davidians who remained at the commune at the start of 1993.

Doomsday loomed large in David Koresh's theological rantings, and the name of Mount Carmel was changed to the ominous 'Ranch Apocalypse'. Increasingly the self-proclaimed messiah spoke of the 'end', of the apocalypse and of the 'great test' that was approaching. Mass-suicide may certainly have been at the heart of these veiled allusions. In one sermon he told the cult: 'If you are not willing to kill for the Message, or in turn to die for it, then you are not worthy of it and will go to Hell and be severely punished by God.' By 1993 many former cult members had attempted to warn the authorities of the growing danger at Ranch Apocalypse. The 'mass self-destruction' threatened by Koresh himself was believed to be close at hand, and many of the ex-members still had friends and relatives in the camp. A small group of former Branch Davidians began to campaign for official action to be taken, but with few positive results.

At last it was the evidence of arms dealing and the disturbing reports of child abuse that spurred the authorities to act. It was the Bureau of Alcohol, Tobacco and Firearms that would stage the raid. Armed with a search warrant, snipers and armed and armoured police officers, the ATF moved in to Waco to expose the dirty secrets of the paramilitary cult. The date was 28 February and surprise, the crucial weapon in any sudden raid, was immediately lost. A large posse of news-hungry media men and women had gathered to witness the long-awaited raid, and it was one of these reporters who accidentally tipped off one of the Branch Davidians as he drove back to Ranch Apocalypse. As soon as he arrived, all hell broke loose, and the Day of Judgement that had long been prophesied seemed to have arrived all too soon. Everyone ran to well-rehearsed battle-stations, and all able-bodied adults, men and women both, picked up their allotted firearms and got into position. The cry 'The Assyrians are coming!' rang through the compound. (Koresh styled the outside world as the biblical enemies of the Hebrews, the Babylonians or Assyrians.) From their viewing slits and firing positions, the Branch Davidians scanned the horizon and saw a convoy of cattle trucks being towed towards the compound followed by an incongruous fleet of media trucks. The cattle trucks were full of ATF agents.

The raid, when it came, was transmitted via satellite across the globe as it happened. The ATF agents were hoping to prove themselves with the arrest, but as soon as it began it went horribly wrong. Heavily armed, well-trained and with sky-high morale, the Branch Davidians began firing through the main doors at the ATF agents there. Other agents, attempting to enter the complex at other points, including the roof, were caught in a hail of automatic gunfire. The sheer ferocity of the ambush overwhelmed the agents. For 45 minutes the terrifying gun battle raged, every available cult member pouring bullets into anything that moved outside the buildings. From the water-tower a couple of anti-tank guns, massive .50 Boys rifles, punched giant holes into the parked trucks. Snipers tried to suppress this fire. The Mighty Men lobbed out grenades, which exploded near the outer walls and forced anyone still out in the open into cover. Four ATF agents had been killed by the Branch Davidians, while 16 more had been wounded. Return fire had killed six of the cult members.

With the hasty retreat of the ATF from the compound, the raid turned into a siege. It would last for 51 days. From now on the FBI would take control of the situation, but that was no guarantee of a satisfactory conclusion to the Waco siege. Attorney General Janet Reno, who masterminded the eventual end to the long stalemate, could only offer one of several best-case/worst-case solutions. The raid bungled, the FBI now tried unsuccessfully to convince Koresh to lead his violent band of followers out of Ranch Apocalypse and into jail. It was a no-win situation. The Branch Davidians had just witnessed the fundamental prophesy of their leader played out before them – they had been attacked by the forces of evil and had been victorious. Their hard and unrelenting lifestyle could be continued for up to a year (so government sources estimated) and perhaps even beyond that considering their stomach for uncompromising hardship. In fact, it was the hardship of everyday life at the camp that made the siege so difficult to break. No amount of discomfort visited on the cult seemed to affect them. The electricity was cut off. Bright lights were shone into the camp throughout the night to disrupt sleep, and loud music (even the sounds of rabbits being slaughtered) was played repeatedly with the same intention. All failed. The psychology of David Koresh and the Branch Davidians was being seriously misjudged.

In the first four weeks a number of cult members were allowed to leave the compound, 21 children and 11 adults all told, but no one else emerged or looked as if they wanted to emerge from the camp. Over 100 hours of telephone conversations with Koresh got the FBI negotiators nowhere, and the experts on biblical interpretation who were brought in to provide some insight into Koresh's fevered mind drew a similar blank. The siege could never progress – it would remain a stalemate. The cult members were right where they wanted to be and had most of the resources they needed to stay there. Absolutely no incentive existed for them to leave. Their 'home', their 'family' and their 'God' were all within Ranch Apocalypse. Waiting for them outside was only imprisonment. Koresh warned his flock during the early days of the siege that any who left the camp would forfeit their chance to reach Heaven with him. Certainly he challenged the loyalty of waverers, questioned their devotion and exploited their feelings of guilt. He let those leave who could only burden him, some of the children and the older, weaker or less fanatical followers. Only the hard-core was left.

Of all those who had joined the Branch Davidians over the years, these 80 were the true believers, the ones who had stayed with Koresh despite his mood swings, his bizarre orders, the paramilitary training, the long hours of hard work and the unintelligible Bible study marathons. Others had faltered, broken rank and left the cult. Some had even tried to cajole the authorities into investigating it. And when the end finally came, when the forces of evil rode up to the gates of Camp Apocalypse, those without faith enough to weather the approaching storm left along with the children. It was the faithful who remained. These 80 – of whom 17 were children and who probably did not understand – almost certainly knew that they were going to die at the camp, although they may not have known how or when. They must have realized that death was the most likely outcome. Perhaps they anticipated a final raid, greater than the first, that would end with a great loss of human life and that would signal Koresh's apocalyptic opening of the Seventh Seal: the end of the world.

Janet Reno knew that conditions inside the camp were abominable, human faeces was regularly tipped out of the door, and there were still six decomposing bodies on the site. She had envisaged the mothers at last relenting and shuffling out of the camp together with their children when conditions finally reached inhuman levels. However, Reno did not understand that *these* mothers were not regular mothers. Their love and compassion had been cruelly hijacked by Koresh, and the children would be forced to suffer in silence, just as they always had been. The Branch Davidians were never coming out. They would rather starve themselves to death than be defeated. So at some point, Reno had to send in the FBI. Unfortunately, another strike team was out of the question. The overriding concern of the Attorney General was to save the children, and it was likely that a replay of the first armed raid would mean first having to kill the entire armed population of Ranch Apocalypse. This was, of course, unacceptable.

Janet Reno's advisors did still have one, as yet untried, option left to them – tear gas. On 19 April loudspeakers blared out across the camp's perimeter: 'This is not an assault! Do not fire! Come out now and you will not be harmed!' The only viable solution was being put to the test. Would tear gas or, more accurately, CS gas, force the Branch Davidians out of their stronghold? Just as importantly, would it prevent them from committing the feared mass-suicide? At six o'clock in the morning, five minutes after the announcement and a telephone warning, the first of several specially configured M60 tanks smashed a hole in one wall of the complex. CS gas was injected into the buildings in an attempt to force out the cult members. As the tanks withdrew, they left large open holes for use as exits. No one left. As soon as the warnings had been received, Koresh ordered his followers to don their gas masks. Instead of fleeing, they moved deeper into the complex in an effort to evade the gas. Those who saw the tanks pumping out CS gas opened fire with no effect. For several hours the staged gassing operation continued, more holes and more gas in an ever-tightening denial of the building to the cult members. Soon they would have to come out. Several panicky hours in a gas mask would cause fatigue, disorientation and discomfort, the military aides had told Reno. But no one emerged. 'There was a lot of activity in front of the windows,' remembered FBI agent Jeff Jamar, and he suddenly thought, 'maybe people can't get out. They're blocked or there's some-one blocking the doors'. He sent tanks in to smash large holes in the wall next to the front door. Still no one came out.

Just after midday observers saw smoke curling up from one corner of the complex. A spotter plane flying overhead also reported that a large fire was blazing behind the water-tower. Other fires were also spotted – there appeared to be four in all. No one knew what had started these fires, but as the blazes took hold, a small number of Branch Davidians emerged from the buildings. Nine people were flee-ing from the fire – they were to be the only Branch Davidians to emerge alive from the camp. All the rest perished in the inferno that followed. Within the hour Camp Apocalypse had been reduced to a blackened, smoking ruin and the unenviable task of locating bodies and of determining the fire's cause began.

Over the next few days the FBI accused the Branch Davidians of initiating a mass-suicide pact that had involved setting fire to the com-plex. The survivors denied that any such pact existed. They were adamant that the FBI had begun the fires either by some misjudge-ment of the flammability of the CS gas, which experts agree is quite unlikely, or that one of the tanks exploded a propane gas cylinder used in one of the makeshift barricades. An even more likely proposition is that one or more of the kerosene lanterns used in the complex had been knocked over, causing the fatal fires. In the longer term, however, the evidence for arson pushed these accusations to one side. Wit-nesses had seen separate fires, each burning independently of the others. Forensic investigators discovered a number of metal lantern-fuel containers that had been pierced with some pointed object, prob-ably a screwdriver. Gallons of lantern fuel had leaked out onto the floor of the complex, feeding the fire and keeping it alive so that the worshippers might die. Exactly who started the fire and why will always be unknown.

The Waco tragedy has several aspects: the pain of the children, beaten and bullied, and of the young girls inducted into the House of David by their compliant parents; the horror of the gun battle with its casualties; and the final apocalyptic inferno that was witnessed by millions on TV across the globe. Can we say that the 80 Branch Davidians who died in the fire were murdered, committed suicide or were the innocent victims of a tragic accident? The answer gives us a crucial insight into the minds of Koresh and his followers. In a basic sense, few if any of the Branch Davidians actually killed themselves. Most of the bodies *were* discovered with bullet wounds to the head, some inflicted from behind. Koresh himself died from a head wound in the forehead. This evidence strongly suggests that the cult members shot each other out of sheer desperation. Rather than be burned to death they chose an easier, faster end. But did they choose? The FBI was adamant that the Branch Davidians had plenty of opportunity to leave the complex during the hours of CS gas spraying, if not past the barricades, then through the holes punched in the walls. When the fire took hold some of these exits remained open. Those escaping were a minority, faced with the choice between perishing in the fire and fleeing. That the majority followed Koresh deeper into the complex, away from possible exits during the gas spraying and even during the start of the fires, suggests that they were aware of the situation. As we have already seen, they would rather die than abandon their leader and face the outside world that they now believed was evil incarnate. Who started the fire – the FBI or a small element of Waco cultists (perhaps some of the Mighty Men) – is immaterial in this consideration. The Branch Davidians willingly faced the holocaust and like all the members of Heaven's Gate, and some of those participating in the Jonestown massacre and the Solar Temple deaths, committed suicide. The 17 children who died with them were innocent victims, pushed into a situation by parents who believed that the life and destiny of Koresh far outweighed the lives of their own children. The children were the real victims of the Waco tragedy.

Special Agent Jeff Jamar hesitates to use the phrase suicide in connection with Waco. 'It was mass-murder,' he says. 'It wasn't mass-suicide. Those people would have done whatever he said. If he told them to "leave, I'll stay here and burn", they would have left.' In that apocalyptic climax, with his flock tightly packed in the very last defensible positions of his fortress, Koresh or his closest lieutenants, must have realized that the cult had no realistic future. Its prophetic destiny was being realized at long last – the cult had fought the enemies of God and was now about to succumb. For egomaniacal Koresh, who cherished media attention and fed off the adulation and worship of others, there were only two choices: life imprisonment or the immortality as a martyred prophet, the Son of God who died in a 'blaze of glory'. We can never know if he actually made a conscious choice or if he sent his advisors out to start the deadly fires, but the ending was a haunting reminder of the biblical Armageddon to which he so often referred. One way or another, his great and terrible prophecy was fulfilled.

The legal ramifications of cult suicides are rarely addressed, but may yet find a place in the unravelling of cult abuse and mind control. A charismatic cult leader can persuade a member that he speaks with the authority of 'God', but then who is to blame if he persuades that follower to commit suicide? Is he a murderer? An accomplice? As more and more mind-control cults come to prominence through outbreaks of shocking violence (most often perpetrated against their own membership), investigators must ask: how responsible are these cultists for their own actions?

In the Footsteps of Koresh

As the Waco siege unfolded, a group of onlookers gathered on the hill overlooking the site. Their camp became the focus of a spiritual vigil: they were not members of the press or Federal agents, but 'groupies'. Sympathizers had gathered to lend their support to Koresh's fanatical stand against the forces of law and order. They were neo-Nazis and 'militiamen'. In Chapter 2 we saw how the Ku Klux Klan and a strong neo-Nazi element has come to fester within the hard right of American fringe politics. Alongside the distasteful racists is a much broader group of right-wing organizations all professing adherence to the same set of strong and uncompromising beliefs. Often organized into local (and unofficial) 'militias' the disparate groups of activists have been dubbed simply 'The Militia'.

No one seriously connected the militia movement with Waco and the Branch Davidians until 19 April 1995, the second anniversary of the fiery end of the Waco siege. On that day, America rocked to the news that a gigantic bomb had been exploded in Oklahoma City. The target, the Alfred P. Murrah federal building, had been utterly and instantly demolished with a frightening loss of life. At least 168 people including 19 children were killed in the blast. Hundreds more were injured by the immense explosion, which was heard over 40 kilometres (almost 25 miles) away. Investigators discovered that the bomb had been packed into a van that was later parked outside the building. The immense scale of the terrorist attack stunned Oklahoma City and the nation. Yet no one claimed responsibility for the devastation and murder. Speculation ran riot in the first few hours, and the prime 'suspects' were Islamic terrorists or Branch Davidians acting in revenge for the 'murder' of David Koresh. 'Obviously, no amateur did this,' commented Frank Keating, governor of Oklahoma. 'Whoever did this was an animal.'

A suspect was soon apprehended, however, a man who seemed to have definite sympathies with the Waco cultists. His name was Timothy McVeigh. As the FBI began to put together a profile of McVeigh, they discovered that they had in their custody a man with a deep-seated hatred of and resentment against the American government, and a man who had been enraged by the deaths of the Branch Davidians at Ranch Apocalypse. He had frequently stayed with two anti-government activists, one in Michigan and the other across the border in Kansas. These two brothers, James and Terry Nichols, defied the Federal government at every possible turn. James Nichols refused to apply for a driving licence, for example, although he continued to drive, and every dollar bill he handed over in payment was always carefully defaced with an ink stamp. His younger brother had refused to license both his car and his marriage and was frequently in court for his attempts to circumvent what he perceived to be government interference in his life. Both men found the idea of government taxation particularly obnoxious. The Nichols could have been considered just overly paranoid eccentrics were it not for the fact that they made bombs. It was their bomb-making activities and their close friendship with Timothy McVeigh that led the FBI to arrest them.

Discovered on James Nichols's property in Michigan were explosive blasting caps, black powder pyrodex, safety fuses and enough ammonium nitrate fertilizer and fuel oil to create a bomb almost equal in size to that which had destroyed the Alfred P. Murrah building. McVeigh and Nichols frequently experimented with bombs, and the sounds of the explosions often echoed across the fields. In addition, all three men were ardent gun fanatics. Terry Nichols was charged with complicity in the Oklahoma bombing, and his friendship with McVeigh illustrated the nature of his links with a diffuse militia community.

The Nicholses were not alone. They were only part of a much larger paramilitary movement in Michigan and Kansas, and the Michigan militia, in particular, received much attention following the bombing. The militia is primarily a pro-gun organization, professing to be an army of civilians ready to defend the people of the US against the government should the need arise. Its members, just like the members of other militias – in Montana, Georgia, Arizona, Texas and elsewhere – run paramilitary camps, training programmes and military-style exercises. The American citizen's right to bear arms forms the cornerstone of the militias' sinister theology; without guns, the groups argue, there can be no freedom. Who protects the people from the government? Distrust and hatred of Washington, President Clinton and the federal government in general, drives the movement on. It cultivates an atmosphere of fear and paranoia.

April 1996 saw another siege in progress, not against a religious commune this time, but around a militia camp in Montana. The Freemen anti-government militia had come to the attention of the FBI when locals from the nearby town of Jordan, tiring of the militiamen's antisocial habits, formed an armed posse and prepared to confront them. The 60 Freemen had been running a tax evasion and forgery school for like-minded individuals at their Justus Township ranch. LeRoy Schweitzer, the group's obsessed leader, had been arrested prior to the FBI siege and appeared in court in combat fatigues. His colleague, Daniel Peterson, who was arrested with him, shouted across the courtroom: 'You watch folks! When it goes, it'll be worse than Waco!'

McVeigh became an emblem for the militias across America in the wake of the Oklahoma bombing and his trial was followed closely by the anti-government activists. As the trial neared its end, the Internet was buzzing with pro-militia sentiments. One anti-government activist called McVeigh the '[Lee Harvey] Oswald of the 1990s', and the electronic support was matched by a deluge of more mundane mail sympathizing with the mass-murderer. The Waco siege and its unfortunate outcome had galvanized the militias, giving them not only an incident around which they could unite but also proof that the federal government was attacking the liberties of freedom-loving Americans. The militia felt that the Branch Davidians were merely exercising their God-given right to bear arms. They had not, said the militias, killed anybody (although they had once shot at the news-paper delivery man and also tried to kill George Roden) with their guns or bombs. According to these paramilitary groups, there was no evidence for any criminal activity at Mount Carmel. The Branch Davidians had simply made a conscious effort to cut themselves off from American society and to create a community that obeyed its own laws without harming others.

The heavy-handed ATF raid and the siege of Waco that ended in the death of 80 Branch Davidians sickened and angered those in the militia movement. For some, who saw it as a public show of despotic force against innocent men, women and children, it was the final straw. It certainly inspired Timothy McVeigh and Terry Nichols to retaliate against the government. A crucial witness told the FBI: 'Tim wanted to wake up America to the danger of our Federal government and their intrusion on our rights. He was hoping to accomplish some sort of mass uprising.' Although the action had the full approval of the anti-government ultra-right, it produced nationwide revulsion, rather than the nationwide revolution that had been envisaged. McVeigh and his supporters were right-wing terrorists fighting to defend an uncon-cerned American public against an imagined totalitarian US govern-ment. In this, they resembled the RAF and Action Directe: radical fringe theories were underscored with a campaign of violence against the very public that the group is ostensibly trying to 'liberate'.

The National Rifle Association (NRA) had always represented the doubts and fears of the militia, but it is seen today more as a toothless giant that is out of touch with the radical edge of the movement. NRA membership is at an all-time low, and many observers have put the blame for this lack of enthusiasm at the door of the militias. Unwanted associations with the activities of the paramilitaries, with McVeigh and with the abhorrent Oklahoma bombing have turned off many long-time or would-be NRA members. The Association is fighting to retain its credibility in a world that seems to be on the point of being overwhelmed by a tidal wave of over-the-top hatred and bitterness. Currently, the spokesperson for the militia movement is Linda Thompson, an Indianapolis attorney, who operates from the office of an organization called the American Justice Federation. She provides a voice for the militias, which, at present have no proper leadership or hierarchy. They have no central office, regional network or official mailing address. Their anarchistic calls for autonomy have kept the spectre of a nationwide paramilitary mobilization at bay and the movement's profile relatively low. Only the Oklahoma bomb has more recently focused attention onto these groups.

The militias' hatred of the government stems from President Clinton's drive to curtail both gun ownership and the ease with which guns can be bought, carried, concealed and used by civilians. A significant proportion of civilian gun owners have switched their political allegiances from the government in Washington and to an idealized society of freedom and liberty cherished by the militia. The majority of militia members and supporters are vociferous and resentful, but only a tiny minority has ever taken violent action. McVeigh and Nichols are two of these, and in the wake of the Oklahoma bomb, a number of other militia members deemed the time ripe to come out of the woodwork and issue statements. A group calling itself the Sons of Gestapo derailed a train in October 1995, and one person died and 12 others were seriously injured when the Amtrak express carrying 248 passengers plunged into an Arizona river.

In 1996, following the detonation at the Olympic Games in Atlanta of a bomb that resulted in the deaths of two people, a group calling itself the Army of God actually declared war on the government. Although the group denied planting the Atlanta bomb, it did claim responsibility for bombing an abortion clinic and gay club in the city earlier in the year. The group's letter, received by two Atlanta TV stations, promised 'total war on the so-called federal Government and death to the New World Order'. The Army of God derives its name from a manual of terrorist attacks on abortion clinics and indicates how an alliance of hate is slowly forming in opposition to the government. Its grievances, in comparison with real guerrilla movements fighting pitched battles for survival in Latin America and Africa, are more imagined than real.

Firearms magazines are just one of the methods the militia members and their supporters use to keep in contact. The Clinton administration has tightened firearms restrictions to such an extent that civilian gun owners across America feel themselves increasingly on the defensive. As a result, most gun magazines have adopted a radical anti-government stance. They may also include debates, not only on the shrinking rights of gun owners but also on vigilantism and news of criminal legislation and moves to improve it. For a magazine like Guns & Ammo, for example, the social content of the magazine goes far beyond the simple 'handgun trends' remit advertised on the cover. Rebecca John Wyatt, an outspoken writer and handgunner, regularly puts forward the views of a whole section of right-wing firearms enthusiasts, with such questions as: 'Why does the government need to regulate our God-given rights?' The tone of other firearms magazines is equally and consistently anti-government, and between work-a-day reviews of new handguns on the market appear highly emotional tirades against Washington and the American justice system. According to Wyatt, the US government is composed of 'self-serving, obsolete, bureaucratic agencies ... fighting for their money-grubbing lives'.

Militia groups also communicate with one another across the Internet and by means of short-wave radio broadcasts, such as Radio Free World. Anthony J. Hilder, who owns and runs Radio Free World, typifies the very extreme end of the militia movement. His message, preached daily, is a highly disturbing and irrational mix of science fiction, conspiracy theory and apocalyptic Christian fundamentalism. It is truly dangerous and has been picked up with varying degrees of belief by groups across America. It is this buoyant new trend within the gun-owning right that is responsible for this discussion of the murky world of the militia here, in Chapter 7, rather than alongside the other terrorist or white supremacist groups that were featured earlier in the book.

Just as David Koresh predicted an all-consuming apocalypse that would engulf the world yet spare the faithful, many militia members are on a similar countdown to doomsday. The federal threat to gun ownership has been regarded as the beginning of the end. When the weapons of the citizenry are at last seized by the government, the movement insists, Washington will start a terrible oppression and slaughter of the American people. They believe that a monstrous conspiracy threatens humanity, and that the United States is actually in the evil clutches of a conspiratorial élite, called the Illuminati, according to some, or one of several other names, according to others. The Illuminati, discussed in detail in Chapter 3, is seen as part of an ongoing masonic conspiracy, and the Bavarian secret society of that name is believed to have survived down the ages under a host of different guises. Today, it acts through Clinton and Congress. Bar codes are believed by the militia to contain hidden information useful to the conspiracy; dollar bills are encoded and contain their innocuous metal strip for some ulterior purpose; even road signs have been co-opted as secret message boards by the secret Illuminati cabal. Fear and paranoia fuel every aspect of the militia movement.

Anthony J. Hilder believes that the Hollywood film industry is under government control and that movies such as *Close Encounters of the Third Kind* and *Independence Day* are little more than propaganda exercises. According to Hilder and others, the US government is developing a whole new generation of terrifying super-weapons that will be unleashed on an unsuspecting public. Secret military bases act as the test sites for these weapons, and witnesses are scared off or persuaded that they have seen UFOs. The shadowy 'men in black' are the agents of this misinformation. Area 51, the top secret military base in the Nevada desert, is the location in popular UFO mythology of captured alien spacecraft. UFO theories create a smoke-screen behind which the US government is supposed to be hiding, and big budget movies about 'first contact' with alien life provide an added layer of believability to the theories. This feared threat from an evil and corrupt government has been dubbed the 'Panic Project'. Militias following this line of argument believe that a fake alien inva-sion of Earth (currently being rehearsed on US bases) will be the cover for a take-over by the Illuminati. Only the militia can defend the people from this imagined threat. Faced with the Panic Project, the fanatical militia members have a simple answer: 'Shoot the sons of bitches!' McVeigh and Nichols went one better with their two-ton bomb.

Colonel James 'Bo' Gritz is a leading figure in the new militia reli-gion. Bo Gritz fought with special forces during the Vietnam War and returned to Southeast Asia on a secret mission in the early 1980s to search for American prisoners of war. His bravery and commitment are of the first order, and in 1992 the highly decorated Vietnam vet-eran ran for the office of president. Although he failed to win office, he did not abandon his desire to save his country from the threats he perceived all around him. Like other militiamen, Bo Gritz is con-vinced that Washington is conspiring against the American people and regularly infringing civil liberties. According to these radical beliefs, the federal government will permit an invasion of ground troops under the command of the United Nations, the very embodi-ment of evil in the world. The United Nations is on a mission to dom-inate the whole world (by implanting silicon chips inside people's heads so that they can be constantly monitored) and is, in fact, the seven-headed beast as described by the Book of Revelation. 'And power was given [to the beast] over all kindreds, and tongues and nations. And all that dwell upon the earth shall worship him' (Rev-elation 13:7–8). In the militia system of belief, the second beast, which exercises 'all the power of the first beast before him, and causeth the Earth and them which dwell therein to worship the first beast' (13:12), is represented by the United States government.

Chad Erikson, a strident militiaman, voiced fears shared by every member of the movement: 'We fear natural disasters, we fear economic collapse, we fear the One World Government that is to arrive on the scene, we fear government of oppression.' To counter the growing threat, and to weather the prophesied apocalypse, Bo Gritz has estab-lished the Almost Heaven survivalist commune at Kamiah, Idaho.

According to the Federal Emergency Management Agency, Kamiah is in one of the safest places in America. With no freezing winters and no potential nuclear strike targets in the area, Kamiah has become an apocalyptic retreat for those men and women who want to survive the holocaust. 'It's show-time,' smiled one of the female members of the group, 'and it's a great time to be alive'.

While the end of the world is brought about by the evil United Nations and its servants in Washington, the Almost Heaven cult will wait for the Second Coming. Its members train continually in survival techniques and firearms use. The Colonel Gritz's special forces training is disseminated among his followers with an almost religious obsession. Certain of the doomsday scenario about to be played out, the militia members envisage a period of anarchy and primitive barbarism in which only the best trained and best armed will have any chance of survival. The American militia are determined to survive this anarchy. According to the Almost Heaven sect, a messiah will appear on earth and all the prophesies of the Bible will be fulfilled. 'We are going to have perfect government, after the coming of the messiah,' Gritz predicts.

With the end of the millennium approaching at break-neck speed, the belief in an imminent apocalypse has taken hold on a frightened and indignant community. Biblical accounts of the end of the world describe a period of great destruction, when the Seven Seals will be opened, pouring death and misery on the world. Following this carnage the Messiah will appear and lead the faithful into Paradise. In past times the way to salvation, to survive 'The End' and reach Paradise, was through the devout worship of Christ. Those who 'had not worshipped the beast, neither his image, neither had received his mark upon their foreheads or in their hands ... lived and reigned with Christ a thousand years' (Revelation 20:4). The militia have resolved to survive the terrible wrath of God not through prayer, but through armed might. Extensive training in demolitions, firearms, sharp-shooting, hand-to-hand combat and tactical driving techniques will equip the militia members for the trials to come. Envisaged almost as a post-holocaust dystopia, a *Mad Max* fight for survival amid the ruins of civilization, only the strongest will prevail. The militia are determined to be among the strongest.

People's interpretations of the Book of Revelation vary immensely. David Koresh saw one thing; Bo Gritz and the militia see something else. Klaus Werner, an eccentric stalker of the British Royal Family, has his own, unique interpretations. To Werner, Queen Elizabeth II is Revelation's 'beast', and he has developed elaborate arguments to support this idea. Some of his placards depict 'Elizardbeast' with '666' (the mark of the beast) drawn across her forehead. Special Branch has taken Werner's obsession seriously. Anyone who truly believes that the Queen is the embodiment of Satan may not stop short of murder in order to fulfil the predictions of the Bible.

Aum Supreme Truth

Until 1995 it was thought that religious mind-control cults had certain limits beyond which their violent activities would not go. Violence perpetrated against cult members manifested itself in a small number of recurring ways: in torture, abuse and, in the most fanatical of cases, mass-suicide. However, an armed élite of cult members close to the leader shot to death other devotees in the Waco, Jonestown and Solar Temple incidents, which proves that cult violence could almost certainly manifest itself in other, more direct, ways.

Japan has innumerable religious factions, splinter groups and cults, but Japanese society has always epitomized sombre sobriety, inhabiting a crime-free haven safe from all the real and imagined terrors of the modern, post-industrial world. Clashing with this rose-tinted vision of a society 'in control', however, Japan rides the high speed, ultra high-tech wave of information-age economics that has left so many other Western nations behind. Its first major taste of cult violence took the nation – and the world – by surprise. A microcosm of Japan as a whole, the cult that hit the headlines in March 1995 was more science fiction than fact. It called itself Aum Supreme Truth, and it had just deployed weapons of mass-destruction underneath the streets of Tokyo.

On the morning of 20 March 1995 five members of Aum Supreme Truth joined the throngs of commuters who were packing into the subway trains at five different stations underneath Tokyo. The separate trains boarded by the men were expected to arrive at Kasumigaseki station at approximately 8:15. Kasumigaseki is the political centre of both the city and the nation: it is home to the National Diet parliament building, the headquarters of the police force and the location of every one of the government's ministries. Each of the cultists carried a bag containing a lethal dose of sarin nerve gas and a sharpened umbrella with which these bags would be pierced. From just after seven o'clock, the mass-murderers began to carry out the plan that they had rehearsed time after time at the cult's headquarters. As a predetermined station was reached, the cult members placed their bag on the floor of the carriage and stabbed it repeatedly before elbowing their way off the train. Their mission complete, they made their way up the escalators to the surface, where Aum cars were waiting at the respective stations to whisk them away.

Meanwhile, underneath the concrete and glass of Tokyo, the sarin liquid oozed out of the leaking bags and began to give off a nauseating and overpowering stink. Noses began to run, commuters coughed and spluttered, some gagged violently. Over the next two hours the effects of the nerve gas began to take hold, as victims started to vomit and even to convulse uncontrollably. Some felt faint and had difficulty focusing. For two hours chaos reigned along the five subway lines. At the next station stops passengers in the affected carriage tried to get out onto the platform and up to the surface. No one knew what was happening. Some commuters struggled off the trains several stops later, a few died where they sat, twitching and foaming at the mouth – killed by the sarin. The gas affected adjoining carriages and washed invisibly along platforms and tunnels, affecting passengers and staff alike. But the snapshot nature of the emergency, seen at one station for a few seconds before the train thundered off, carrying its deadly cargo of sarin to the next stop, precluded a full-scale alert.

One doctor who was helping to treat the thousands of choking, convulsing and blinded victims diagnosed the effects of sarin poisoning at around 10:30 that morning. From then on, the military and police were mobilized to try to secure the affected subway lines. The enormous scale of the catastrophe, initiated by five individuals acting in unison, amazed and shocked the authorities, the nation and the world. That morning 12 innocent people died. Over 5500 others were injured by the effects of sarin poisoning, and the psychological damage inflicted on those survivors was immeasurable. Many were crippled and at least two victims survived the ordeal only to slip into permanent coma. One unfortunate woman was hospitalized with searing eye pains – her contact lenses had fused to the surface of her eyeballs, and surgeons were forced to remove both her eyes.

Police believed that the Aum Supreme Truth cult was responsible, and on 22 March a massive police raid on its Mount Fuji headquarters compound discovered enough material to manufacture sarin on a huge scale. The authorities turned the camp upside down in their search for evidence, but were unable to apprehend Aum's enigmatic leader, Shoko Asahara. Although they also failed to find any direct evidence linking the cult with the subway attacks, they did uncover the amazing secret history of Aum, a history of brutal repression, science horror, murder and mass-murder.

Aum had resources that other killer cults could only dream of. Sufficient chemicals had been stockpiled to kill perhaps 10 million people. All the technology required for the production of biological weapons and military assault rifles existed at the cult's headquarters. It owned a Russian military helicopter and had made extensive plans to procure more Russian weaponry, up to and including a nuclear device. The severe regime to which Aum cultists had surrendered soon came to light when emaciated followers were discovered locked in isolation chambers, devoid of any comfort or light. Some of these prisoners wore bizarre headsets wired to transmit Asahara's brainwaves into their heads. Hidden behind ornate Buddhist temples and prayer rooms, were secret chambers that had been converted into computer-controlled laboratories and drug factories. This was a confident, technologically literate, incredibly wealthy and domineering organization that worryingly had other offices in Tokyo, in other parts of Japan and abroad, in nations as disparate as South Korea, Russia, Australia and the United States.

Only when Shoko Asahara and his lieutenants were finally apprehended in May 1995 could the Japanese police finally build up a picture of Aum Supreme Truth and attempt to explain the motivation behind the appalling subway attacks. Shoko Asahara cuts a strange figure – he is almost blind, with a round, chubby face, flowing black hair and beard and wears purple robes. The only partially sighted child at the blind school in which he grew up, he bullied and dominated his classmates. Asahara's ego continued to grow, and as he matured he cultivated a charismatic and charming demeanour. His dabblings in yoga and alternative medicine led him into the realm of alternative religion, but he always remained a quack doctor, a con-man and would-be healer. All the time, he stayed one step ahead of the authorities. Aum Shinrikyo (Supreme Truth) was established by Asahara in 1987, following a visit to the Dalai Lama in Dharmsala, India, in February of that year. Previously known as the Aum Association of Mountain Wizards, Aum Supreme Truth soon took on the trappings of a personality cult, with many of the remedies, exercises and classes offered by Shoko Asahara actually revolving around his role as a spiritual guru. The prophet vowed to 'rescue people from their suffering' and 'lead the world to enlightenment'. 'Aum' is actually a Hindu sound, used as an aid to meditation and adopted by the cult leader. It is said to contain the supreme truth of the universe.

Donations from new members and the large fees demanded for ineffectual remedies and classes formed a sound financial base on which Asahara could build. He sold his hair clippings, his blood and even his bath water to mesmerized followers eager to taste the 'magical properties' that were supposed to course through the prophet's body. Asahara's central role as *sonshi* or guru became the linchpin around which a diverse mix of beliefs coalesced. Aum was a complex blend of Buddhism, New Age therapy and the teachings of Hindu and Buddhist Zen masters. From Christianity (and Nostradamus) Aum borrowed the concept of an impending apocalypse, a Doomsday that would purge the earth of non-believers. The apocalyptic message proved popular with recruits and soon came to dominate the cult's hotchpotch theology. In the ruins of the atomic holocaust that the guru predicted would destroy civilization in late 2003, Asahara's followers would rise up as a race of 'super-humans'. Aum could teach its followers wondrous powers, including levitation, out-of-body travel and super-intelligence. It was the training provided by Aum that would prepare its members for Armageddon and assist them in reaching 'enlightenment'.

In 1988 a purpose-built centre was constructed especially to house the cult's religious and spiritual activities. In keeping with Asahara's lofty predictions for his organization, the compound was located at Kamikuishiki, on the lower slopes of Mount Fuji, Japan's most famous landmark and its highest mountain. Construction continued unabated for years, and the camp always retained an unfinished, ramshackle appearance. Like many cults before it, Aum seemed to take on a paranoid and anti-social air with its relocation to Mount Fuji. The compound further isolated Asahara and his devotees from the mundane world, which they increasingly came to reject.

Now increasingly dependent on their megalomaniacal guru, the Aum cultists were willing and eager to devote not just their savings and belongings to the cult but also their entire lives. And soon the domination began. All the well-known techniques of mind control were employed to keep the cult members in line. Sleep deprivation, beatings, strictly controlled diets and the dislocation of a member from his family and friends were used. A simple philosophy underscored these methods: comfort and pleasure make one weak and are therefore bad; pain and discomfort make one strong and are therefore good. It is brutal philosophy that has been used successfully in army training camps around the world. Applied to a religious cult like Aum, the philosophy hardened the resolve of its members, created an intense group loyalty and a willingness to endure inhuman hardships. Interestingly, all of these qualities were found among the Branch Davidians who lived in such dire conditions on the Mount Carmel ranch at Waco. Men, women and children alike were exposed to this tough and disciplined regime.

While some recruits had brought their families to live alongside Shoko Asahara, others had come alone. A good deal of Aum's upper echelon membership were professional people. Engineers, chemists, doctors, office workers, computer technicians and a host of different scientifically trained men and women joined Aum. Asahara welcomed the scientists into the cult, and they, in turn, were eager to put their knowledge to use in his service. Brain-wave machines, 'astral projectors', chemical and biological weaponry and the chemical study of Asahara's bodily substances (blood, DNA, hair and so on) became full-time projects for the skilled cultists. The astrophysicist Hideo Murai became a prominent member of the guru's council of 'mad scientists'. Together, they told Asahara of all they could achieve with their combined know-how, of particle accelerator weapons, lasers, atomic bombs and chemical agents – they would provide Aum with the necessary means to defend itself during the predicted

Armageddon. All this power became vested in one man – Shoko Asahara, the school bully who nurtured feelings of hatred and revenge against modern society. Once a partially sighted loner, a vindictive and bitter outcast, Shoko Asahara was now the master of his own small kingdom. Its citizens were loyal devotees, willing to carry out his every whim. Many of these young men and women were well educated and technologically able.

In a country like Japan, it seems incredible that young men and women, previously devoted to intensive study and to the highly competitive rigours of the Japanese education system and years in university, could then 'drop out' to follow an egotistical con-man and his dreams to weather the approaching apocalypse. Experts agree, however, that it is that very discipline and competitiveness of the education system that may have made Aum seem so attractive. Built on a precarious tower of fantasy and bogus treatments, the cult provided the one thing denied to modern Japanese adolescents: an alternative. Recruits could rebel against their families, friends and 'the system' and still take along with them all the post-modern trappings of high-tech society. Japanese animated movies (*anime*), cyberpunk fiction, virtual reality machines and computer games had all influenced the cult's hierarchy. Science fiction shot through much of Aum's thinking, just as it had the Heaven's Gate group. Here, however, the science had a far more tangible form. Here, the cult scientists had the finances and the time to research the most unusual and fantastic things. In Japan it was estimated that in 1995 Aum had perhaps 10,000 supporters, and in Russia, the cult's second home, it had upwards of 30,000. In 1990, when Asahara still had pretensions of legitimacy, he and 24 of his disciples stood for the Japanese parliament but polled barely enough votes to account for the Aum membership. For Asahara, like Colonel Bo Gritz in the US, this final rejection seemed to confirm every suspicion that the cult had of the 'corrupt society'.

Following his electoral defeat, the guru began to prophesy doom for the Japanese. He predicted that Mount Fuji would explode and that the end of the world was imminent. Only Shoko Asahara, as 'Today's Christ', could save the world. His apocalyptic visions quickly changed the pace of life within the organization, and an emphasis was placed on surviving the forthcoming holocaust, even if this meant travelling to distant stars. Hideo Murai was once asked why Aum possessed the capacity to manufacture nerve gas. 'The answer is simple,' he said. 'In order to inherit this civilization, we must not be destroyed.' Aum was ready and able to defend itself with the deadly nerve gas sarin, which had first been tested by Nazi scientists in the concentration camps. When three judges were about to rule against the cult in the summer of 1994, Aum carried out the world's first terrorist nerve gas attack. It failed to make headlines outside Japan, although, in retrospect, it provided an ominous warning of the horror to follow. The gas had been released on 27 June 1994 near the apartment building in which the judges lived. There were over 150 victims of sarin poisoning (including the three judges) that night, and seven people did not survive. No one suspected that Aum had been behind the attack, however.

Aum was now rushing headlong towards its ultimate destiny. Several development programmes under way at the cult's complex would have stunned the outside world, had it known of them. Financed by Aum's massive corporate empire, which consisted of 37 companies by 1995, the projects ranged from the full-scale manufacture of assault rifles, to the production of the anthrax virus, microwave weapons and earthquake machines! Its greatest 'triumph' came in the development of chemical weapons, such as mustard gas and sarin. This experimentation and production took place at Satian 7, one building at the Mount Fuji complex that always had a heavy guard. There, purpose-built laboratories, computer-controlled equipment, close-circuit TV and sealed hatchways were installed and ran at full tilt until the end of March 1995. There were a few frequent accidents there, and locals in the village of Kamikuishiki complained of foul odours and of persistent flu-like symptoms.

Aum had even bigger ideas, and Asahara was determined, with the support of his scientist-generals, to procure the most lethal weapon available. A great deal of money and effort was expended in trying to purchase a nuclear warhead from the Russian *mafiya*. Fortunately, nothing concrete came of the deals. Other members of Aum were dispatched to Zaire in Central Africa, their mission was to bring back samples of the horrific Ebola virus, the virulent disease causing a victim's internal organs to liquefy and seep from any available orifice. No one has yet been able to confirm or deny the cult's success in this endeavour.

Coordinating the various activities of Aum were a number of separate 'ministries', the most powerful of which were Hideo Murai's Ministry of Science and Technology, the Ministry of Construction (which was charged with procuring a nuclear warhead), Ministry of Health and Welfare (which manufactured bacteriological weapons) and the Ministry of Justice (which handled the numerous lawsuits that so frightened Aum's opponents). It was the rumour of a massive raid on the Kamikuishiki facility by the up-to-now reticent police that spurred Asahara to initiate the subway sarin attacks. Outside the Kasumigaseki subway station lay the main headquarters of the Tokyo police, which threatened, at last, to ruin his vast multinational religious-cum-criminal empire.

Accordingly, the five cult members – Ikuo Hayashi, Masato Yokohama, Kenichi Hirose, Toru Toyoda and Yasuo Hayashi – were then dispatched with the blessings of their guru and god Shoko Asahara to commit mass-murder on 20 March 1995. One of them had previously been a surgeon, three of them were physicists, and the fifth had made his living as an electronics engineer. Their actions catapulted Aum from relative obscurity into the full glare of the global media. Unwilling to act on many previous occasions, the Tokyo police were now forced to move in on Aum and carry out the raid on its Mount Fuji compound.

Meanwhile, along the hundreds of kilometres of under-city subway, the nervous commuters continued to travel, ever vigilant of suspect packages, strange smells or the unnerving coincidence of two passengers coughing simultaneously. The fear that sarin might suddenly begin leaking into the carriage at any minute made subway travel almost unbearable. This long-term panic was termed 'sarinoia' by the media, and it perceptibly altered the mood of the city. On 5 May Aum cultists did strike again. This time at Shinjuku subway station. At 7:40 in the evening a bag left in the men's toilets spontaneously ignited, and after staff extinguished the fire with water, it gave off thick, choking fumes. After analysis, investigators discovered that Shinjuku station had narrowly avoided being gassed by lethal hydrogen cyanide. In July, after Asahara and the majority of the Aum leadership had been imprisoned, there were four more failed hydrogen cyanide attacks on Tokyo's subway system.

Aum today is a crippled and dying beast. Shoko Asahara has been indicted with 23 counts of murder as well as a host of other crimes relating to Aum's illegal activities. More than 350 of his followers have also been jailed, while others have turned against him and are ready to testify against their prophet. His lieutenants were charged with crimes ranging from murder and kidnapping to forgery, drug production and property fraud. The guru who was unofficially responsible for the murder of 27 people – victims of sarin or of Asahara's own execution squad – is also responsible for the disappearance of perhaps 30 more cult members in Japan and Russia, some of whom were caught trying to flee Aum. In Australia, Germany and New York the authorities began their own investigations into Aum's operations and were frustrated by the lack of Japanese cooperation. On Aum property at Banjawarn Station in the Australian outback, for instance, police discovered the skeletons of 29 sheep, all tethered in a circle. Tests later confirmed that they had died from sarin poisoning. It was there that the cult tested their deadly compound before beginning their assault on the Japanese populace.

Aum Supreme Truth is the nightmare reality of cult watchers and law enforcement authorities around the world. It surpasses every expectation and every assumption about what a modern mind-control cult is. Aum's bizarre foray into weapons development, drug use and chemical, biological and nuclear materials would not have disgraced the pages of a science fiction novel. Yet the truth has proved far stranger than fiction. Aum has exaggerated almost every aspect of a modern mind-control cult. What distinguishes Aum Supreme Truth from other groups is its proactive attempt to take mass death to the general public, whereas the typical doomsday cult will vent its violent feelings in a mass-suicide. For those of us living our lives outside a cult, this is a worrying new feature. Coupled with the cult's ability to leapfrog traditional cult armaments such as blades and guns, the appearance of biological germ agents, nerve toxins and nuclear warheads on the apocalyptic cult front should terrify us all.

Modern technology is out of the hands of élites and is now freely available, in libraries, on the Internet and on college courses. With a modicum of academic training and a few textbooks and training manuals, Aum has shown that it is possible for an amateur to manufacture the chemical or biological weapon of his choice. It may be neither easy nor cheap, but it is possible.

Until the terrible sarin attack on the Tokyo subway, terrorist attacks were in some ways predictable. Terrorist experts have always understood that the terrorist wants to bring about political or social change. To do this he must minimize civilian casualties and turn the attack into a media event. It is press coverage rather than corpses that a terror group really desires, since only through public anger or public disaffection can the political or social changes be achieved. Aum Supreme Truth cared nothing for public sentiment. Their war was a religious one; it was a crusade against a corrupt society that had no redeeming features. Contrary to what terrorist experts had learned to expect, Asahara's followers planned and executed their mass-murder with the specific goal of causing as many casualties as possible. There was no mercy, no pity and no vestige of humanity in the minds of the five killers and the scientists and cult activists who sent them.

Unlike the apocalyptic cults that have perished in previous years, Aum had decided to create the Armageddon that would engulf the world. Asahara risked being made a fool if the end of the world did not occur as his teachings had predicted. There seemed to be no sign of an approaching nuclear holocaust, so Asahara decided to use his growing arsenal of weaponry to change all that. 'We will start a war in August,' he had proclaimed in 1994. His intention had been to kick start the apocalypse, to bring about the end of the world and to survive it, along with his followers.

The cult failed. Will the next?

Conclusion

How can we best understand the phenomenon of the cult, the secret society – the brotherhood? What makes previously level-headed individuals abandon their lifestyles to take up the restrictive life of secrecy and violence that constitutes one of our 'brotherhoods of fear'?

There are several factors. With some of the organizations we have discussed, the decision of the candidate has already been made for them. I am thinking here, in particular, of the African tribal brotherhoods that are part of everyday life, despite their propensity for real or mock violence. For the rest of the dark brotherhoods in this book, however, there *is* an underlying thread that connects them together, and that *is* hope.

Hope keeps people alive, it keeps people motivated and active. Without it they become disillusioned, pessimistic and suicidal. It is the cult, secret society, covert organization or terror group that can provide the disillusioned member of society with some sense of purpose. These groups are fatally attractive because they give the candidates who apply for membership a real (or false) *hope*. Hope of what exactly is determined by the social conditions of the age. In medieval Europe, with crushing poverty and ignorance, the Catholic Church offered everyone, even the lowliest swineherd, farmer or craftsman, the chance to enter heaven. Such was the terrible economic situation of the medieval peasant that any hope, if it existed at all, had to rest in the next life. The Church proved fundamental to this belief. It provided not only a way for the lowliest peasant to sit at the side of God, but it reinforced the belief that the only way to advance and to prosper was through death and the afterlife. Medieval European civilization could, in consequence, be classed as a massive cult of sorts. Its 'membership' believed whole-heatedly in the predictions of the cult 'hierarchy' (the Church) and would follow almost blindly its dictates. For the membership of a frightened and devout religious cult, the existence of evil witches, their familiars and accomplices seemed very real. Proof of their existence came from the cult leaders (the Church), and also fitted in seamlessly with what the uneducated peasant had already been taught about theological matters.

Witchcraft, although a fantastic creation of the Inquisition and the other magistrates who pursued it, became for the cult members a horrible reality. Most societies seem to purge themselves of their unwanted membership, or at least provide their followers with a way to let off steam and vent their pent-up anger and frustrations. Adolf Hitler and his SS thugs did this and so did the papal Inquisition.

What about more modern 'brotherhoods of fear'? With the phenomenon of the racist society (the Nazi Party aside, which seems to fit the definition of a modern doomsday cult in almost every way), the theme of 'hope' holds true. White supremacist movements have at their core a frustrated, uneducated white group of young men who see their lives and their country being overtaken by 'foreigners'. The fascist movements give these youths hope that things can go back to how they were (however impossible). They want jobs, money, girls and freedom. Stuck at the lowest end of the economic scale, along with most of the nation's poverty-stricken foreign immigrants, the fascist youth finds himself competing face-to-face with the very group of people he blames for his predicament. Conflict, violence and murder are his methods of expression.

The revolutionary terrorist is driven by the same subconscious emotion – a longing for hope. Studies by criminologists around the world have created a profile of the revolutionary terrorist. He or she (since many, if not an equal number, of these urban guerrillas are female) has had a difficult childhood. They will be the products of a middle-class background and of a university education, yet they will have rejected their parents outright. Whether we are talking about members of the RAF, Red Zora, the Weathermen, Action Directe or something as seemingly innocuous as the British Socialist Workers Party, the members of these terror groups have a fractured relationship with family life and normal day-to-day existence in general. Many years ago a friend of mine, shy, uncomfortable and homesick, was quickly recruited by the revolutionary Socialist Workers Party at Queen's College London. It was a well-known tactic of the organization to target those new university students who seemed to need most help in adjusting. Hope provides the far-left terrorist with a way to come to terms with his frustrations, anxieties and feelings of dislocation and abandonment. Authority, the primary bugbear of any left-wing terror group, is an object of hatred, and this hatred stems from a psychological need to rebel, to work to attain an existence where there is no us and them – just us.

Criminal elements from the savage brotherhoods of crime have no such desires, yet they are still driven to conform to the rigorous dictates of the criminal syndicate by the hope of something better. The individual mafioso, whether in Colombia, Moscow, Sicily, Singapore, Tokyo or Chicago, is seeking to better himself. Usually it is always the poorest and most desperate members of a city's population that make the transition from a life of poverty to a life of crime. Membership of a harsh and deadly regime provides at least some hope that the situation may improve, and they have nothing to lose by turning to crime. In the very roughest of neighbourhoods, membership of an organized crime syndicate can provide a gang member with much sought status and a step up from the local gangs. Organized crime becomes a 'way out' of the ghetto.

Lastly, the members of today's religious mind-control cults hope to find a better life within their chosen cult (despite the often brutal regimes) than without it. Life today can be so fractured, so chaotic or disordered that any order, however strict and disciplinarian, can seem attractive. Modern religious cults seem to be a new and dangerous phenomenon, but although they are today more numerous, they are not peculiar to the twentieth century: the medieval Assassins, the Indian Thuggee and the Greek cult of Eleusis all predated Jim Jones and David Koresh. Psychiatrist H.A.K. Sukhdeo of the New Jersey School of Medicine worked with survivors of the Jonestown massacre: 'Our society is so free and permissive,' he declared, 'and people have so many options to choose from that they cannot make their own decisions effectively. They want others to make the decision and they will follow.'

The mind-control and doomsday cult phenomenon is best understood in relation to the sociologist Alvin Toffler's concept of 'Third Wave' society. This post-war, post-industrial consumer society is driven by information technology and total freedom of expression. We can be whatever we choose, but many in our society *cannot* choose, and require guidance. Toffler himself believes that every mind-control cult 'sells community, structure, and meaning at an extremely high price: the mindless surrender of self'. It is authoritarian leadership, too, that the religious cults peddle. The desire for guidance, for control in a seemingly out-of-control world, pushes people to seek out groups such as Aum or the People's Temple. Such a desire must also, in some part, motivate both the left- and the right-wing extremists, the terror groups who are willing to kill in order to restore strong and just government.

What is clear, despite the rational explanations of cult recruitment given by Toffler and others, is that some members of the human race have an unfortunate propensity to commit violent crime. The brotherhoods, cults and secret societies that have littered human history have given these individuals the opportunity to institutionalize this dark passion. We are far from ridding the human race of this subconscious urge. In fact, if cult-watchers and law enforcement groups are correct, we may yet see the greatest proliferation of violent sects, religions and secret syndicates that the world has ever known.

Further Reading

Baigent, Michael, Leigh, Richard and Lincoln, Henry, *The Messianic Legacy*, Jonathan Cape, London, 1986

Baigent, Michael and Leigh, Richard, *The Temple and the Lodge*, Jonathan Cape, London, 1989

Barret, David V., *Sects, 'Cults' and Alternative Religions*, Blandford, London, 1996

Basedon, Herbert, *The Australian Aboriginal*, F.W. Preece & Sons, Adelaide, 1925

Becker, J., *Hitler's Children: The Story of the Baader-Meinhof Gang*, Granada, London, 1977

Booth, M., *Triads, The Chinese Criminal Fraternity*, Grafton, London, 1990

Braschlev, William, *The Don: The Life and Death of Sam Giancana*, Harper & Row, New York, 1977

Brogan, Patrick, *World Conflicts*, Bloomsbury, London, 1989

Bull, Angela, *The Machine Breakers*, William Collins & Sons, London, 1980

Clutterbuck, Richard, *Terrorism, Drugs & Crime in Europe After 1992*, Routledge, Chapman & Hall, New York, 1990

Cornelius, Robert, 'A to Z of Cults', *Life*, 14 May 1995

Doyle, Edward, Lipsman, Samuel and Weiss, Stephen, *The Vietnam Experience: Passing the Torch*, Boston Publishing Group, Boston, 1981

Elliott, Paul, *Warrior Cults*, Blandford, London, 1995

Frazer, Sir James G., *The Golden Bough* (abridged), Macmillan, London, 1959

Godwin, John, *Unsolved: The World of the Unknown*, Doubleday & Company, Garden City NY, 1976

Gould, Robert F., *The Concise History of Freemasonry*, Gale & Polden, London, 1951

Hole, Christina, *Witchcraft in England*, BCA, London, 1977

Howard, Michael, *The Occult Conspiracy*, Rider & Co. Ltd, London, 1989

John-Wyatt, Rebecca, 'Vantage Point', *Guns & Ammo*, January 1996

Jensen-Stevenson, Monika, and Stevenson, W., *Kiss the Boys Goodbye*, Bloomsbury, London, 1990

Kaigh, Frederick, *Witchcraft and Magic of Africa*, Simson Shand, 1947

Kedward, Roderick, *The Anarchists*, Macdonald, London, 1971

Knight, Stephen, *The Brotherhood*, Panther, London, 1985

Haworth, Abigail, 'Sarin', *Life*, 14 May 1995

Kaplan, David E. and Marshall, Andrew, *The Cult at the End of the World*, Hutchinson, London, 1996

Leppard, David, *Fire and Blood*, Fourth Estate, London, 1993

Lethbridge, T.C., *Witches: Investigating an Ancient Religion*, Routledge, London, 1962

Mackenzie, Norman (ed.), *Secret Societies*, Aldus Books, London, 1967

Mbiti, John S., *African Religions and Philosophy*, Heinemann, London, 1969

Moss, R., *Urban Guerrillas: The New Face of Political Violence*, Temple Smith, London, 1972

Murray, Margaret, *The Witch-Cult in Western Europe*, Clarendon Press, Oxford, 1921

O'Brien, Joseph F. and Kurins, Andris, *Boss of Bosses*, Simon & Schuster, New York, 1991

Parrinder, Geoffrey, *West African Religion*, Epworth Press, London, 1961

Pasley, F.D., *Al Capone*, Faber & Faber, London, 1966

Posner, Gerald, *Warlords of Crime: Chinese Secret Societies – The New Mafia*, Macdonald & Co., London, 1978

Roberts, J.M., *The Mythology of the Secret Societies*, Secker & Warburg, London, 1972

Rose, Ronald, *Living Magic*, Rand McNally, New York, 1956

Saga, Junichi, *Confessions of a Yakuza*, Kodansha International, 1995

Segaller, Stephen, *Terrorism into the 1990s*, Sphere Books, London, 1987

Shirer, William L., *The Rise and Fall of the Third Reich*, Secker & Warburg, London, 1960

Short, Martin, *Crime Inc: The Story of Organized Crime*, London, 1984

Sifakis, Carl, *Encyclopedia of Assassinations*, Headline, London, 1993

Sterling, Claire, *Octopus*, Norton, New York, 1990

Summers, Montague (tr.), *The Malleus Maleficarum of Heinrich Kramer and James Sprenger*, Dover Publications, New York, 1971

Toffler, Alvin, *The Third Wave*, Pan Books, London, 1981

Turner, V.W., *The Drums of Affliction*, Clarendon Press, Oxford, 1968

Vaksberg, Arkady, *The Soviet Mafia*, St Martin's Press, New York, 1992

Wade, Wyn Craig, *The Fiery Cross*, Simon & Schuster, New York, 1987

Williams, Randall (ed.), *The Ku Klux Klan: A History of Racism and Violence*, Southern Poverty Law Centre Special Report, Montgomery AL, 1982

Woodward, Kenneth L., and Hamilton, Kendall, 'Day of Judgement', *Newsweek*, 3 May 1993

Index